School Daze: 10 Years
Of Heartache

School Daze: 10 Years Of Heartache

◆

Excerpts from a New York Teacher's Diary

Maxine Moline

iUniverse, Inc.

New York Lincoln Shanghai

School Daze: 10 Years Of Heartache
Excerpts from a New York Teacher's Diary

iUniverse books may be ordered through booksellers or by contacting:

iUniverse
2021 Pine Lake Road, Suite 100
Lincoln, NE 68512
www.iuniverse.com
1-800-Authors (1-800-288-4677)

Because of the dynamic nature of the Internet, any Web addresses or links contained in this book may have changed since publication and may no longer be valid.

The views expressed in this work are solely those of the author and do not necessarily reflect the views of the publisher, and the publisher hereby disclaims any responsibility for them.

ISBN: 978-0-595-48208-5 (pbk)
ISBN: 978-0-595-60299-5 (ebk)

Printed in the United States of America

This book is dedicated to my mother who has been for me, and many others, a great teacher and mentor. This book is also dedicated, with my greatest sympathy, to all the children who have been harmed in any way by school systems; including those who have been raped, maimed, or socially promoted without being educated.

My husband and I ran a home-based business that brought in more money in a good month than I made from teaching all year. Does anyone know how much of a turnoff that is.

Contents

FOREWORD. xi

BACKGROUND. xiii

LETTER TO THE PRESIDENT 1

THE NYC SITUATION AS I SEE IT. 6

AROUND THE SYSTEM AND BACK AGAIN 17

IN THE BEGINNING 40

THE SCHOOL RULES. 52

VIOLENCE 57

STRESS 70

THE RUBBER ROOM 82

PRINCIPAL'S REVENGE. 85

MY CLEVELAND EXPERIENCES Hedley High School,
Cleveland Ohio (August 1996 to May, 1997) 97

THE TURNING POINT Cooper High School, Brooklyn
(September 1998–June 1999). 121

TIME TO GET OUT OF THE GAME 150

THE FINAL CHAPTER? 187

POTPOURRI. 217

EPILOGUE 227

FOREWORD

I spent over 10 years compiling the information in this book. Most of the book was written in 1999 from notes that I took over the years. Additions were made in 2001, and again in 2007; these added sections are indicated with the use of superscript [01] and [07] respectively at the beginning of the added sections.

⁰¹BACKGROUND

I want to go through a little background on the school system to enable the reader to have a clearer understanding of the chapters that follow.

I taught full time for a year in Cleveland, 5½ years in New York City (NYC), and 2½ years at Northeastern High School in a rural town in upstate New York (2004–2007), for a total of 9 years. During those 9 years I taught high school students, except for a miserable semester that I spent teaching in an intermediate school in Brooklyn.

Student population
White students make up a mere 15.5% of the 1,071,074 students in the NYC public school system. Hence, the majority of the students who are affected by the inefficiencies of the system are blacks and Hispanics. In most of the communities where I taught in NYC the majority of the inhabitants were blacks and Hispanics, at least 30% of whom were living below the Federal poverty level. These areas had high infant mortality rates, high incidence rates for chronic diseases, high incidence of children with asthma, and sadly high rates of HIV infection and death due to AIDS.

The town in which I taught in Cleveland was 92% black, the median family income was $21,581, and almost a quarter of the population was below the Federal poverty level. Poor health indicators accompanied poverty—high infant mortality rate, high rates for chronic diseases, and high rates of homicide and suicide.

⁰⁷The area in which I taught in rural New York was 97% white, and located in one of the poorest of New York State's 62 counties—a median family income of around $35,000. In contrast only about 14% of the population was living in poverty, and with the exception of respiratory diseases (most likely due to smoking), the health indicators were close to the State averages.

Types of High Schools
In the NYC public school system there are 4 types of high schools:

1) Academic high schools—These are your standard high schools with a focus on general academic subjects. These high schools are supposed to prepare students for college. Students attend academic high schools based on zones which

are based on address. Anyone who knows anything about education in the United States of American (USA) knows that zoning is mainly for the purpose of segregation. The landmark case *Brown vs. Board of Education* made racial segregation in schools illegal. However, zoning laws legally maintain racial segregation of NYC schools. According to the *Village Voice* (February 5, 2002), the NYC school system is one of the most segregated in the country. There are people who will spend a fortune on getting into a certain community in order to take advantage of education at a particular school. Others will use the address of friends or relatives in order to register their child in a certain school. There are cases wherein students who live in the school zones have difficulty getting in because their spaces are taken by students from other areas who have managed to get into the schools.

2) Vocational high schools—These are schools that in addition to academics offer trade skills. In NYC these schools offer training in aeronautics, auto-mechanics, electronics, nursing, business skills, etc. The vocational high schools have the advantage of not being zone schools hence they can send disruptive students back to their zone schools. To my knowledge there are no vocational high schools in NYC that are so sought after by students that they can be overly willing to expel disruptive students. Hence expulsion is reserved for the most extreme cases.

3) Specialized high schools—There are 4 such high schools in NYC, and students gain admission to them based on their score on an entrance examination (exam). These schools are for so-called gifted students. I don't know how much gifted has to do with it since a major test preparation institution offers a course that students can start taking as early as the 6th grade in order to prepare for the entrance exam. I maintain that if you can prepare for it then it's not an aptitude test. I have nothing against people preparing for and doing well on exams; matter of fact I think that is the best way to go. However, let's call it as it is, and stop pretending that the Scholastic Aptitude Test (SAT) and other such exams are measures of brilliance or genius. I won't even start talking about intelligence quotient (IQ). The fact that you use a test to measure IQ means you are measuring what the person who designed the test deems to be intelligence.

4) Alternative high schools—These high schools represent a stroke a sensibility in the NYC public school system. These schools are designed for students who don't fit in at the other types of high schools. The expectation is that these students will benefit from an alternative learning environment because they performed poorly, or didn't perform in the other types of high schools. The Board of Regents (responsible for creating the annual exams on which students' mastery of

New York State (NYS) high school curricula is based) in their infinite wisdom, has decided to wage a fight against these schools' desire to have waivers in order that they may give their students continuous assessment in lieu of the Board of Regents' exams. Based on the limited experience I have had with these alternative high schools, I would say the Board of Regents (Regents) could learn from the administrators of these schools.

School Budget

You could spend a life time learning about school budgeting in NYC. The entire school system is stuck somewhere in the 19th century, and much of what should be computerized is still being done manually. The system of accountability for the billions of dollars spent by the school system is complicated and archaic. With this in mind there are some basics that can be summarized.

1) Most of the money goes to teacher salary. Anyone who knows anything about budgets knows that with the exception of startup ventures, which require a great deal of one-time capital expenditures, the major part of a budget is the personnel. There are those who maintain that one way to ensure greater efficiency in the system is to make sure that teachers are actually teaching. There are a lot of teachers in the system being paid to teach, but actually spend a great deal of time doing other things. The system has to pay substitutes or full time teachers to cover classes that should be taught by such teachers. There are teachers who get paid to teach but don't bother to do so. Usually this results from years of frustration with no assistance from school administrators.

I would love to see a NYC school system where every teacher has an opportunity to actually teach in their licensed area, in a single classroom, with all the resources they need, and the full support of school administrators. In my experience the major factors stopping this from happening are all symptoms of poor management, namely disruptive students in the classrooms, inappropriate teaching assignments, and mismanagement of resources.

[07]One of the actions that the NYC Board of Education (the Board) took to try to improve on management of schools was to break up some of the large schools into smaller schools. So now a building that used to house 1 school now house up to 6 schools. In these small schools the majority of teachers, especially those who teach science, end up teaching more than one subjects in 2 or more classrooms. One way these small schools could make things better for teachers is to operate on a semester system where students do half their courses in the fall semester and the other half in the spring semester. These students would take the Regents in January and again in June.

2) There is insufficient accountability for the money allocated for other than personnel services. I have seen more waste in the schools I have worked in than I care to report here. I have seen the wanton destruction of school property by students, with no consequence whatsoever. I have seen the destruction of thousands of dollars worth of textbooks. I taught in one school in Brooklyn where the students threw the books in the back of the classroom under the tables, there was a leak in the classroom that had gone unnoticed for who knows how long, and all the books ended up with water damage. I am not sure how the previous teacher managed to have missed all that. Then again, based on the mathematics grades that he gave to students who performed disastrously on the *Citywide Assessment* I can't say that I am surprised.

No discussion of NYC school budget would be complete without mentioning the issue of 'excessing', which can only be described as STUPID STUPID STUPID. The amount of money schools get is based on the number of students in attendance. In September schools are assigned money based on the number of students the Board estimates they will have based on the number of students they had in the previous school year. ([07]Note: A few years ago the Board became the NYC Department of Education. The Board went from being a quasi City agency to being a City agency which answers directly to the mayor. The Board will be used in this book since it was the entity in operation when the events in the book took place.) In January schools' budgets are reassessed based on the number of students actually in attendance. Schools that have fewer students than the estimate lose money, and hence have to adjust their operating budgets accordingly. This usually means that some teachers will be excessed. Based on the contract between the teachers' union and the Board, teachers hired in September are guaranteed a job for the entire year. Hence a teacher that is excessed from his or her position remains in the current school until reassigned by the Board.

The Board allows schools to hire teachers without State certification to teach in shortage areas. However, the position held by the teacher is listed as a vacancy by the Board. Excessing is done based on certification and seniority. One of the first things a new teacher in NYC learns is that there is no guarantee he or she will be in the same school with the same students for the entire year. Such a fact can disenchant the most resilient of new teachers. Whatever savings the Board accrues by the use of this crude budgeting method cannot be worth the harm it causes new teachers.

Teachers' Union

Each local school system that I have encountered had a local union that belonged to the larger national teachers union, the American Federation of Teachers (AFT).

In NYC the local union is called the United Federation of Teachers (UFT). The woman who was president of the UFT for a long time, Sue Fussel, has moved on to the position of president of the AFT. The current UFT president has done more against teachers than she has done for them. I have seen more teacher-bashing under the new president than ever before. When Sue was president she would have eaten up anyone who dared to attempt teacher-bashing without reasonable cause. I have heard the new president supporting teacher-bashing.

Unions are formed with the objective of protecting workers from the hazards of ludicrous management policies, layoffs, and termination without proper cause. Of late unions have become just huge political machineries that are constantly being primed with monies from the salaries of their default members. Once you become a teacher in NYC, you are automatically a member of the UFT, and union dues are deducted from your salary.

I currently work for an agency in NYC; this makes me a default member of a popular union in the City. When I filled out the documents to become a member of the union, the dues section asked how much I wanted to pay for union dues. I put down $10 per month. When I got my check stub they had taken out over 20 dollars per 2 week pay period.

When I worked in Cleveland, I was informed by the Board of Education that based on the teaching certification I had I would not qualify for certain union-negotiated benefits. When the union representative gave me the papers to fill out to join the union I asked him what the union would do for me, he never gave me an answer, and so I did not joined the union. I had medical, dental, optical and prescription benefits through the school system.

Orientation

One of the things I came across in other fields I worked in which I did not encounter in teaching until I taught in rural New York (2004) is the new employee orientation. The UFT started a mentoring program, which I suppose is supposed to serve as a surrogate for the employee orientation. Based on the little experience I have had with mentoring, I would suggest that the Board would do well with starting a new employee orientation program to go with the UFT's mentoring program. How else is a new teacher supposed to know the basics such as the standard disciplinary procedures—how to handle disruptive students, how to handle fights, when and how to get parents involved. What about investment options such as deferred compensation, pension, bonds, and college savings. Not to mention health benefits, and time and leave allocations. I did not know anything about any of the things I mentioned at the point in time when I was tossed into the school system. I learnt it all as I went along, and I learnt most of it from asking others.

What is usually given on a continuous basis (at least once per year) is information on teacher's progress in meeting certification requirements. It's no wonder all the newspapers ever write about is teacher certification, that's all the system focuses on, and hence that is all the system knows.

Teacher Certification
In order to enter the teaching profession teachers have to be certified. There are various types of certificates. The easiest to get is the NYC certificate, which has the least job security. This certificate allows someone who has a degree in a given discipline to teach in that discipline while working to meet the requirements for the permanent NYS Certificate.

The next step up is provisional NYS certificate, wherein the teacher meets requirements set forth by New York State Department of Education. Currently the requirements for NYS provisional certificate are as follows:

1. Bachelor's degree

2. 18 graduate credits in education

3. 1 year of student teaching in the license area

4. 36 credits in the subject area of the license (this requirement is usually met by the bachelor's degree.

5. 6 credits in a foreign language

6. Language Arts and Science Test (LAST)

7. Assessment Teaching Skills—Written (ATS-W)

8. Approved course in child abuse identification

9. For non-citizens, declaration of intent to become a United States citizen

There were many teachers in NYC who taught for years as uncertified teachers because they met all the requirements except for '9'. The Immigration and Naturalization Service in NYC had extremely long waiting periods for applicants for United States residence, and were notorious for making a mess of immigration paperwork. This was due in no small part to the fact that the agency had extremely high staff turnover rates, and the funding that they received was not in proportion to the number of applicants they had to process.

[07]The State has since removed '9'. In the early part of this decade, the Board went into a hiring frenzy, with strong overseas recruitment. Someone I know questioned the logic of hiring so many teachers from overseas, while keeping '9' in place. Other shortage areas such as medicine had long since removed the residency requirement. The State also added fingerprinting, which was always a requirement in NYC, and a course in school violence prevention was also added. I took this violence prevention course, which informed me of the extent of the proliferation of school violence. Based on my experience since taking the course, I seriously doubt that taking this course will do much to prevent school violence. In 2004 the State made yet another set of sweeping changes to its requirements for teacher certification. I hold a certificate awarded before those changes, hence I will not include them here.

Beyond the provisional certificate is the permanent certificate, for which the requirements are:

1. All the requirements for the provisional certificate

2. Master's degree

3. 2 years of satisfactory teaching experience

4. Assessment of teaching skills-Performance (AST-P)

5. Content Specialty Test (CSP)

6. United States citizenship

In lieu of the changes made to the requirement for the provisional certificate, the State changed '6' to United States citizenship or permanent residency. Certification may seem like a difficult process but it is quite easy for a graduate from a teacher-training program to enter the school system with a provisional NYS certificate. For the average New Yorker, this being an immigrant city and all, this is not really that easy, especially since the Immigration and Naturalization Services in NYC probably has some of the longest waiting periods for residency and citizenship.

Of course once the educational requirements have been met, most teachers usually look towards gaining tenure. Tenure provides job security for the teacher who has invested many years of service, and plans on investing even more.

In NYC teachers who have met the requirements for certification are usually appointed to a school, usually the school in which they currently serve. Once this appointment is in place the teacher has to stay at the school for a period of 5 years. As you can expect, teachers usually make sure they are in a school that they feel at home in prior to getting their appointment. Being appointed to a school that you hate, or a school where you are hated is a fate worst than death.

Teaching

Most teachers prepare for and teach 5 classes per day. Ideally these classes should be in the subject area in which the teacher is certified. For most subject areas this is the case. This is not usually the case for science teachers. I had chemistry certification however I taught chemistry for 11 out of a total of 21 semesters. I have heard of all sorts of ridiculous assignments. There was a recent news report (October, 2001) of a math teacher teaching chemistry who started a fire by handling alcohol with an open flame. For a chemist the knowledge that flammable liquids should be kept away from open flames is second nature. You gain this knowledge after many hours of laboratory (lab) work in which you conduct experiments, which involve both a flame and a flammable liquid.

Of course lesson planning is a big part of a teacher's job. A well-planned lesson can make the difference between a really great day at work and a truly miserable one. Of course it's quite difficult to plan really good lessons when you are teaching out of your subject area. Whereas I can walk into a chemistry class, and teach a great lesson at the drop of a dime, I could spend an entire day preparing an earth science lesson, and still do a poor presentation. It's hard to be stellar when you are teaching by reading the material, and then passing it on to the students, or as a dear friend aptly phrased it, "being one page ahead of the students". I once taught technical drawing, meteorology and aerodynamics. I learnt a whole lot because these were all subjects that were foreign to me prior to my teaching them. I felt quite sure the students I was teaching technical drawing to were probably better at it than I could ever be.

The teacher has some administrative responsibilities, however with the increased use of technology in schools these have been significantly reduced over the last few years. The administrative responsibilities are still a big deal. Teachers have to take attendance for each of the 5 classes that they teach. Technology has made this task easier because the attendance sheets are collected once per week. Each teacher has a class that is considered his or her homeroom class. In some places, such as NYC, this class is just like any other, except the attendance of this class is collected daily. This attendance sheet is used to determine if the student is present for that day or not. Hence at about midmorning, teachers will see the students in their homeroom; all homeroom classes are during the same period—I believe this is the third period for most schools. Elementary school teachers have the same students all day, so they simply take attendance once and this attendance sheet is collected.

In some places the homeroom last 10 to 15 minutes, and may be just a group of students who are assigned to the teacher for administrative purposes. The teacher takes attendance, makes announcements to the students, hand out materials that need to be handed out, collect materials that are to be collected, etc. At Hedley High School in Cleveland each classroom had a television, which was used during homeroom to aid in the dissemination of information to the students.

Discipline

Most schools have a system in place to deal with disciplinary problems. All the schools I have encountered had a referral system. The referral system involves documentation of the incident on what's called a referral form. In most instances this referral form comes in duplicate or triplicates; though I have seen the form as a single sheet. The purpose of having duplicates and triplicates is to allow the teacher to keep a copy of the referral for his or her records. At Hedley High School the referral form came in triplicates. The original and the yellow copy were sent with the student to his 'unit office', and the teacher retained the red copy. Later after the unit office had taken action, the original was returned to the teacher indicating what action was taken. The yellow copy was retained by the unit office. I assumed the yellow copy went into the student's file. This way if the student got into big trouble and the school's administrators decided they wanted to have the student transferred to another school, then they could pull the student's file, and voila—out would pop the giant stack of referrals for everything in the book and then some. [07]At Northeastern High School there were 4 parts to the referral and the fourth part was sent home to the student's parent or guardian.

Many poorly run schools either don't have a disciplinary system in place, or they do but they don't use it. I think the latter is more likely. In such schools discipline is left up to the teachers, and when the teachers attempt to discipline students they get no support from the school's administrators. Most school systems also have a code of conduct, which dictates what disciplinary actions are to be taken for a variety of offenses.

Student Assessment

A system of assessment has to be in place in a school system. In NYC the assessment tools are the Regents exams for high school students, and the Citywide Assessment for elementary and intermediate school students. As anyone who has been reading the newspapers knows, NYC students have had failures on both types of assessment. When I started teaching in 1992, the Regents had the Regents Competence Test (RCT) in various subjects. These competence tests assessed level of competence in the subject areas. The Regents exams were reserved for the better students in the school, those who were considered college bound.

The former chancellor of the Board, R.C. Coley, mandated that all students take Regents level classes. To make matters worst, schools are being judged on their exam results, and principals are losing their jobs based on the performance of their students on these exams. There are those who suggest that teachers should get merit pay based on their students' results on these exams. If people knew that the same teachers in the same schools would get the merit pay year after year they may seriously rethink this stupid idea.

What no one has bothered to do is address the exams themselves, and assess whether or not they are good assessment tools. The other issue is the fact that linking students' grades to job retention for supervisors, and projecting that they will be linked to teacher salary makes great motivation for people to engage in unwholesome activities in the name of boosting students' grades. I will touch on both these issues in the chapters to come.

Let me conclude by saying that my students have gotten passing percentages on the Regents ranging from 0% to 100%. When I did private tutoring every student I tutored for the chemistry Regents passed, on the other hand I taught summer school one year wherein none of my students passed the Regents. [07]At Northeastern students take the Regents exams in January and in June. I had 100% of my students pass the June administration of the chemistry Regents exam during my first year there.

Clearly my passing percent will depend on the type of students I have—students whose parents are paying me $30 an hour to tutor them 1–2 times per week, students who I tutor all semester long, or students who are sweating it out in summer school to take a subject that they failed in the regular school year.

LETTER TO
THE PRESIDENT

In May of 1999 I wrote this letter to Bill Clinton. At the time of the letter I was at Cooper High School in Brooklyn and the victim of a principal's vendetta, and Bill Clinton was President of the United States of America. As a teacher I had done the unthinkable, I stood up to the principal, for that I had to be severely punished.

I did not mail the letter, but I think it makes a fitting start to this book.

May 27, 1999

I listened with interest as the Secretary of Education outlined his plans for improving education in our schools. The Secretary, like most other school administrators, seem to think that if they increase the number of requirements and make teacher certification more difficult to attain, that will solve the problems our schools face.

Quite frankly, I feel that adding more requirements to teacher certification will just ensure that time teachers should spend improving their lessons will instead be spent in classrooms taking courses for professional development. In 6 years of teaching I have met only one teacher who spoke highly of those teacher-training courses. For the most part, these courses are taught by people who have never experienced the realities of an inner city classroom, or who experienced it but were unable to cope. In one such 'teacher-training' class, the instructor got quite upset because a teacher asked her how she would handle a real world situation, and she wasn't able to give an appropriate answer. I spent my time in the school system suggesting that staff development should take the form of peer teaching. Most of the effective strategies I have practiced over the years I learnt from other teachers. I think I may have learnt 2 strategies from my over 20 credits of graduate education courses, and hundreds of hours of professional development. What these courses and workshops have been very effective at doing is boring me to tears and making me wonder about staying in teaching.

Case in point—when I entered the NYC school system as a teacher in 1992, the requirement for State certification was 12 credits in graduate education courses, now the requirement is 18 credits plus 6 credits in a foreign language. Yet from all indications the quality of teaching in NYC schools has deteriorated significantly in the last 7 years

Teachers don't need upgrading. What we need is the cooperation of parents and administrators. Give teachers the tools and the appropriate environment and they will get the job done. Most teachers I know would love the opportunity to really teach to the best of their abilities. As it stands now, we just do the best we can under the given conditions.

Students should not be given the idea that it's okay for them to disrespect and harass teachers without reprise. Teachers should not be thrown into hostile situations without any assistance. Teachers should not have to teach in rooms that are lacking in all the facilities needed to make them inhabitable. How do you conduct science lab in a classroom not equipped for lab work. How do you have students use chemicals when there is no sink for them to wash their hands when they are finished experimenting with toxic chemicals. You are forced into a situation where the teacher does the experiment and the students watch.

Anyone who feels that students are not fully aware of the inadequacies of their environment has lost his marbles. These students watch television, and they know what things are like in other places. It is demoralizing for students to accept that school administrators do not care about them. In my school, my students sat on stools for the entire year, aching and complaining. Then in the penultimate week of classes chairs were brought in. Students at my school have to walk 4 blocks through traffic from their school to a college to attend classes, while almost an entire floor at the school houses school administrators—the school has a little over 600 students.

I have to tell you Mr. President, what ails the school system in this country won't be fixed by increasing teachers' academic credentials. The only thing that will result in is a large number of frustrated, highly qualified teachers.

The NYC school system has a large number of dedicated, hardworking teachers. With time, these same teachers will become burnt-out, frustrated, fed up, space holders if they have to keep banging their heads against a wall of non-supportive school administrators. Not to mention parents who seem to feel it's okay to transfer their children's welfare into the hands of teachers. Discipline is the job of the parent, and school administrators should be obligated to assist. Too often the parents and the school administrators leave discipline in the hands of the teachers. I don't want to tell you some of the things I have seen teachers do and say to children in the name of discipline; these things should never happen.

Parents must be held responsible. This country's social system needs to make it a part of its responsibility to teach mothers and fathers how to be good parents. Few parents even bother to attend their children's schools. In an average school year, it's normal for me to meet less than 20% of parents of the children I teach, even though I normally mail out 2 progress reports per year to go with the 6 report cards that the school sends home. In addition, parent teacher conferences are held twice a year in NYC, once at the end of the first marking period in November, and again in March at the end of the first marking period of the second semester.

Parents must be responsible for their children, but many parents are lacking the skills needed to improve. We are not born with parenting skills we have to learn them. Smart schools have started holding workshops to help parents improve their parenting skills.

In a city like NYC with so many immigrant families sending their children to our schools, it's important that the school system be explained to parents. If the school does not explain it to the parents then the children will. As can be expected, any explanation the child gives to the parent will be in his or her favor. A lot of these immigrant parents are from countries with school systems where it's okay to leave your child's welfare up to the school system.

One teacher stated it quite accurately when he said that if we spend most of our time teaching critical thinking to students, then they would learn everything else with ease. It has always amazed me that when students are faced with critical thinking questions their brains seem to shut down. As a student, critical thinking questions were the ones that excited me the most because they offered challenge.

I summarize by telling you that quality is more important than quantity, both in respect to teachers and students, and if you want to improve educational outcomes in American schools:

1. Assure efficient and effective management of schools by qualified administrators. Take the money you would spend on improving teacher education and use it to hire more qualified administrators. In NYC administrators' hourly rate is less than that of a teacher, so is their maximum salary. See a problem there? (The last school administrators' contract changed this, but the administrators gave up tenure and with it their job security).

2. Give teachers the tools and environment they need to perform. If you are not sure ask teachers. 100% of teachers I know have a problem with the fact that their opinion is never sought regarding what is taught and how it is taught.

3. Take steps to make teaching a respectable profession. There should be some strict penalties for disrespecting a teacher. ([01]Case in point, the 107th Congress put forth almost 50 bills all aimed at improving teacher qualifications, but there were only 2 that I could find for protecting teachers. One of the bills [*S.316*, February 13, 2001] was to amend the *Elementary and Secondary Education Act* of 1965 to protect teachers from violent acts and frivolous lawsuits.) In my current school, teachers have been treated with utter disrespect by students, administrators, school secretaries, and other school staff. The *New York Globe* wrote, "What's the difference between a New York teenager and a teacher?" The answer was "The teenager dresses better". The demoralization I spoke about for students also work for teachers. NYC has a mayor who called teaching "the best paid part time job", and encouraged students to cut classes to attend a baseball game because he (the mayor) learnt more from baseball than he did from school. [07]That NYC mayor is now campaigning to become the next president of the USA, I wonder how he feels about education now.

4. Support those who bring positive changes to the school system. The Chancellor of NYC's school system, Mr. RC Coley, is doing a very good job. I have seen some decent changes since he has been in office, but he seems to be alone on most of his agendas. He gets little support except from administrators who find their jobs on the line. (In December of 1999, the NYC Board of Education voted 4-to-3 not to renew Mr. Coley's contract when it expired in June of 2,000. There were tons of reasons given for the decision, but anyone who knows the politics of NYC knows Mr. Coley was ousted because he disagreed with something the Mayor wanted. The ousting of Mr. Coley was, in my opinion, the biggest error of the Board since I have been in the system, and the Board has blundered several times.)

5. Something needs to be done to stamp out nepotism in American schools. I am in a school that has a principal who is totally out of control, but he and the Superintendent of the district are friends. He spends quite a bit of time threatening and harassing teachers and trying to

intimidate them into passing on students who are failing. He gets away with this by ensuring that only teachers without State certificates remain in the school.

THE NYC SITUATION AS I SEE IT

June 1999

In June of 1996, the Board did a huge first, it did something that benefited teachers more than it did the Board—various retirement incentives were offered. Also in 1996, many teachers and administrators left the NYC School System for Long Island, upstate New York, and other states to fill slots left vacant by retiring teachers. It is important to point out that a large number of teachers and administrators who at the time were working in NYC actually lived in theses places; namely Long Island, Upstate New York, and New Jersey.

Mainly as a result of this mass exodus of teaching professionals, the NYC School System has changed dramatically over the last 3 years, and things promise to get worst before they get better.

The Department I was in at Queens' Langley High School lost 3 out of 6 teachers. 2 teachers retired, and I left for Cleveland. This wasn't too huge a lost for the Department because the teachers who remained were at the top of their game—one recently awarded *Teacher of the Year*. The big lost was the assistant principal (AP) for the Department. He was the best AP I ever came across. He left for Long Island. He got a similar position, which was closer to home, paid more, and promised less stress.

Berger High School in the Bronx took a huge hit, the school lost almost all its experienced teachers—16 teachers and APs left.

In my humble opinion there are 3 major factors responsible for the weakening of the NYC public school system.

1. The current mandate that all students must take Regents level science and mathematics.

2. Widespread departure of experienced teachers and administrators.

3. Large influx of new teachers and administrators.

Requiring all students to take Regents level mathematics and sciences is a good idea. However, it's an idea for which the NYC public school system is not quite ready. When Chancellor Coley came along and made that decision most of the older experienced teachers made comments like: "he's crazy", "he's dizzy and confused", "this will never work", "there are less than 100,000 students in the school system where he's from, maybe it will work there, but it certainly won't work here".

I was the only teacher I knew at the time who was for Mr. Coley's idea 100%. I still feel it's a good idea, which given time can work. I believe though that all parties concerned need to recognize that a lot of dedication, effort and money will have to be invested into getting it to work.

It's hard to prepare students for Regents level science when you are lacking lab facilities. Even if you were able to get a large number of students to pass the Regents without doing lab work it defeats the purpose, because a major part of Regents level science is the lab component.

While we are on the subject of passing Regents I want to inject here my opinion of Regents exams. I believe Regents exams are a rather poor tool for assessing students. Nevertheless Regents exams are representative of the types of exams that students will have to take to move ahead in life, and that includes getting into—

College—Scholastic Aptitude Test (SAT), and the American College Testing (ACT) Program's test
Medical school—Medical College Admission Test (MCAT)
Graduate school—Graduate Record Exam (GRE) and Graduate Management Admission Test (GMAT)

I have 2 major problems with the Regents exam as an assessment tool. (1) There is little or no feedback from the Regents. Each year thousands of NYC students take the Regents exams, and most of these students fail. There is no assessment done by the Regents to see just what areas of a given test gave students the most difficulty. As a result teachers get no feedback to enable them to determine what areas they need to improve, or place greater emphasis on. The result is year after year the Regents set the same exam questions, and year after year students fail.

[07]The Regents has made sweeping changes to the exams. One of those changes is a section on the answer key called *Map to Core Curriculum*, which maps questions on the exam with key ideas in the curriculum and a set of State standards. The complaint teachers have now which I share is that the current curriculum does not indicate the extent to which different areas of the curriculum should be

covered. Teachers frequently spend less time on topics based on how much information is provided in the curriculum. Then students go to the exam and find that the questions on the exam require a greater depth of knowledge. It's easy to see how this is unfair to the students. Also, the Regents chemistry curriculum is so broad that in order for it to be feasible it requires oversimplification of a lot of basic concepts. In some cases, these oversimplifications amount to misinformation. This is particularly so for the calculations and the abstract concepts.

[07]Some teachers have started doing their own post-exam evaluation. This presents a very sticky situation if this leads to violations of Regents exam protocols. At the last professional development day at Northeastern High School, the assignment for most of the teaching staff was to do a question by question analysis of the Regents exams. I think this is a really great idea (I was the one who suggested it after attending a conference where a chemistry teacher presented his findings from such an activity), and one that can work really well, provided it is a properly administered district directive.

I often compare the Regents with the exams given by the University of Cambridge in England. The Cambridge exam system has rigorous feedback wherein teachers get a question-by-question analysis, which enable them to make appropriate modifications to their teaching. Of course the major difference between the 2 exam systems is the Cambridge exams are graded by the University of Cambridge, while the Regents exams are graded at the schools by the teachers who taught the subjects.

2) The grading and proctoring of the Regents exams at the schools by the teachers who taught the subjects presents endless opportunities for cheating. I have seen more cheating by teachers and students in NYC than I care to detail here. Cheating is even more widespread now that the Regents are mandated, and schools are being judged based on their exam results. Also with the large influx of new teachers who may not necessarily know how to pick up when students are cheating on the exams, the problem is being compounded.

This year I had to deal with cheating in every exam I proctored. I had to boycott the 'bathroom trick' twice (the bathroom trick is where one student asks to use the bathroom so he/she can leave answers on a piece of paper in the bathroom, about 10–15 minutes later another student will ask to use the bathroom so he/she can go and get the answers that were left in the bathroom). In both instances the other teacher who was in the room with me was totally baffled by my decision to go outside and bring in an informed escort to take the second student to the bathroom.

Then there are the instances in which teachers help students cheat. They do so by telling students answers during the exam, turning a blind eye while students are copying, erasing wrong answers on students papers and shading the correct answers, and telling answers to students who use the bathroom excuse so they can go outside and ask a teacher for the answer before going back into the exam room.

[07]The State paid a visit to Northeastern during the January administration of the Regents, and their major complaint was that proctors were not actively monitoring students during the exams. The principal announced this over the intercommunication system, and made it clear that it was his fault for not stressing this fact. The school issues the directive from the State regarding the rules for conducting the exams at least a week in advance. I have always found it strange that I didn't see other proctors in the room with me actively monitoring students the way I was. The teachers were usually busy working the problems on the exams, and complaining about ones they didn't think should be there. There was one Northeastern student who told me that he cheated his way to passing grades on all his Regents exams. He said it as though it was a mere joke, but I suspected he was telling the truth. I grew more convinced when on the day of the chemistry exam he went for a seat behind the girl with the highest grade in the class. I quickly took action to change that, and I guess that was his first failing grade on a Regents exam.

Let's face it, if given the opportunity to cheat students will do so. When the topic of cheating comes up in discussions with other teachers, I always find that I am usually the only one in the room that can honestly say that I have never cheated in an academic setting. This is not an indication that I have superior morals or any such virtues, I was just so pompous and confident that I felt that if I didn't know the answer then no one else in the class did. I was always in the top 10 or top 10%, because I was not willing to accept anything less. In the fifth grade I cried bitter tears because I got fifth place instead of first place, which I felt sure was mine. I was never even daunted by the fact that I was new to the school and the youngest student in the class.

In addition a lot of schools allow students to do Regents science exams without completing the required number of lab hours. Schools usually selectively choose students who they feel will pass the exam to accord this privilege. Harmless as this may seem, it represents another form of cheating. Then there is the earth science Regents exam which has a practical as well as a written exam. In this case teachers cheat by adjusting the grade on the lab section so that when added to the grade for the written exam a passing grade will result. Sometimes the grades are tallied, and then the papers of those students whose grades are a few points short of the 65 points required for passing are graded again.

Then there's the common practice of finding a point for the student who gets a 64 as his/her grade for the exam. In a lot of cases answers that would clearly be incorrect under normal circumstances will be considered worthy of 1 point. Over the years these practices have for the most part been passively accepted and endorsed. In fact they are so entrenched that students have come to expect teachers to help them cheat. It always seem to baffle my students that I insist on not being anywhere near where they are taking their Regents exam, and am quite comfortable recording a 64 for a student's Regents grade.

What's interesting about all this is that if the Regents exams were conducted in the manner intended there would be little or no opportunity for cheating. However, I have yet to see a school that conducts the Regents exams according to the directions established by the Regents. What actually happens is schools make up their own directions, which they give to teachers who proctor the exams. As a result the procedures for conducting and grading the exams differ from school to school. I shudder to think what the Regents results would be like if there were no cheating.

Most of the students in the NYC School System don't have the skills required to do well on Regents exams. I am talking about basic skills, namely reading comprehension, arithmetic, writing, critical thinking and reasoning. I believe all schools should have a basic skills course that all students have to take each year that they do a Regents level class, or until they have demonstrated proficiency in basic skills as determined by a properly administered basic skills test.

What has been happening is that high school teachers complain about skills that students are not learning in intermediate school to prepare them for high school; intermediate school teachers complain that elementary schools are not doing a good job of preparing students for intermediate school; and elementary school teachers affirm that they have been teaching these basic skills as instructed by state endorsed curricula.

It would seem to me that it may make a lot more sense for schools to say, "Okay some of our students are lacking these basic skills that prevent them from progressing, let's forget about who should have taught them and when, and lets just address the deficit the minute we realize it". There is enough money for every NYC Public School to institute a basic skills course for every student who needs it. It might be in the interest of the City and State to allow credit for such a course. Like anything else this course would need to be teacher approved and piloted in a few schools before it becomes a City-wide mandate. Considering the current teacher shortage, it might be difficult to find the personnel to teach such a course, but if such a course were instituted, it would be well worth the effort.

Don't get me wrong, I am not saying basic skills are not being taught. The problem is most of our students seem to progress through elementary and intermediate schools without learning these skills. How do I know this? It's simple, once you learn these basics skills you retain them the rest of your life. These skills become second nature, like swimming or riding a bike. There's a vast difference between what's being taught in our schools, and what's being learnt. For instance I looked at a second grade mathematics curriculum and was shocked to see congruence and probability, yet students struggle to deal with ratio problems in chemistry, and NYC students' average on the mathematics section of the SAT reasoning test is 467 (2007 data). A great deal is being taught, but very little learning is taking place. Over the years students have gotten the notion that they don't have to learn to get a passing grade.

Education, like life in America, is loaded with excess. It would be more profitable to give students just enough to make sure they absorb it all, than to give them in excess, and they absorb little or none of it. It's as if the system is designed so that the majority of students will fail. We can build probes to monitor distant planets; we can certainly fix a school system in need of change.

If you know the basics all advanced learning is easy. One of the major basic skills that our students lack is reading comprehension. A lot of students who do poorly on mathematics and science Regents exams do so because they have trouble understanding the questions.

I had one class wherein I taught the students how to break down the questions on the RCT in Science. Ultimately my students started to criticize the manner in which the questions were written. What stood out for me was when the most unruly boy in the class criticized the Regent's use of the word 'paperboard' instead of 'cardboard'. We felt we were more likely to understand the question if they used the word cardboard instead of paperboard. Like my student said, "what on earth is paperboard?" All but the weakest students passed the exam at the end of the year, and those who failed only missed it by a few points.

One of the things I would do at the start of the school year was to tell students that the Regents exam is easy, and that I can teach them how to pass it. Then I would listen to hear them say with enthusiasm, "So teach us". I would tell them that to pass the Regents all they had to do was listen to me and follow my directions. That one moment was a forecast for the year. The students who were serious about passing the Regents would listen to me and do as I instructed.

When I learnt reading comprehension, the dictionary was my companion, that way any word I didn't know I could look up the meaning of. Most students I have met don't even own a dictionary, let alone have one as their companion. Students have gotten used to teachers who give them all the answers. In NYC schools it's expected that the day before a test the teacher will give students the answers to the questions that will be on the test. It may sound ridiculous, but this is what happens, it's usually called a test review, and the questions and answers are written on what's called a review sheet. Students are upset and disappointed because I do the review of the test after the test and not before. I tell my students the topic or topics to be covered on the test, and I tell them this at least a week in advance. The rest I leave up to them.

With teachers and administrators leaving NYC en-mass for greener pastures things will certainly get worst before they get better. The reason for my pessimism is the large influx of new teachers and administrators; many of whom are not quite up to the job. I have met more new teachers this year than I did in my entire prior 4 years with the school system.

Also, unless NYC does something to try to hold on to teachers and administrators, once these new employees get some experience and State certification, they too will move on. Just this year I know of one teacher who has moved on to another state on getting his NYS certificate, and I know of several others who plan to do so as soon as they get theirs.

With the current nationwide shortage of teachers states are recruiting teachers from wherever they can get them and NYC seems to be the locale of choice for recruiting. School officials from Maryland recently held a job fair in NYC. Let's face it, teaching in NYC is a very impressive entry on any teacher's resume; combine that with NYS certification, and you are quite a marketable commodity. The feeling is that if you can teach in NYC you can do well just about anywhere else.

Not only are other places recruiting from NYC, they are offering very attractive incentives. Moving Upstate or to Long Island promises an increase of about $10,000. Maryland offers a down payment on a home along with a signing bonus. Boston offers a hefty signing bonus. With all that has been going on in NYC most teachers are looking favorably to these places that promise a better quality of life, and at the very least ease of parking, fewer parking tickets, and little or no tolls.

The other major problem is the large influx of new Assistant Principals and Principals; many of them were classroom teachers who were pushed into administration without adequate preparation. What this means is that the next few years promise a large number of poorly run schools, which will result in disenchanted teachers and accompanying low test-scores. The last thing a new teacher needs is to be in a poorly run school, unfortunately the first school to hire a new teacher, particularly a new teacher without a NYS certificate, is usually a poorly run school; it has been termed 'paying your dues'.

Coming from a country where there is considerable equity in the high school system, I was shocked by the lack of equity in NYS, especially when schools in NYC are compared to schools in the suburbs. These comparisons were made with alarming frequency by those teachers who lived in the suburbs, and schooled their children there. Needless to say no one bothered to address this.

The poorest schools get the worst teachers, what a horror! In an educational system where teachers are assigned to schools by the Board, if the City were taking a creative approach, the better teachers would be sent to the poorest schools. It's a sure sign of failure of any system when children are allowed to suffer. There can be no pardon or excuses for such a crime against humanity.

I can recall the way I progressed while under a very good AP versus while under a very poor AP. While at Berger High School in the South Bronx (which was my first teaching position in NYC) I worked under an AP who was totally ineffective. He was so ineffective and devoid of any level of authority that it was the norm for students to say "fuck you" to him, and turn and apologize to me if it was done in my presence. While at Berger, most of what worked in my classroom was the result of new and innovative ideas I came up with on my own. Some of my ideas were actually copied and instituted school wide. I was fortunate in that before going into teaching I had been employed in middle management in private industry, and as a result I had some management experience to fall back on.

At Langley High School in Queens I met one of the best administrators I ever came across. Most of what worked in my classroom resulted from advice I received from him. A lot of my current teaching methods are derived from what I learnt from him. Unfortunately for NYC, he like many other good administrators left for Long Island.

When I started teaching, I knew nothing about how to teach, and I had no intention of making teaching a career. What I did have was my usual conviction that whatever I do I should at the very least do to the best of my abilities. I decided to take the good things that I had seen teachers do over the years, adapt and improve on them. I decided to employ those strategies that worked for me when I was a student.

I forgot one very crucial fact; the NYC school system was so different from the one I was educated in that I may as well be from another planet. And, God forbid I had standards and expected something from my students, the horror of it all.

When I taught Regents level subjects I expected all my students to pass—indeed I was an alien species. Pretty soon I was down in the gallows of despair with the other teachers saying stuff like, "If I get 5 passes I'll be happy"—5 students passing in a class of up to 34 students. Of course there was usually about 30% absenteeism. Some students would show up for transportation passes at the start of the month then disappear until the next month's issue. Like students who go to SAT preparation class the first day just to get the book, and never show up again. Teachers don't mind, fewer students mean less stress for the same salary.

When my chemistry class took the Regents, and only 7 out of 16 passed, I was shocked and disgusted. One of my students commented, "You expected us all to pass." This from the student ranked number 2 in the school. Needless to say his score of 79% on the Regents was much less than expected. It's as though students are weighed down by an enormous anchor of repression that stifle their true potentials.

One thing that worked for me as a student which also seemed to work for my students was when I gave them assignments, showed them how to do it, and then let them work on their own or with each other. The lowest ranked class would soon begin to exhibit progressive behavior. They liked the idea that they were doing for themselves. It worked even better when I pretended I didn't know anything, and placed the onus to find out smack on the students' shoulders.

Also this enabled me to assess students' progress and give individual attention. It also allowed for peer tutoring. It's amazing how well students learn from each other, even when it's just a regurgitation of the same thing the teacher said.

Maturity is as alien a trait in the NYC school system as are manners and discipline. Sometimes the students are so immature that if I close my eyes real tight I would think I am in a kindergarten classroom. They throw papers, spitballs, lunch tickets, and at Langley High School they threw screws from shop class. One day while I was teaching at Langley High School, a battery came sailing across the room and smashed unto the chalkboard. Fortunately on the side of the board opposite where I was. Nevertheless I was shocked into stupidity, which means I just froze; I was saved by the bell.

The bell is my enemy when it signals that I have to go to the 'front lines', as I recall one teacher calling it. The bell is my friend when it signals the end of a period of torture.

Then there's the constant whining:

"Miss he took my thing"

"Miss he's 'dissing' my country"

"Miss he's throwing papers at me"

"Miss I don't feel like doing any work"

"Miss I want to go home early"

"Miss he took my book bag"

"Miss he took my pen"

"Miss he called me a name"

"Miss this niggar's gay" (niggar is used by all races of students alike, this I can't but find rather amusing)

"Miss he's bothering me"

Once I decided I would tape my students so I could let them listen to themselves. The cacophony of voices that resulted was pandemonium. It sounded like the rattling of a NYC subway train amidst chattering of people in different languages magnified 10 times. I could not believe this was what I taught in daily. If noise is considered a stressor, then guess what.... .

I had a rather uncomfortable situation with one really disruptive class. There was a gay student in the class; I will call him Paul. The students would pick on Paul every day. They made comments about Paul's sexuality in a seemingly endless assault. The deans and counselors were forever taking students from my class for harassing Paul. To make matters worst, the school made the mistake of blocking students, which meant that Paul was sharing all his classes with his harassers. As if all this wasn't enough, Paul would taunt the students with his mannerisms—flicking his tongue and making provocative comments. This I estimated was his way of getting back at his tormentors. Paul's behavior only served to fuel the fire resulting in threats—"See you after school Pauline", and consequently more dean involvement.

Not only are students immature, but they also lack something mentally. Their brains don't seem to make what many people would consider logical connections. According to one teacher, it's all a result of the students never being challenged mentally. This could be. After all, if you were always spoon fed, you would not suddenly know how to feed yourself. Infants learn to feed themselves by taking a spoon and practicing, mothers don't spoon feed their children until they are 5 or 6 years old, and then suddenly expect them to know how to feed themselves without making a mess.

Then there is the lack of reading comprehension skills. Students have difficulty comprehending what they read, even those who can read fluently. It's surprising how few students walk around with a dictionary in their book bag. If the students don't know the meaning of a word they ask the teacher. The teacher is expected to be the know-all, the limitless information giver. My response is always the same—"Go look it up." I often tell students to look up information for extra credit. I was rather impressed when I saw that my Asian students (mostly from China) had electronic dictionaries that translated English to Chinese.

Thinking is such a novel thing to students. If asked a question that requires some thought, the tendency is to skip it or guess the answer, and not even an intelligent guess at that. I have taught in high schools in all 5 boroughs of NYC. In all that time I found one student with excellent computational skills. He was an Asian student at Bronx High School of Science (actual name of school). He would come up with his own methods of working problems, and proceed to do the calculations in his head. I provided tutoring for him in chemistry, because his parents were concerned that he was just passing—scoring just under 70% on his chemistry exams. After 2 tutoring sessions with me he got a 93, and his grade never fell below 90% thereafter. He really didn't need me, though his parents retained my services for some time.

Thinking is not the only absentee skill. I have found basic mathematics skills severely lacking too. A number of teachers have concurred with me on this.

Most times the students' parents are decent, hard-working people who have no idea the shame that their children bring to their names. I once smelled cigarette smoke on a student's breath and threatened to tell his parents. From his reaction I could tell his parents knew nothing about his habit.

I know there are those who will insist changes are taking place. Yes, on paper a lot of changes are taking place, but in practice the old saying applies, *The more things change the more they stay the same.*

AROUND THE SYSTEM
AND BACK AGAIN

I have taught in every NYC borough, and taught students of various ages, races and ethnicities. I love teaching in NYC. I don't think I would trade teaching in the NYC school system for any other school system. I don't say this because I think highly of this school system; on the contrary, I think the school system is terribly flawed. I enjoy teaching in NYC because I love NYC students. I love the cultural diversity, I love the boundless zest for life that emanate from these students. It's amazing to me that NYC students are treated with such utter disregard by the school system, yet they manage to make the most of it, and bring joy to themselves and their teachers.

I taught for 5½ years in NYC, and most of the experiences I had in which students openly disrespected me took place during the years I taught outside of NYC.

In NYC, most of my hassles and disrespect did not come from students but from school staff—from principals down to school secretaries and security guards.

What follows are brief descriptions of my experiences at various schools across NYC's 5 boroughs—Bronx, Brooklyn, Manhattan, Queens and Staten Island.

Berger High School, South Bronx (September 1992–January 1995)

My most memorable experience from Berger High School is of the way in which students were willing to work with me, and the level of success that resulted. We (my students and I) averaged about 70% passing in both class and Regents. I spoke about my students everywhere I went, I was so proud of them. I would watch in amusement as other teachers expressed shock on realizing I was talking about the South Bronx. I had one particular group of student who will remain forever etched in my memory. I taught them biology; they took the biology Regents and passed. Then I taught them chemistry, they took the chemistry Regents and passed. Then they moved on to physics, which they insisted they wanted me to teach. Unfortunately I was not willing to venture into teaching physics, I know the subject, but I'm just not very fond of it.

I endured a nightmarish experience when the Principal of the school, Nelly-ann Thomson, decided to make my life a living hell because I wasn't willing to teach a zero period (7:15 am) lab class. Another Berger High School memory which will remain with me forever is the day a 9th grade student brought in a letter from his parent informing me that he had AIDS, and as such would be required to be out of school at various times throughout the semester for treatment. (According to data from the NYC Department of Health's AIDS Surveillance Program the South Bronx has the highest incidence of AIDS in the Bronx, and one of the highest incidences in the City.) When something like that happens—and believe me I had several such occasions while teaching in NYC—you end up in a place beyond shock and disbelief, and your mind just draws a blank.

While at Berger I also witnessed the rapid degradation of one of my better students. His mother died, and it seems it affected him immensely. He became totally uncontrollable, he no longer took pride in his hygiene or attire, and he became satanic and dyslexic. Hey that's what I witnessed—he wore black always with skeleton and other grim graphics, and he wrote backwards. It was so bad that I was on the verge of calling and reporting child neglect, but I feared that such a report might do him more harm than good.

Bissell High School, Bronx (July, 1993)
I was a substitute teacher there for a few days. I don't really remember much about this teaching experience. What I do remember though was a female student coming into class and exclaiming, "A student got shot, there's blood all over the second floor". To this day I still recall the frightening image that formed in my mind on hearing "blood all over the second floor".

Bissell High School is in the heart of the Spanish community in the northern part of the Bronx. It's a school that had been exemplary but has been on a major decline.

Hoffman Evening High School, Manhattan (November 1993–January 1994)
I didn't like Hoffman, mainly because of the filthy condition of my classroom. There were mice. It was common for students to exclaim that they saw a mouse run by. As I write this (fall 1999), Hoffman High School is in the midst of well needed renovation, they recently installed new windows, and they are in the process of painting ceilings and repairing the outside of the building. Hoffman is

actually a very old school with beautiful woodwork on the inside. I only recently began to notice the beauty of the building, and it's truly a splendid edifice.

While at Hoffman I taught a student who was a Black Muslim. I remember he would stay behind after class and lecture me about the manner in which the science he was learning figured in the Muslim teachings. He had a wife who was expecting, and he was steadfast in his religion. I was very proud of his dedication. He, unlike most of the other students, wasn't taking chemistry because he needed it to graduate he was taking it to learn new knowledge to apply to his religion. I ran into him in the summer of 1998. He walked up to me, reintroduced himself, and proceeded to lecture me as he had done on numerous occasions 4 years earlier.

Evening school is a very difficult thing for students. I am amazed at how many students attend school in the day, go to work in the afternoon, and then attend evening school from 6–9 pm. Where do these students get time to study and do homework; fact is most of them don't. There should be some amount of restriction on how many hours students can work per week during the school year. Also there should be an enforced limit on the age at which students can attend night school. It's ridiculous for students who are 14 and 15 years old to be out attending class from 6–9 pm at nights, then taking the train home. [07]At Northeastern High School, most of the students went straight from school to work where they stayed until 9 pm in some cases. The sad thing is students work to save for college. College tuition has been on an uncontrollable upward course for the past 10 years. Some colleges have increased their tuitions by over 300% in that time, outpacing parents' salaries, scholarships, grants and Federal student loans.

Quite frankly I think evening school should be eliminated as an option for high school students. The resources could be better spent educating the parents—helping non-English speaking parents to learn English so they can better understand the school system, teaching parents basic skills so they can improve their lives and hence the lives of their children, maybe even teaching parenting skills.

Children should be made to understand that they must meet certain minimum standards, and they must do so within the regular school year, during day school hours. Many students depend on the availability of summer and evening school. If these options were not available, then there would be some serious attitude adjustments.

If the NYC school system were to set high standards, and insist that students meet them, then the students would perform to those high standards. What students in NYC know is that if they fail a class in the regular school year then they can take it at night or in the summer and they will do even less work and get a passing grade. This has a lot to do with the attitudes of evening and summer school teachers (myself excluded) who seem to use a very relaxed grading policy. I have heard comments such as "the only thing a student has to do to pass my class is sit down and be quiet", "all a student has to do to pass my class is not get on my nerves", "I give all my students passing grades", "I pass them on so I don't have to see them again", "I pass them, after all how many times can they fail". Students have learnt quite well—if there is a subject you need to graduate, but it is too difficult for you, don't expend the energy to improve, instead, cut class and take a failing grade. Then in the summer or evening school session, take the class again, make sure you don't have too many absences, and you will pass, simple dimple.

Whittemore High School, South Bronx (July, 1994)

I was called in to replace a teacher who quit after 1 day. The experience lasted less than a week and the only good memory I have of it is that they had a new science lab—I was teaching science classes in the lab. I was given a beautiful science curriculum called the Summer Science Institute, which in my humble opinion is one of the best science curricula introduced into NYC in recent years. It was actually developed at the University of California, and it comes with a day-by-day instructional guide.

Why was this experience nightmarish? Let's just say that bad students and a disciplinary code that is not enforced will turn the best curriculum to mush. From my first day at the school I was convinced the students belonged in a special education class. If there were chandeliers in the room they would have been swinging from them. I immediately started filing complaints with the school administrators; nothing was done to address the situation. I tried to discharge unruly students; they were put back in the class.

On my third day at Whittemore I was observed. The AP, a Ms. Harvey, came in during the last 15 minutes of my first period class. She sat down; students still 'swinging from the chandeliers', she offered no assistance. She wrote up an evaluation that said my lesson was unsatisfactory. I told her that I was not willing to sign the report which she shoved at me, because I felt it was a bit unfair of her to give me an unsatisfactory based on the last 15 minutes of a class that was an hour and a half long. She didn't care about what I had to say. She walked out in a huff.

Would you believe this same AP observed me teaching a few years later in evening school and tried to offer me a teaching job? Of course at that time I was making plans to get out of teaching in NYC. She told me how impress she was with my teaching, and how much teachers like me were needed in NYC. I thought, "it's a pity the NYC school system doesn't appreciate teachers like me".

Anyway, less than 15 minutes later the Principal came up with the Superintendent. (I actually found out later that the man who was standing at the front of my class with the Principal was the Superintendent. He did not introduce himself to me or my students, and that was the first and last time I ever saw a superintendent in my 5½ years of teaching in NYC.) Later, Mr. Lyons, whom I knew from Berger High School, came by to persuade me to sign the observation report.

There are no hard and fast rules for conducting classroom observations, but still, there is a right way and a wrong way to conduct them. The right way is the one used by good administrators, and the method used when the aim is the benefit of the teacher. The wrong way is often the method used by poor administrators, which is usually of little or no benefit to the teacher and often does more harm to the teacher than good. When an administrator dislikes a teacher and wants him or her removed from their school, the wrong way is the method of choice. I say 'their school', because most school administrators I have met behave as if the school and everything in it belong to them. To put it mildly, the reasons for giving an unsatisfactory can be trivial and petty, even bordering on the absurd.

The purpose of the AP of Supervision is the improvement of instruction, and the sole purpose of classroom observations is to enable the AP to help the teacher improve classroom instruction. I took some supervisory courses while I was teaching, and I learnt this in one such course.

An ideal observation involves what's called a pre-observation conference, which represents part of a continuous dialogue between teacher and AP. During this pre-observation conference, the AP discusses with the teacher which class is to be observed. For instance, it's really pointless to observe a chemistry teacher teaching an earth science class if that chemistry teacher has 4 chemistry classes that you can choose from. You might think that this is stating the obvious, but I have actually been observed several times teaching subjects other than that which I am certified to teach.

During the pre-observation conference it's also customary to discuss what aspects of the classroom instruction will be the focus of the classroom observation. What such a strategy does is it prevents the teacher and the AP from overwhelming each other. This step-wise strategy is rather useful for new teachers because it does wonders for a teacher's overall professional development.

The next step is the actual observation at the time and date agreed on, which will focus on those aspects of classroom instruction agreed on in the pre-observation conference. This ensures that the teacher doesn't feel any undue stress at the prospect of a classroom observation. The stress of being observed without warning can cause a teacher who would otherwise conduct a great lesson to just mess up.

Next is the post-observation conference wherein the teacher and the AP discuss the observed lesson, still with a focus on those aspects of classroom instruction that were agreed on during the pre-observation conference and focused on during the observation. They may also discuss what aspects of the teacher's teaching need improvement, and hence need to be the focus of the next observation. They may even plan a date for the next pre-observation conference. At this time if the observation report is written up, the teacher will be asked to read and sign it, or in another day or 2 the teacher will receive a written report to sign, and given a copy for his or her file. The other copy is place in the teacher's file at the school.

Teachers have a right to request their file and see what's in it. School administrators are not supposed to place anything in a teacher's file without the teacher's knowledge. This can never be taken for granted though. As a result when a teacher determines that he or she is on a school administrator's shit list, it's in the teacher's best interest to check his or her file on a regular basis.

Mr. Talbot, the Mathematics/Science AP from Berger High School, was quite famous for telling teachers they didn't need to read the observation report. He would say, "Just go ahead and sign it". If my memory serves me well, he told me that for all 10 reports he gave me to sign. Ms. Hardy, a fellow teacher, who was also my union-appointed mentor, recounted an occasion in which Mr. Talbot gave her a blank sheet of paper and told her to sign it and he would write the report on it later.

The NYC standard is for the untenured teacher to get 3 observations each semester. After tenure, observations take place a minimum of once per semester. At Cooper High School in Brooklyn, I worked for a year and received only one written classroom observation. The AP was always saying, "Oh, you know, when I walk into your classroom to hand you papers I am also observing your teaching". That does not benefit me if there is no feedback.

Anyway, to get back to the story, I signed Ms. Harvey's observation report and she went on her merry way. When I got home I called up the summer school office and told them I was quitting. The woman I spoke to begged me to stay, explaining that they were short of science teachers. There's always a shortage of science teachers in NYC, and an even greater shortage of good science teachers. I told her under the circumstances there was no way I was going back to Whittemore High School. The next day the Summer School office called and assigned me to Wheeler High School in downtown Brooklyn. They were only too happy when I told them I would give it a try.

I later found out that a number of other teachers tried teaching the classes I gave up on at Whittemore and all of them ended up quitting. It was a special education teacher who actually stayed for the summer.

Wheeler High School, Brooklyn (July—August, 1994)

I took over the 2 biology classes from a Jamaican teacher. She had everything very well organized. She even told me where to get great food and entertainment in the area.

I remember a lot about Wheeler, which is kind of unusual for a summer school experience. I recall it was a very hot room even with the windows open. I also recalled the horrible condition of the room. I was amazed at how hard the students worked under those conditions.

I remember 2 students in particular. One was a skinny boy with dreads who insisted he wanted to marry me. The other was a skinny, light-skinned boy with a slightly oversized head, who amazed me by the eloquence of his speech. I recall one day he mentioned that he was unable to perform to his usual speed because he was 'firing on one cylinder'.

I had some horrible experiences at Wheeler too. I came in on reorganization day (which is the day set aside for summer school teachers to enter students' grades so they can be sent to their home school) and forgot my bubble sheets (sheets on which students grades are to be bubbled in) at home. The principal told me I'd better go home and get them or he would see to it that I never worked in summer school again (as if that was a terrible thing). I had to go from Brooklyn home to the Bronx and back to Brooklyn by train. In addition to that my salary was docked for the time I took to travel to the Bronx and back.

Let's not stop there. I was observed by a Don Seeley who wrote me up an unsatisfactory observation. I was just so hot and bothered that I didn't even make an issue of it. This Don Seeley later wanted to hire me to work at the high school where he served as AP because he was so impressed when he observed me teaching evening school later that year.

It amazes me that in their anal retentiveness supervisors don't seem to realize that it's almost impossible to expect the same level of detail and commitment from a summer school teacher as you would from that same teacher during the regular school year. The summer school teacher is usually teaching in a building with which she is unfamiliar—the lucky teachers are the ones who get to teach summer school or evening school at the same school where they work during the regular school year. As a result of this the teacher has much less resources at her fingertips. I certainly know I would probably be laughed to scorn if I were to ask for the use of a school's laser disc player during the summer.

To make matters worst the teacher is teaching in temperatures above 90°F in the worst classroom the school has to offer. Add to this the fact that you are teaching students who are there because they failed the course as taught by a teacher who had available about 90 days and access to resources. Incredibly enough, the same course content that took 90 days during the regular school year is to be completed in less than 30 days in summer/evening school.

While we are on the subject, let's spend some time talking about summer school teaching, and why it's just a huge waste of taxpayers' money.

I taught summer school in the summer of 1999 wherein less than 15% of the students who took Regents exams passed though most of the students had taken the exams in June of that same year. Let's not stop there, most of the students who passed were students who took the exams as 'walk-ins' (students who did not attend summer school).

The majority of teachers teaching summer school are those who don't make enough money during the regular school year. This is an indication that they are either new or uncertified teachers. We almost lost our hair at the end of one summer school because such a large number of teachers had no idea what they were doing. The principal held several meetings to no avail teachers were still in the dark regarding what to do and how to do it.

As I mentioned before the summer session is more intense, and it's not uncommon for the summer exams to be harder than those given in June. In the summer school classes that I taught in 1999 there was 100% failure for the chemistry final exam (which is set by the City of New York), and 100% failure for the chemistry Regents exam. This was a first for my experience. I only taught the students for 12 days of the summer semester. They started out with no teacher, had one teacher who stayed for about 3 weeks then left, then I came along. Understandably it's hard for me to judge them objectively. However, the results were not a lot different for the other chemistry classes that had teachers from the beginning.

I proctored one of the August 1999 mathematics Regents exams, and was shocked at how many students left without a strong attempt on parts II and III. They sat for 2 hours and came up with nothing, so when they told me they tried but they just couldn't do it, I had no choice but to believe them. Unfortunately not doing parts II and III meant an automatic failure.

Teachers' grading policy for summer school is extremely relaxed. According to one teacher he gives students grades based on whether or not they give him a hard time. Which means all a student has to do to get a passing grade in his class is sit down and be quiet. When I mention that I like to stick to the grading policy set by the school administration, I was told to consider the fact that if I fail a student in summer school I am likely to see that student again in September. Quite frankly, I don't mind seeing the same student twice taking the same course. I actually had one such student. I had her in evening school in the fall and then again in the spring. She barely made a passing grade the second time around, though I was using the same materials that I used in the fall—I gave the same homeworks, the same exams, and even the same class assignments.

Over the years I have found that students who are willing to work hard and abide by my strict rules of operation are usually happy to have me twice (usually not for the same subject). On the other hand, students looking for the easy way out usually endeavor to get a program change when they see my name on their class program schedule.

The administrators who work summer school are usually those not making enough money during the regular school year. Teachers used to make more per hour than administrators, so an administrator had to be pretty hard up to sweat it out in the summer heat to make less money than the people he or she was supervising. The recent supervisor contract increased the hourly salary, but that did little for improving the quality of summer school administrators.

This is the part I find most irritating. Students are so used to the idea of passing summer school without doing any work that no matter how hard you try to get the inverse across to them they refuse to accept it. This summer I received this 2-page letter of plea from one such student:

8–12–99

Dear Ms. Moline,

Well after four years of High School I am still here without a diploma. Though it is by no means your fault, it is the horrible truth. My name is Leandra Amando from your first period Chemistry class osis# 111–222–333. I am writing to you not just to plead with you but to acknowledge my concern with the NYC Board of Education. The minimum requirement of credits to obtain one's diploma is 40. I have 42 but different schools ask for different criteria. My school not only requires 40 credits but it also requires a sequence of 3 years of math and 3 years of science equaling 6 credits of each. I have been in honors level classes *as well as AP classes in other subjects but I only have 5 of the 6 required science credits. I failed Chem 2 twice already, this summer school would be my third. I admit the first time I didn't take it seriously, the second I put somewhat of an effort but not much, this led to me not graduating. I was not allowed to even attend the ceremony. This being my 3rd time I tried to pass the final but I believe I was not able to.*

After not graduating I was told by the Head of Admissions at Adelphi University that without my diploma I would not be able to enroll for the fall semester but if I didn't pass in the summer, I would lose my acceptance. On top of this I lost a scholarship for failing to graduate. Now I am aware that this is not your problem, and if I didn't seem to make an effort I would fail but I want to move on I want to start at Adelphi, I don't want to be held back in chemistry for a 3rd time please understand my situation. I want to move on and prove that I can be something not just a failure I am begging all I need is the minimum passing grade. I am only writing to you because I know you care about your students. If you didn't care about them you would not have called the night before the final please after not having a teacher the first few days of school and then having him leave after the midterm I just want to continue my education but in college not high school.

Thank you for your time
Leandra Amando

Please just the minimum passing grade that is all I ask.
718–222–3333

I did glance at this letter, but this is the first time I read the entire letter. Interestingly enough I did give this student a passing grade, he was borderline, and I could see no reason to give him a failing grade so he got a 65 (the minimum passing grade). I don't know if what's in the letter was true, but I hope he has moved on to better things. The Board is overloaded with unimaginative administrators; so too is the Regents and the State Department of Education.

Bissell Evening High School, Bronx (September 1994 to January 1995)

I was quite pleased when I was assigned to teach chemistry at Bissell High School's evening school. I had heard a lot of good things about Bissell, and was in the process of trying to get a daytime position there. It was much closer to where I lived in the Bronx than Berger High School. Sometimes you get to meet people in evening school who are able to have some influence in getting you into the day school. Needless to say I was not successful in making any such connections.

I did have quite a nice experience there though. The discipline was quite strict, to the extent wherein I was able to teach classes with over 40 students with little or no hassle. Also, I had a number of older students; 2 of my students were older than I was.

The oldest student in the class, a 36-year-old Hispanic man gave me a gift-wrapped Christmas present—a purse with a planner in the middle. I still have that purse, and I used to take it with me everywhere I went. It has been 7 years, and that purse is still going strong. It was the only time I received a gift from a student (greeting cards excluded of course).

The only negative thing I can recall was that a supervisor called me at home and tried to get me to give a passing grade to a student who failed one of my classes. I asked if the grading policy had changed from the one I had been given. I was told it hadn't. I told him that in that case I could not change the grade.

Over the years I have been proud of the fact that I have always maintained fairness in the manner in which I grade students. I don't believe a student should be able to talk his or her way to a good grade. It's always uplifting to me that my class grades seem to always match the way my students perform on Regents exams. For the most part my average for both class and Regents has been about 70%, which is a pretty good record for a science teacher in NYC. I knew a teacher who consistently got 100% passing for a Regents science course, and no he was not teaching in a specialized high school. My best results were 91% on a Regents exam, and 100% for a non-Regents summer school class.

[07]At Northeastern, with the exception of my first semester when I averaged 70%, I was averaging over 90% on the chemistry Regents. One semester I had 100% passing; I was very proud of those students because about 50% of the class struggled throughout the entire course.

Saturday SAT Preparation Hoffman High School, Manhattan (October 1994 and March 1995)

I truly believe this program was started as a means of helping a publisher to sell SAT preparation books to the Board. The first Saturday saw a wave of students registering then subsequent Saturdays would see a gradual decline in the number of students. It was a consensus among teachers and administrators that the students only came so they could get the book, yet there wasn't much of an attempt to encourage students to remain in the program.

Consider this, the program was a few Saturdays starting in October, next another set of Saturdays starting in March. How much can you teach students in that time, especially students who are lacking those aforementioned basic skills?

A lot of noise is currently being made about continuous assessment. If you are going to continuously assess students you must have some system in place to ensure continuous uplifting for those students whose performances demonstrate a need for it. Otherwise you will continue to have students who fall through the cracks. I have met several 12th graders who were getting ready to graduate high school, but were illiterate, and I do mean illiterate—reading at an elementary child's reading level, can't spell, have difficulty with simple arithmetic, unable to comprehend what they read, and have difficulty following simple instructions. I wish I were talking about mostly non English speaking students, but I am not.

I remember how eager the students who stayed with the SAT preparation program were, and how much I enjoyed teaching them mathematics. I believe basic mathematics as given on the SAT should be second nature to students by the time they complete high school. Unfortunately this is not the case.

I had a first hand opportunity to observe peer tutoring—I would go over a problem on the board, and the students who understood my explanation would break it down for their classmates. Sometimes the student tutor would repeat my explanation verbatim, and his or her peer would claim to understand it finally.

One sad memory is that this was the last time I saw my best friend, Kay Samuel, alive in a teaching situation. She died of breast cancer in the summer of 1996. Teaching in a poorly run school is a serious health hazard. In my experience I have found teachers tend to get sick and die more often in poorly run schools than in those with strong administration. I think it may have a lot to do with job stress, which has been shown to be a huge risk factor for adverse health conditions.

The other negative thing I remember was that a supervisor came to observe me every Saturday, even though I only had about 6 students in the class. I couldn't help wondering if this administrator couldn't find anything better to occupy his time. The NYC school system works on the basis of who knows who. If an administrator has connections he can have the system create a position for him so he can get paid, even if there's no work to be done.

Langley High School, Queens (February 1995 to June 1996)
I will never forget the level of discipline, which was standard at Langley. The first time I walked down the corridor at Langley High School as a new teacher I saw students snatch off their hats on seeing me. As teachers we did not have to tell students to take off their hats or walkmans. I was able to run the "if I see it, it's mine" line on students regarding hats and walkmans, and it actually worked.

The quality of students at Langley was also quite impressive. One year Langley students came second in the science competition, beating both Bronx High School of Science, and Stuyvesant High School (actual name of school). For the years I was at Langley their Regents results were about 70% passing for both chemistry and biology, and 100% passing for physics.

I met a number of students at Langley who ran their own businesses. Probably the most impressive thing about Langley students was the fact that they were quite modest with their success, especially in the way they dressed. This was in sharp contrast to some schools I taught where students had to have the latest of whatever wear was in fashion, even if they couldn't afford it.

Langley had one of the best school administrations I ever came across. The deans were ultra strict. All I had to do was give the go ahead and a student would be suspended. So when I told students I would have them suspended, it was not just an idle threat. If I had a student in my class who was giving me a hard time, I would tell my supervisor, and he would come to my class, remove the student and read that student the 'riot act'. Then after class, both the supervisor and I would have a talk with the student's parent. Parent involvement was also a big thing at Langley. When I called up a parent, there was immediate improvement in the student. On open school night there were long lines of parents waiting to meet with teachers to find out how their children were doing.

When I taught at Berger, we had early dismissal at least once per month so we could have meetings—departmental meetings, and faculty conferences. I think I went to 2 faculty conferences the entire time I was at Langley, and our department meetings were 15 minutes of meaningful discussion during the regular school day. The science department was 6 teachers and our AP, and we had really great rapport with each other.

Unfortunately, at about the time I left Langley, a lot of other teachers did too, and the quality of the student body was on a very sharp decline.

If I had to rate all my full time teaching experiences Langley would definitely get first prize. I enjoyed teaching at Langley so much that even though I lived on Staten Island I went back to Langley for the 1995–96 school year.

I found this letter that I got from Mr. Egan, the Science Department AP, at the start of the 1995–96 school year:

9/6/95

Dear Ms. Moline:

I would like to thank you for your efforts in teaching the Earth Science curriculum last semester. It was indeed a difficult assignment because you had to pick up classes in the middle of the semester. In spite of your limited experience you were able to do a credible job because of your willingness to accept constructive criticism, and your strong belief in films and demonstrations to help reinforce concepts. This semester, with additional assistance, you should improve significantly.

Once again thanks for all your efforts and we hope that this year will be more successful than the last.

Sincerely

Jeffrey Egan

It's the only such letter I ever received, and I remember just how wonderful it felt when I received it.

Portland High School, Staten Island (July—August, 1995)

Portland High School was a very interesting place for me because it offered me a view of NYC schools that I had not been familiar with. The school was a very large building set on an extremely large piece of land. The School was surrounded by lush greenery with no limit to the amount of space students had where they could hang out and relax. I had often wondered about this of NYC Schools. Most of the schools I taught in prior to Portland were squeezed in between other buildings without even enough space to allow teacher parking let alone have a huge playing field for students to play football or soccer.

I have never been able to understand the logic behind having a school without space for students to play and socialize. Humans are social beings, yet we ask students to spend their entire lives not socializing, then we wonder why they seem not to be appropriately socialized. We expect students to spend all day going from one class to another, in which they sit quietly unless required by the teacher to speak. The only social period is lunch, which is usually spent in a room with over 100 students. I don't know of a single grown up who could abide by such rigor. This fact explains why students cut class, hang out in the halls in between classes, and talk in class while the teacher is trying to teach. These instances represent, for most students, the only opportunity they get to socialize. This could also explain why there are so many fights—likely a result of all the pent up emotions these students have.

One of the things that I have always done is allow students to socialize at the beginning and at the end of each period that I teach. To facilitate this I usually have assignments—homework and 'do now' on the chalkboard. Do now is the name given to the class assignment that students are expected to do when they enter the classroom. Would you believe some students see the do now staring them in the face, and will still inquire, "What are we supposed to do now Miss?"

Anyway, my students and I are usually of the understanding that while they copy and complete these assignments, they are allowed to speak quietly among themselves. I usually end my lesson a couple of minutes before the bell. This gives students a chance to ask questions, as well as socialize while they pack up and get ready to go to their next class.

Students like those at Langley who have extensive extracurricular activities after school seem to do better. However, many students have responsibilities, such as picking up younger siblings, which prevent them from taking part in extracurricular activities. It might not be such a bad idea to have some social programs for students during the school day. Such social programs could be a good replacement for those abundant study halls in which very little studying actually take place.

In cases when I don't have to share classroom with other teachers I usually allowed students to spend their lunch period in my classroom. It represented an opportunity for them to interact with me and with each other in a relaxed atmosphere. Over the years most of my preparation and lunch periods have been spent in the company of students.

[07]At Northeastern students would come in during such periods to review their most recent test. I knew that I had a 100% passing rate on the chemistry Regents for students that I tutor one-on-one, so when I started teaching at Northeastern I set up a grading system wherein student got an additional 5 points for coming in to review their incorrect answers on a test. I don't believe in changing the rules in the middle of the game, hence students were able to take advantage of the opportunity regardless of grade. Which meant a student could score as high as 105%. There were teachers who had misgivings about this method, but I saw the result in terms of how well my students did in the class as well as on the Regents. I have had students who struggle the entire semester, but manage to pass both the class and the Regents because they were always willing to take advantage of these pri-

vate tutoring sessions. I was giving the students for free what I used to charge $30 per hour for.

Needless to say I was very impressed with Portland High School's extensive space, and the student's use of this space. The other phenomena I encountered at Portland were students' abuse of tobacco, and the fact that the building had central air condition. At 7:45 in the morning I would have to wade through the dense fog of cigarette smoke in order to enter the building. I had never seen so many teen smokers before, and I was quite shaken by it. Teaching summer school in an air-conditioned room made a world of difference. The room was so cool that most students wore sweaters, and I always wore a blazer.

At Portland I had my second opportunity to teach the *Summer Science Institute*. The program was wonderful as I said before. It was interactive, hands-on and fun. I would rate that course as the best program of instruction I ever taught, and that class of pre 9th graders as the best students I ever taught. At the time I was also taking a really great course on cooperative learning—the only graduate education course I took which taught me something that I was able to apply in the classroom. I had a great opportunity to practice much of what I was learning. On realizing the beauty of cooperative learning, I have since made a concerted effort to use it every chance I get.

One of the students that stand out in my mind was a pert little Italian girl, who was quite insubordinate in the beginning. On the last day of the course, I had a little session with the students in which they spoke about their feelings about the course, and I told them how much fun I had teaching them. In the midst of all this, that little Italian girl left her seat, ran up to the desk and hugged me. I was totally amazed.

On the last day, one of the things I did was have students write things about themselves on index cards. One of the card entries was 'write 2 adjectives to describe you'. There was one girl there who was quite problematic because the other students didn't seem to like working with her, and she was quite averse to working with others. I solved the problem somewhat by making the groups totally random. She ended up working with a very bright boy named Brian Philips, and they did an excellent end of semester report.

I went around the room calling on students to read their card to the class. Everyone readily read his or her card, except for this girl. She insisted she preferred to show me her card after class. At the end of class when all the other students left (she was usually the last one to leave the room), she came over and showed me her card. The 2 adjectives she had to describe herself were 'fat' and 'stupid'. I was saddened and angry because I knew she wasn't describing her; she was merely repeating descriptions that she had heard from others. I told her that I did not want to hear other people's description of her, but her description of herself. I had her sit for a while to try to come up with adjectives that she felt described her. She did manage to come up with 2 more appropriate adjectives. I have often wondered what became of her. She was getting ready to start high school, and I knew with her demolished self-esteem she was in for quite a rough high school experience.

Hedley High School, Cleveland (August 1996 to May 1997)

Probably my most impressive memory of Hedley High School was of an incident I heard about in which a teacher and a student were involved in a fight. The student, Mark Farvin, was quite a little troublemaker. The students from my 4th and 7th period classes came in that day and gave blow by blow descriptions that indicated the teacher and the student were on the floor fighting it out, and the teacher definitely got the award for the win. Some reports said that the teacher stomped Mark, others said she swung him like a rag doll. I had one question for all the reporters—"Did anyone take any pictures?" Alas there were no pictures.

The student was suspended and the teacher went on about her business. Had it been NYC it would have been the other way around. The teacher would have been arrested and thrown into the **Rubber Room** to await trial, and Mark would have gone on his merry way. Hence the reason I wanted pictures.

Cooper High School, Brooklyn (September 1998 to June 1999)

The man who was principal at Cooper High School was the worst principal I ever came across. He wasn't qualified to manage a set of thumbtacks. Evidence to just how flawed the NYC school system was he went on to become superintendent of one of the City's largest school district.

Teacher turnover was the order of the day at Cooper. When I started teaching there at the start of the 1998 school year, there were a total of 16 new teachers. I can count on one hand how many of those 16 new teachers remain.

The other order of the day at Cooper was social promotion. A willingness to engage in social promotion was subtly promoted as a requirement for having a successful teaching experience at Cooper. Teachers were cornered in administrators' offices, and forced to change grades. If the teacher did not complete the desired grade changes, rumor had it that members of the school administration would do the honors for the teacher.

I was not willing to engage in social promotion, since it goes against everything I believe in when it comes to education. I am sure the final grades I submitted at Cooper were changed. I can't actually prove it, but I can almost guarantee that students to whom I gave failing grades were on rosters at colleges in the fall of 1999.

Milton Evening High School, Brooklyn (February 1999 to June 1999)

The most impressive thing about Milton was the efficiency with which the evening school ran. The students in evening school who attended the school during the day were always complaining about how much they hated the school, which is a good indication that the same efficiency existed in the day school.

This was the first time I taught evening school and was allowed lab supplies. At the start of the semester I gave the lab technician a list of labs I intended to conduct during the semester, along with a list of the supplies I would need for each lab. When I got to the school at 5:00 pm, which was the schedule starting time for the lab, the technician would bring in all the supplies I requested for that day. Just before 6:00 pm, when the lab was scheduled to end, she would return to pick up the supplies. The technician was an elderly woman, who seemed to be working post-retirement.

Fortunately it was not the last time I was given the use of lab supplies. It seemed the Board started to take lab sessions more seriously for Regents classes. When I again taught evening school in the fall of 1999, we were allowed to use lab supplies and conduct labs in the school's science lab, and there was a lab technician available to prepare the labs in advance.

There was no social promotion at Milton. If students had too many absences they were discharged (kicked out). If students did not abide by the rules of the evening school, they were discharged. When I handed in my grades, there was no scrutinizing look to see what sort of passing percent I had.

At Milton, the top student in my second period class was discharged because she was less than courteous to a security guard. I really felt bad for her, and was quite sad to see her leave. She wrote me the letter below asking me to help her, but the last thing a teacher wants to do is go against good administration. She had broken the rules of the evening school, and she had to pay. That's the double standard that's quite standard in NYC public schools—what a student can do in one school and get away without so much as a slap on the wrist, is cause for dismissal in another school.

June 3, 1999
Donna Applegate
Pd.2 Chemistry—Night School

Dear Ms. Moline:

I am writing this letter in concern with me being kicked out of night school and wanting to pass this class. I know as well as you the whole reason of me being kicked out was foolish. I don't want to put you in a bad predicament, however it would be very appreciative if you wrote a note to my guidance counselor concerning my grade with Chemistry 1. As you have seen I've been trying so very hard to pass this class, I will definitely do so. I am deeply sorry if I put you in a bad situation on Tuesday, but I just had to try one last time. I understand if you will not write a note to my counselor but I thought it would be good to give it a try. As you have definitely seen I never give up until I can't try anymore. I am still determined to try to pass this class, however, if I go back to school Mr. Ross informed me that I could be arrested for trespassing, and I can be arrested. I'm sorry for doing this to you but if you can find it in your heart Ms. Moline, you do not know how much I would appreciate it. Thank you for your time.

Sincerely Yours,

Donna Applegate

Bennett Carmichael Summer High School, Queens (July, 1999)

I was a substitute at this high school for about 3 days in July 1999. It was a pretty good experience. When I finally got to the school, which was way out in Queens near the border with Long Island, I thought "so this is how the better half lives". The school reminded me of Portland High School on Staten Island. It sat on a huge piece of property, with more than enough space for sporting activities, and it had central air conditioning. In my view, the major difference between Bennett Carmichael High School and Portland High School was the fact that smoking was not prevalent among the summer school students at Bennett Carmichael High School.

It was a rather easy substitute assignment. All the class assignments and lab work that were to be completed by the students were prepared by the teacher, and everything was ready for me when I got there. All I had to do was hand out the assignments, watch the students work, and answer any questions they had. I actually had the students do some of the problems on the board for the benefit of each other.

Hoffman Summer High School, Manhattan (July—August 1999)

I was called in to replace a teacher who had a family emergency in Haiti, and had to leave. I gathered that the students had been through a number of teacher changes before the Haitian teacher. The principal subtly urged that I stay until the end of the summer. I had already traveled for summer vacation, and had no additional plans for the summer, so I assured him I would stay.

It was a good experience, except it was too short for me to accomplish much. Many of the students on the class roster had pretty much given up and stopped coming, probably because of the teacher problems that they had. Most of the students who were there when I came along stayed for the remainder of the semester.

I was disappointed in the students' progress. I found that I had to almost start from scratch. I was teaching chemistry 1 and chemistry 2, which is first and second semester of the Regents chemistry curriculum. The problem was worst for chemistry 2, because they seemed not to remember much of what they were supposed to have learnt in chemistry 1. Chemistry 2 builds on the knowledge from chemistry 1; to say I had very little to build on would be an understatement.

The students worked very hard. They all failed the final exam that the City gave to be administered, and those who took the chemistry Regents failed. A lot of the students had no need or desire to take the chemistry Regents; they just needed to pass the course to meet their science credit requirement for graduation. The grading policy that the school gave me was based on a weighted average wherein the final exam was worth 10%. I used the grading policy to determine the grades of all students. The other 90% of their grade was based on their attendance in the lab sessions, homeworks, class assignments, and class exams that I gave.

Hoffman Evening High School, Manhattan (September, 1999 to June, 2000)

As punishment for my unwillingness to participate in social promotion at Cooper, I was given an unsatisfactory rating. While I was waiting to have my case resolved I taught evening school at Hoffman.

I again taught chemistry 1 and 2. It was a rather easy assignment. All the lab assignments were being done in the day school, so I just replicated them for the evening session. I used pretty much the same lessons and exams I had on file from the summer, with some minor changes. The students were great, and most of them stayed for the duration. There were a number of students who started the course and were doing well and then left for college. I guess their day school found some other means of giving them the science credit. I felt happy for them, but I am always saddened when I lose good students. I think they are such nice positive reinforcement for the weaker students. The other pleasant thing was that they did a lot better than the summer school students on both the final exam and the Regents.

PS 999, Brooklyn (February 2000 to June 2000)

I really can't remember anything good about PS 999. 2 negative things stand out in my mind. One was of the AP, Mr. Duvivier, telling me that the students I taught earth science couldn't take the grades I gave them to high school. I wondered what motive I could have for wanting to be part of their plan to trick the unsuspecting high schools.

The other is a real stinker. One my final day in the school, the principal called me into her office, and told me that if I wanted a satisfactory evaluation I would have to agree not to return to the school in September. At that point I had already gotten a job in a field other than teaching, and had no intention of ever teaching in NYC again. So I decided that though there was a battle to be fought, it was a battle I had neither the time nor the energy to fight. One of the important lessons my mentor, Ms. Hardy, taught me was to pick my battles very carefully, because not all battles are worth fighting.

Northeastern High school, Upstate New York (September, 2004 to January 2007)

Northeastern was a very different experience for me. There were a number of differences that really stood out.

Coming from school systems in which it was rare to have less than 20 students in a class, I was very pleased when I looked at my class rosters and there weren't more than 20 students in either of my 2 classes the first semester I was there. As I said before Northeastern used a semester system, so I taught the year's curriculum in 5 months using alternating 80 minutes and 160 minutes class/Lab sessions.

The other thing that impressed me was the amount of resources I had access to. The lab section of my classroom reminded me of the lab I worked in when I was in college. There were drawers at the lab desks that I could place items in and assign students to them. When it was time for lab assignments, I would simply give the students the lab instructions, and they would get out the apparatus that they needed to complete it. I had a Dell projector, and was able to do all my lessons in PowerPoint. Everything was computerized, and you can't begin to imagine how much time that freed up. Having resources made a lot of difference; at Northeastern I was able to do many of the things I always wanted to do as a teacher. The result was better student achievement. I guess what I said in **Letter to the President** bore true—'give teachers the tools and the appropriate environment and they will get the job done'.

The third item worth mentioning is the level of disrespect I was subjected to from the students. The majority of the students had very little respect for themselves, the teachers, or the administrators. Whatever obscenities popped into their heads was what they would spit at you. The discipline was way too relaxed, and students exercised maximum rights.

IN THE BEGINNING

I am a self-taught teacher. I was thrown in at the deep end—sink or swim. I needed the money, so I swam through all the filth. When I could see clearly to do so, I got out of the muck, cleaned myself up and moved on.

IN THE BEGINNING

In July of 1992, having been out of work for 2 consecutive years, I decided, against my better judgment to apply for a teaching position in the NYC public school system. My friend, Kay Samuel, had been teaching for about 2 years by then, and maintained that so long as you didn't allow the students to walk all over you, it wasn't all that bad.

I went through the application process, and had my fingerprints taken so they could be sent to the Federal Bureau of Investigation in Washington D.C. By August I was ready to look for work. Between the last week of August and the start of school, I had called just about all the schools in the Bronx. 2 schools requested that I come in for interviews—Berger High School, and Whittemore High School, both in the South Bronx. When my family got wind of the news they were appalled. "How can you go to teach in the South Bronx", they echoed my fears.

I was neat and conservatively dressed in navy for my interview at Berger. When I got off the bus, I counted my blessings, there were no drug addicts shooting up on the street. That, I believe, was my expectation.

Nevertheless, this was no tranquil site. The word ghost town formed in my mind as I tried to find my bearings. All I saw were tall buildings, none of which looked occupied. I consoled myself by the fact that it was mid-morning on a bright sunny day.

The school was a far cry from what I was used to back home in Barmenia. There was no flower-lined walkway that led to the building's entrance. You simply walked off the street and into the building. There were no immaculate hedges; instead the building was surrounded by a fence, which had holes in too many places. The only thing in the enclosure apart from the school building was a parking lot. Where do the children play, I couldn't but wonder. I honestly could not imagine a school without a playing field.

The interior of the building had a personality all its own, it gave no credence to what lay outside. I thought, "This is like in the movies". I walked past a lovely big auditorium; there was a huge curtain on the stage. When I was in high school, such an auditorium was a dream my classmates and I worked hard to achieve. Yet the dream was never realized. My school just never made enough money to build an auditorium. The building was very clean; clean walls, and shiny floors. I kept saying to myself, "My God they polished the floors".

I took an instant distrust of the science AP, Mr. Talbot, with whom I had my interview. A tall white man with bulging stomach, bald head, and glasses that seemed to belong on his face. He wore shoes that reminded me of the safety shoes we wore when I worked in industry. He made mention of having had an accident, that being the only thing he ever said to me that I actually believed. He seemed the great pretender, a misfit, in the tense calm of the surroundings he stood out like a scream. He was willing to accept me as a biology teacher. That meant a job, finally, that fact cancelled out every negative thing I could think of.

The Principal, Nellyann Thomson, whom I met on my second trip to Berger, was a different story. She seemed confident and at home in her extremely large office. I felt as if I was in a company boardroom rather than a principal's office.

Nellyann was a tall black woman who was neatly dressed in a conservative suit, her hair pulled back into a bun. I felt she was wearing too much make-up, but she still managed to command my respect. I came home from my interview thinking it may not be so bad after all.

On my third trip to Berger, the students came, and I thought, "WHAT A FUCKING NIGHTMARE." My first semester was that exactly, a nightmare; a nightmare that nothing in my prior life could have prepared me for.

On my first 2 meetings with the students I pretty much regurgitated what Mr. Talbot had told me to say: "My name is Miss Moline, and I will be teaching you electricity for the remainder of the semester." My God, electricity, what the hell did I know about electricity. I was a chemist. The post of chemistry teacher was reserved for Mr. Talbot. After all, with 6 students, it was probably the smallest class in the school. At my interview I had been offered the post of biology teacher. Somehow that had changed, and the Regents biology class was being taught by day-to-day substitutes.

Most of the substitutes came and left after only one day. Then along came a Jamaican woman. She was a biology teacher with years of experience. Not only did she have a Masters in education, she was working on her Doctorate at Columbia University's Teachers College. Mr. Talbot volunteered information about the new biology teacher to me. I told him if she was Jamaican she would stay, and she did. However, when the semester came to a close in January of 1993, she was excessed—she got a letter stating that the School no longer had a position for her, and she should remain in the school and await further instructions. She was sent to Marcus High School in the Bronx. I saw her at the end of the school year at a workshop. She was enjoying Marcus, and especially enjoying their high percent passing on Regents science exams, and the appreciative nature of the science AP.

Before Berger my only experience with teaching was a part time stint 4 years prior. At the time I was fresh out of University, and working for a food processing plant in Barmenia. The salary I earned working in this food processing plant was so pathetic, I felt inclined to moonlight. I managed to get a teaching position at the most prestigious high school in the area. I taught chemistry from 9 am to noon on Saturdays. The pay was even more shocking than what I was getting from my full time job, but the students were great. I would spend a great deal of time preparing for my lectures, which is basically what they were. I was teaching twelfth grade chemistry, which is the equivalent of first year chemistry at the university level. The students sat, listened, asked intelligent questions, and took notes. I at no time even had to raise my voice.

In the summer of 1999 I visited Barmenia and spoke to the principal of the high school I attended there. The school has had the same principal for the entire 25 years of its existence. I also spoke to a former classmate who was a teacher at the school. I listened in shocked horror as they detailed what's currently taking place in high schools in Barmenia. The schools are being demolished by drug involvement, poor management, and parentless children. Both the principal and my former classmate expressed that they had plans of getting out of the system. The principal expressed that he intended to do one more semester and then he would leave. It's hard to imagine what my alma mater will be like when that 25-year legacy comes to an end. My former classmate very 'Jordanly' expressed that if the principal leaves then he would definitely follow suit in the not too distant future. I visited Barmenia in December of 2001, and found that they were both gone.

It's not just something about America; or as my sister so quaintly puts it, "something in the water". It would seem juvenile delinquency has become an international problem—*To Sire with Love* revisited. What's the reason? What are the answers? Is it a case of too many child protection laws, and not enough discipline? Your guess is as good as mine.

In my first couple days of teaching at Berger I tried the approach I had used in Barmenia. It was totally futile.

I had 4 tenth grade classes of electricity and one 9th grade physical science class, which I taught in a huge classroom on the second floor of the 3-story school building. It was a nice room with polished wood floors. The only problem I had with the room was that there was no chalkboard. I had a white board on which I would write using colored dry-erase markers. I had a major problem with the location of the room though. It was next door to Mr. Talbot's office, and when my classes were being unruly he would come over. If it helped, it would have been okay, except his presence only served to further agitate my students. They had no respect for him, and they certainly didn't pay attention to anything that he had to say.

I'll never forget what he did during one of those periods in which he came in to observe my teaching. He got up in the midst of my teaching, took the marker from me, and started teaching my class. His action upset my students much more than it did me. They started screaming for him to leave. One student got out of her seat and proceeded to push him out of the room, and then others joined in. They pushed him out of the room, and closed the door behind him. Then they requested that I pick up from where I was so rudely interrupted. It was an amazing thing.

Talbot wasn't much of an administrator on the job, and from all indications he didn't do too well at home either. He made mention that his son ran away from home, and was doing drugs. Judging by his ability to be overly content with getting to work at 7:15 am, and not be in much of a rush to get home, I assumed his love life was also inert. He was an irritatingly touchy person. He couldn't seem to talk to me without touching my arm or my shoulder. One day he came into my classroom while I was there alone. He had some supposedly important matter to discuss with me. Amidst his talking to me, his hand found its way to my leg and rested there. I halted all conversation and just stared at that intrusive hand on my leg. He followed my gaze to his hand. He immediately pulled his hand away and apologized; thereafter he curbed his touchiness.

Anyway, what the hell did I know about electricity. Well I had done well in physics, and the material was similar, though a bit outdated. My students went away, and complained that I was teaching them like they were in college. I revised, and dropped my level of teaching, yet there were still numerous complaints. I had to lower the teaching level until I was virtually spoon-feeding the students before the complaints diminished. The complaints never actually ceased, but I decided I was willing to bear the complaints, but I wasn't going to drop standards any lower. As I later learnt, the students had even gone to the extreme of petitioning Principal Thomson to get rid of me. Evidently I expected too much from my students in the way of intelligence and maturity.

Even with my lowered standards in a very easy course, which the students were also learning in shop (Berger was a vocational high school where the focus was electronics) the passing rate hovered just above 60%.

Throughout my years of teaching, I was consistently amazed by the inefficiencies of NYC high school students. Even those who managed to make it to college ended up having trouble. Remediation is the order of the day. As one teacher told it, the students go to college and pay to take remedial courses so they can learn what they could have learned for free in public high school. In 1999 the City University of New York (CUNY) voted to end remediation in its senior colleges beginning in January of 2000 (CUNY Office of University Relations, information obtained from CUNY web site). According to the resolution, students in need of remedial classes will have to take them at CUNY's community colleges or at the senior colleges during the summer sessions.

The common complaint from students who managed to survive Berger and get into college was "we never learnt how to study". I thought back to when I was in school. I was never taught how to study; I read books that gave studying tips, and I developed a method that worked for me.

I don't think students in NYC realize that they need to do for themselves. They have come to expect everything to be handed to them on a silver platter. Why should they expect any less? The system provides books, transportation, food, counseling, condoms, and every means possible for students to make it through high school without even trying.

Needless to say, in my second year at Berger, Principal Thomson put in place a system wherein the first week of instruction for each semester was to focus on the topic, *How to Study*. We were even given instruction regarding what to teach—parts of the textbook and how to use them; and when and where to study. Indeed the silver platter had to have all the trimmings. How amazing that with all the money that's spent providing books for students in NYC schools these students would not know the parts of a textbook and how to use them. Believe it or not, a lot of students still don't know this.

I think after we started teaching *How to Study* as the first order of business each semester, students did learn how to study. Of course, as I could have told anyone prior to *How to Study*, the students still didn't study. You can lead a horse to water, but you can't make him drink.

Students are baffled by multiplication and division. Yes, I am referring to high school students; hundreds of them that I have met. For instance, students can't seem to understand that a number such as 5 can be divided by 10. They simply think it's impossible. Those who don't think it's impossible, think the answer is 2. Forget about asking students to multiply by fractions, or do anything with fractions for that matter.

If a test is given, students can't compute the value of each question based on the number of questions given, and the fact that the test is scored out of 100 points. How hard should it be to compute the value of each question if there are 20 of them on a test, especially when most of the tests you are given have 20 questions.

Mr. Mason, a former Langley High School teacher recalled a student asking that very question. He turned it back to the student, "you figure it out, if there are 20 questions on the test, what's the value of each question?" The student sat down and agonized over the problem for at least 10 minutes; ultimately giving up. Mason, with the intention of challenging the student, said, "Each question is worth 3 points." The student thanked him, and went merrily on his way.

Quite frankly, I think a lot of students don't know they are failing a class until they see it on their report cards. Far be it for us to expect them to do something about it, worst of all something as novel as studying.

As I mentioned Berger was my first full time teaching experience, and I had no formal teacher training to fall back on. All my prior work experiences were in private industry. I taught by trial and error; surprisingly most of the things I tried worked. I think the reason a lot worked in my classroom was because I had high expectations for my students. I knew that if I didn't have high expectations for my students then it would be time to stop teaching.

One of the things I tried was implemented throughout Berger the following year. In my first week at Berger, Talbot showed me all the form letters that were sent home when students misbehaved. Coming from a school system that was big on elaborate systems for rewards rather than punishment, I asked him, "So what do you send out when the students are good." "Well," he said, "they are bad so often we didn't even think of coming up with such a form". I asked him if it would be okay for me to come up with such a form. He said it was okay with him. So I came up with a form where I could check off various wonderful things that the students had done. I did a mass mailing of the form letter; all but my most excessively absent students got one.

One student, a big serious boy named Marlon, came into class one day almost on the verge of tears. He said, "Ms. Moline you made my mom so happy." "What are you talking about?" I asked. I had actually forgotten about sending the letters. "That letter that you sent," he said, insisting on getting my acknowledgement. I smiled at him and he smiled back.

The following semester Talbot handed us a form letter to send home for students—it looked painfully similar to my form letter. The following year Nellyann handed out an improved version of the form letter—it was being promoted throughout the School.

I was watching Jeopardy at home one evening, and got the idea that it would be an excellent way to review with students. I went to work and tried it out with my chemistry class, and they loved it so much I had to keep doing it. Now I notice that a major textbook publisher even has a book of questions for chemistry Jeopardy. I also do tic tac toe and bingo as variations on the Jeopardy game. Students get to block each other from winning by correctly answering questions. In classes where I hear sexist criticisms I do battle of the sexes where I split the class into 2 groups, boys versus girls.

Also in my first semester at Berger I was asked to fill out certificates to be handed out to students who were doing well. I filled out certificates for all but my most excessively absent students. I heard criticism; there were teachers who felt I made a mockery of the award ceremony. I remember sitting in the auditorium and hearing all the whispers when my students went up for their awards—"George Nueva got an award you've got to be kidding me—for what".

You see what they didn't understand was I had a plan. I was doing trial and error, and I was going with whatever worked. By all accounts I always had some of Berger's toughest students, yet they were perfect students in my classroom. When I saw them in action in other classes I couldn't believe I was observing the same students.

Near the end of my second year at Berger I told my students I would give really good prizes to students who got 90% or above on the chemistry Regents. One student got a 93% and was awarded a walkman. I think if the students realize how serious I was about the prizes I would have had to give out more prizes.

On average about 50% of students would pass the science Regents and the science classes at Berger. However, an average of about 70% of my students would pass my class and the Regents—of course this meant my results were responsible for lifting the School average. So, it would seem the things I tried really did work.

Maybe my students were trying to impress me, which is why they did well in my class. I remember I gave this student a really expensive pen because he did well on an exam, and he was quite embarrassed. He was afraid of being seen as a nerd by his peers. The bright students at Berger that we knew about were in the small minority. To let it be known that you were intelligent was to live with being called nerd, and being pestered constantly by your peers. Hence bright students who wanted to be cool and fit in would pretend to be really dumb. I tried to change that impression in my class. I constantly rewarded students who did well, and the kind of prizes I gave made other students want to do well. I recall having a party for my top students at Berger, and we had to keep the door locked because other students wanted nothing better than to get in the room.

I once asked my students at Berger if a nerd is someone who does well in school, and is successful in life. They accused me of being a nerd, it proved my point, and I never had to deal with anyone calling someone nerd in my classroom again.

At Langley High school I had an earth science class that was very weak. There was an Asian student who stood out among the rest. He was Korean, and his name was Zhihong Han. Then there was this troubled student, Servion Valentino, who was forever pestering Zhihong. When I commended Zhihong on a job well done, Servion would blurt out something like, "I want some shrimp fried rice." He would get all the other poor performing students involved in his antics with the intention of embarrassing Zhihong. Zhihong would merely turn around, look directly at Servion, and state, "I am not Chinese I am Korean". I was always so impressed by this, because it did wonders for highlighting Servion's ignorance, and it proved Servion's teasing had not accomplished what he intended it to.

It's amazing the things students will do to fit in. At Langley High School I had a class with a large number of immigrants. Actually there were only 2 Americans in the class, both of whom had foreign-born parents. I had students from all over the world, a little bit of the United Nations you could say—Italy, Bangladesh, Dominican Republic, China, Peru, Ecuador, Honduras, India, Croatia, Russia, and Chile. Almost all the students who were recent immigrants from Hong Kong, China changed their names. On my roster they had names like Hua and Han, in class their names became Alice, Sally, Tom and John. It was the most amazing thing.

What was interesting about the Asian students at Langley was that for them fitting in meant getting really high grades. It seemed that to do poor academically mean being an outcast. Though my Asian students were from Hong Kong, and their spoken English was not very good, they never scored below 90% on any of the tests I gave, and they were the top students in the class.

Anyway, let's get back to the beginning at Berger High School. When I started working at Berger I caught them at a good time construction wise. I heard the school was in a pretty bad state, and the Board spent a few million dollars to refurbish the school. As I said before, the building was quite beautiful inside. There was one thing that was sorely lacking. Though there was a brand new science lab, the science storeroom was a great big mess, and the students were not allowed to do science labs. The standard was for the science teacher to conduct the lab work, and the students would sit in their seats and observe. If the class was really good, one lucky student would be afforded the privilege of assisting the teacher with the experiment.

In my second semester at Berger, Talbot turned over the Regents chemistry class to me along with the Regents biology class, and a physical science class. I decided there was no way I was going to teach Regents level science without having my students do hands on labs. I convinced the school administration of this, and they put forth a part time lab technician position, which I applied for and was granted.

I completely revamped the lab storeroom, and labeled and arranged all the supplies alphabetically. Then I set up a system whereby teachers were able to sign out and return supplies. Once this was in place, I pulled out the lab textbooks that had never been used, and distributed them to my students. Hence science labs returned to Berger. I faced a lot of criticisms for my efforts. There were those who guaranteed me that the students would set fire to the lab; others were counting the days until the students flooded the lab. There wasn't a single incident.

The previous semester when I taught electricity and physical science, every time I asked Talbot for supplies his answer was always "we don't have any". He would indicate that maybe if I were at one of the better schools such supplies would be available, but not at Berger. When I cleaned up the storeroom I realized that all the supplies that I inquired about, and was told we did not have, were right there in the storeroom.

I would assign the lab close to a week in advance, and my students would prepare the lab report beforehand, so all they had to do on the day of the lab was write in their results, perform the necessary calculations, and draw their conclusions. I got some of the most elaborate lab reports from my Regents classes. It's not an exaggeration to say I got college level lab reports from my students.

I guess my students had gotten used to my fiery temper, so they did not piss me off by showing up without their reports prepared. They also knew that if they did, they would have to do the lab and the write up that day or get a zero for the lab, which I would average into their grade.

About a semester after I did my stint as part time lab technician, the school hired a full time lab technician, an Asian named Mr. Chang. He was a blessing for me; he did a wonderful job of preparing labs for me, and providing me with materials for classroom demonstration. It took me a while to get used to the fact that I didn't have to do it all myself. Once I got a handle on Mr. Chang's role, I was able to further improve my efficiency.

Not only did I have my students perform hands on labs, but I also made sure each topic had a classroom demonstration, which the students were required to participate in. It was a beautiful thing, and the following year it led to the best Regents chemistry result the school had had in years.

In my second semester at Berger, Talbot talked me into becoming Computer Coordinator; this with everything else I was doing. Now when I look back at those events I do believe it was all parts of his ploy to overburden me with the hope that he would force me into quitting. Someone should have schooled him regarding the resilience of Barmenian women.

Being Computer Coordinator meant it was my job to liaison with the City-wide computer person, and get teachers to introduce their science classes to a computer program that allowed students to practice science skills in preparation for the science RCT. Talbot got me to accept the job by telling me that as computer coordinator I would receive an increase in my salary. This turned out to be just another one of his lies.

If the School were being properly managed, the program would have been managed through the electronics department. Instead I was running the program with my limited computer knowledge, and limited knowledge of the school system. The printer in the computer room was always malfunctioning. The head of the academic department, Kevin Nolte, who also taught classes in the computer room, apparently went about telling his students that I had no classroom control. According to him my poor classroom control was the reason the printer malfunctioned. It didn't matter that no one was able to explain to me the details of the printer problems. I explained that I did not need the printer on while I was conducting the computer classes, but they insisted on leaving the printer on anyway. As a result of these antics I had a tough time getting the other science teachers to take their classes into the computer room. I guess criticisms didn't roll off my colleagues as easily as they did my slick back.

As I said before I believe Talbot had me teach 3 different Regents subjects, while serving as lab technician and Computer Coordinator as his way of making sure I would decide not to come back to Berger for a second year. Well, when the year ended, not only had I managed to hold my own with all my responsibilities, I had managed to have the best overall results of the mathematics/science department.

Seeing this Talbot decided to change his strategy. He decided to get rid of me by eliminating chemistry from the department's offerings. He expended a great deal of energy convincing everyone in the Department that earth science was the way to go.

One of the main reasons I stayed in teaching after my first semester at Berger was my being assigned a mentor named Ms. Hardy. She taught me a lot of survival strategies, and she became a trusted friend. It was Ms. Hardy who cued me in on the master plan that was unfolding. She told me that we should pretend to go along with Talbot's plan. I was a bit apprehensive, because she was asking me to go along with a plan to get rid of my job. Then she explained to me that Talbot's plan was poorly thought out—the school had no earth science text books, no earth science teaching aids, no earth science lab materials, and most important no licensed earth science teacher.

Hardy went on to explain to me that she would convince Talbot to bring his great plan to Nellyann's attention—what an idiot he went eager as a beaver with his plan to Nellyann. One afternoon, shortly after my conversation with Hardy, Talbot gathered the members of the science department and escorted us to a meeting he had convened with Nellyann.

I think Hardy must have cued Nellyann about the situation, because when Talbot laid out his plan before Nellyann she asked all the pertinent questions about earth science books, teacher and teaching materials—"DO WE HAVE ANY?" When Talbot clammed up and fell into his own pit, Nellyann almost jumped him from across the conference table. Of course none of us came to his rescue. Hardy, who had pretended to be a big supporter of Talbot's plan, stepped back and left Talbot alone in the limelight.

Essentially Nellyann told Talbot she had no intention of getting rid of Chemistry for which she had both teacher and supplies, and replacing it with earth science for which she had neither.

Talbot and Nolte weren't the only ones who gave me a tough time in those early days at Berger. There was Lebrate, the old, Italian shop teacher who kept telling students that what I taught them in electricity class was wrong. I confronted him about it and made him realize that he was the one out of touch with reality.

One thing I can never be accurately accused of is teaching students inaccurate information. If I don't know something, I will research it, or I will simply tell students that I don't know the answer. The student will then marvel, "you are the teacher and you don't know!" I will then challenge the student to look up the answer to his question in return for extra credit. In my 9 years of teaching I only had one case in which a student got extra credit by this method. Of course, something as simple as Ohm's law, which is what Lebrate claimed I had wrong, I have known since the 9th grade.

I was forever being harassed by security guards. It would hardly matter how I dressed or what I did. They kept insisting that I looked like a student—I was kicked off elevators, out of offices, out of my classroom, asked for ID, etc. Of course my feeling was always that even if I were a student that was no excuse for me to be treated with such blatant disrespect. It reminded me of the NYC police officer who commented "these children are animals", because I reported seeing 4 students steal the coat of another student and kick him off the train.

No, these children are not animals, they are merely doing the things children do, and amongst them are the mischief-makers and the bullies. These children depend on us who call ourselves grownups to provide them with guidance. Any shortcoming on the part of these children represents our failure as grownups, our failure to provide guidance, and institute discipline. As far as I can see there are wide-scale failures on our part, and things won't change as long as we continue to hide behind name calling, and blaming children for their failures.

THE SCHOOL RULES

Talbot had a document which contained a set of classroom rules and a grading policy. Based on the manner in which Talbot promoted the use of the document I could tell he was the one who developed it. I guess writing such documents is something Talbot was actually quite good at; I have not seen anything as concise and elaborate at any other school. Ms Hardy always said that Talbot should have been AP for administration at Berger. Talbot had the gift of gab, especially on paper. The AP for administration, Mr. Lyons, was the opposite; he loved to teach and hated pushing paper. One of the signs of poor management is inappropriate job assignment. In many cases people who perform poorly on the job do so, not because they are deadbeats, as we like to think, but because they are misplaced. A good administrator can zoom in on the strengths and weaknesses of the people he or she supervises to ensure they are placed in positions that maximize their strengths, rather than accentuate their weaknesses.

"These are the school rules, I intend to follow them, and you should too." I recited those rules so many times while at Berger that I think if I tried I could repeat them almost verbatim right now. Here goes:

1. *All students must come to school regularly _to learn_.* I always stressed, to learn, although I knew learning was the last thing on the students' minds when they came to school. They came to be with friends so they could share secrets, talk about entertainment and sports, and see who can afford the latest clothing and footwear. They came to be with boyfriends—hugging and kissing in the hallways, having sex in stairwells and closets, and necking in class with no respect for the teacher's presence. They came to get away from abusive homes, and homes in which they were being faced with adult responsibilities. They came because school was the only place they felt they could command and get respect. They came because school was a source of consistency in their troubled lives. They came to get free meals and transportation passes; and letters that enabled their parents to get public assistance. In winter they came because it was too cold to hang out outside, and home was the last place they wanted to be. They came to have a decent roof over their heads, even for a few hours. They came to stay out of trouble. They came because their parent or guardian forced them to. They

came because it was a part of their parole agreement, and they knew their parole officer would be checking up on them. Indeed, very few came to learn. Those who did were successful against all odds. They had to deal with being the minority in the school, and being called nerd on a regular basis. *If you are absent, you must bring a note from your parent to be shown to all your subject teachers.*

2. *One cut* (A cut was the term used to describe a situation in which a student was present in school but didn't go to class. We had a lot of cutters at Berger High School.) *is equivalent to 2 unexcused absences.* This rule I put in: *7 unexcused absences will result in failure for the marking period.* (A marking period is about 6 weeks in length. In NYC high schools there are 3 marking periods in each semester, and 2 semesters in the school year. When all the holidays and weekends are removed, the school year from September to June is 180 days. [07]At Northeastern there was 4 marking periods in a semester; this was a result of the semester system.

3. *If you are late, you must sign the late sheet, or you will be marked absent. 2 unexcused tardys is equivalent to one absence.*

4. *Sit in your assigned seat; otherwise you will be marked absent.* Assigning seats worked wonders for me. In a few weeks I would know all the students in my classes. By the time I completed my second school year at Berger, I knew most of the students in the school by name.

5. *All students must have a loose leaf notebook, so they can take out and put in pages.*

6. *Homework is to be done on loose leaf paper, and kept in the homework section of your loose leaf notebook.* I forgot to tell students that homework assignments should be handed in, and it was the actual graded assignments that should be kept in the homework section of their notebooks. As a result I was forever finding students with completed homework assignments in their homework section, which had not been graded.

7. *Do not bring games, radios, walkmans, or beepers to school.*

8. *Unacceptable classroom behaviors include cursing, talking without permission, and leaving your seat without permission.* When I started conducting lab classes, I included eating in class as an unacceptable behavior.

9. *Do not call out answers, raise your hands and wait to be called on.*

10. *Ask teacher about extra credit work.*

Except for failure due to excessive absences, there were no penalties for disobeying the rules. As a result not many students obeyed them.

There was a teacher, Mr. Warner, a rather unusual human being. He always wore a scowl on his face along with his glasses with the very thick lens. The sight of him always made my skin crawl. I didn't know why until I heard he had just returned from his nth nervous breakdown. Mr. Warner could be relied on to ask the pertinent question, "What do you do if the students refuse to take off their hats and Walkman?" This question he would ask when Principal Thomson mentioned seeing students in classrooms with hats and Walkmans on. Warner never got a satisfactory answer.

Those were the rules I would recite to the students at the start of every semester. I don't think the students liked the idea of having to obey rules in their domain, where respect was due them. To say they were not very obedient is an understatement.

Parent involvement would have been a strategic inclusion, but that was not the case. Students were given a copy of the rules to take home for their parents to read, and sign. The signature section was to be cut off and returned to the teacher. I always assign that task as homework number one. As a result I got back most of those signed slips. It's easy to imagine that most parents did not read the document before signing. A lot of the parents did not read or speak English very well; a lot of students did the honors for their parents by signing the sheet with or without permission from their parents. After all why should a little signature keep them from gaining credit for the first and easiest homework of the semester?

I dare say schools would probably fare better if they insisted that parents come in for a meeting that first week of school, at which time school administrators can go over the rules with parents and discuss how parents can assist the school in maintaining discipline.

It was purely by accident that I came across what was almost a panacea for the students' disobedience. The cafeteria was my safe haven in the middle of the school day. I would go there to get away from students, teachers, and the classroom with its bleak reminders of chaos. It was in the cafeteria that I met a retired Italian teacher, a short, soft-spoken, elderly gentleman, whose name eludes me now. He told me the secret. He said, "put a little zero on their Delaney card (a 1" x 2" card, arranged in a Delaney Book according to seat assignment; the back of the card has dates that are used by the teacher to check attendance)." Once I convinced the students that the zeroes would result in points being deducted from their grades, it worked like a charm. Ultimately, all I had to do to quiet a class was pick up my pen. I never actually took points off for the zeroes, but I used the zeroes at my discretion when applying the grading policy, which was as follows:

0—Student never attended class

43—Student is excessively absent

50, 55—Other failing grades

60—Intermediate grade given only in the second marking period of a semester (remember there are 3 marking periods per semester) to a student whom the teacher expects to pass at the end of the semester.

65 to 90 in 5 point interval and grades over 90—Passing.

When I averaged students' grades, I used the zeroes to decide what grade to give. For example, a student with an average of 73% would end up with a grade of 70% if his Delaney card had a lot of zeroes, or 75% if the zeroes were absent or sparing. Until I taught at Cooper High School, no one ever questioned my grading policy. If anyone asked I would have justified the grade by saying the student's average was reduced for poor class participation.

In order to give a grade I would always apply the grading policy that I received from the school administration. If I weren't given a grading policy I would make one up, that would account for exams, homework assignments, projects, lab work, and class assignments. I always made sure everything the students did counted towards their grade. I am the only teacher I know who would manually calculate students' grades. I think being a mathematics and science enthusiast, I am quite aware of just how easy it is to make subjective mistakes with numbers. I have never trusted the method most teacher use, which is to simply look at the grades and decide on an average grade.

My mother recently retired from teaching. I remember watching her 'make up' final grades for her students. She would pick up the big package that was the student's written final exam; she would then put the package aside, and write down a final grade for the student. She didn't even read the first page of the student's 10–20 page paper. I would marvel at such a practice. When I probe her about the possibility that a student who did poorly during the school year could try to make up for it by doing well on the final exam, she would just brush aside my concerns. I promised myself that if I were ever a teacher, I would be a lot more objective in the way I do my students' grades. This is not to say that my mom did her students any disservice. I think she knew her students well enough to know their capabilities; they did 2 years of hands-on work with her prior to the final exam.

The situation in NYC public schools is quite different. A lot of students get over because of teachers' insistence on grading them subjectively. There are also cases in which students are shortchanged in the grades they receive because of this subjective grading. Some students have been lulled into thinking that if they pass the last test of a making period that means they will receive a passing grade for that marking period. Some teachers used that kind of logic, but that was strictly forbidden in my classes.

The other thing I would do is keep students informed of their progress—missing homeworks, etc. Sometimes I would allow students to make up missing work early in the semester. I would also remind students every now and then about how the grading policy worked. Students were always asking me, "are you going to pass me Ms. Moline?" as though all they had to do was ask and a passing grade would be given to them. The majority of times my answer to "are you going to pass me?" was "yes, in the hallway".

Using the zeroes on a student's Delaney card to aid in the determination of his or her grade wasn't legal, like it wasn't legal to throw a student out of your class because he got on your damn nerves. Most teachers did things like that; we did it to keep our sanity. Daily we existed in a 'them or us' situation. We used whatever worked. There was one teacher, Mrs. Jenkins, who used a magic marker to mark on the floor the positions the students' chairs were to remain in.

There are times when teachers break under the pressure. They tell students stuff like, "shut the hell up". Then there are those teachers who call students names other than their given names—*white trash, nigger, schmuck, deadbeat,* to name a few. This I am pleased to say, I am not guilty of. The Principal of Berger High School was forever appealing to us in faculty conferences, "please do not call the students any names other than their given names".

Having left Berger under uncomfortable circumstances at the end of my fifth semester, I went to teach at Langley High School in Queens. While at Langley, one teacher, Mr. Mason, recounted an encounter he had with a parent on open school night. He said that he told the parent all the horrible things the student did in class. The parent sat quietly and listened. At the end of his summary, the parent remarked, "but that's no reason to call my son an asshole."

VIOLENCE

I am pleased to say I was never hit by a student. Others, unfortunately, weren't so lucky. Most New Yorkers can probably recall the teacher and her elementary school student who made the news. The teacher was so afraid of the violence of the little girl she was afraid to go to work.

Confrontations between students are very common. I have had a number of incidents in which students got into physical confrontations in my classroom. For the most part my remedy for verbal confrontations is to have students apologize and shake hands. This ensures that a confrontation doesn't escalate into a fight in my classroom.

Fights and verbal confrontations are always disruptive. However, what I found very bothersome were the little antics students employed in what can only be construed as a bid to terrorize the teacher. Usually this attitude is a symptom of something more distressing that's taking place in the student's home life. Servion Valentino bears proof of this. He was a student who was obviously distressed. He would exhibit extremely abnormal behavior. He made continuous desperate attempts to get his classmates' attention. Even when his classmates, tired of his antics asked him to stop, he carried on. I grew tired of his antics, and of constantly sending him to my AP. I could not ignore the fact that he was crying out for help. Such a blatant scream for attention and affection can be nothing less than a cry for help. I spoke to my AP, and he called Servion in. Behold he found Servion was living in an abusive home and was under the care of a psychiatrist.

Throughout my time in the school system, my biggest fear was that of a violent confrontation between a student and me. In response to this fear, I always made it clear to students, "whatever you do, DON'T TOUCH ME", and "if anything is thrown and I get hit, I will see to it that the entire class gets suspended". Also, at the start of the semester I would tell students my definition of a fight: If 2 students start arguing and one or both students get out of their seat, that's a fight.

Ms. Hardy said that if students challenged her she would take out her little knife, and slap it down on her desk. Then she would ask, "Do you think your cojones are bigger than mine?" At this point all the students would freak out in shocked horror as she made a mock attempt to take off her pants. Whatever student had started the argument would immediately back down.

I had referral forms ready so that if 2 students started arguing, I would write up a referral, call security, and report a fight. This I would do with all the students in the classroom maintaining the truth, "that was not a fight". With all that a number of fights have taken place in my classroom.

The first fight was at Berger. It took place between a boy named Christian, and the daughter of one of the School's English teachers. The incident only escalated into a fight because security took too long to get there. I later found out that Nellyann went around gossiping that it was my fault that the fight occurred. According to the rumor, the fight was due to my poor classroom management skills. Well, if my classroom management skills were poor (which I guarantee they were not), then it was because I had an AP supervising me who could not hold his own in a classroom, as you will learn later.

My second fight was at Langley. I had no opportunity to see the build-up to the fight; it took place right at the start of the period. I went against my better judgment, and broke up the fight. I was very angry with myself. I had made a firm decision a long time ago never to intervene in a fight between students. I had gone back on my decision and put myself in danger; this after 3 years in the school system, there was no excuse.

My decision never to intervene came from what happened to a teacher who intervened in a fight between students. This incident took place at Berger. 2 students had a festering altercation, it seemed. One student, who was in special education at the time, jumped the other student in the hall. Mr. Stone was teaching in his room with the door open when the fighting students stumbled in (I always teach with my door closed, this being part of the reason). Mr. Stone tried to part the students, and was rewarded by a push that landed him on the radiator. He was injured, and hospitalized. The UFT reprimanded him for his actions. It was emphasized, DON'T GET INVOLVED, CALL SECURITY. Mr. Stone was lucky he wasn't seriously injured. The student who was jumped was not so lucky however, he had one of his lungs punctured, and he was hospitalized in serious condition.

This was one case of violence that touched me deeply; the fact that I got involved by default only made it worst. The student who was stabbed in the chest was in one of my classes. His name was Dalton Sanchez, and he was a sweet child; tall and skinny with mischief up his sleeves at all times. He knew the first name of the student who stabbed him; the attacker was also in my class—the same class as Dalton. I was called to the nurse's office by security. I went in and looked down at poor Dalton sitting on the exam table, bandaged and pale. The sight of his pale frame laid out on the cold steel exam table made my heart skip a beat.

I did recall the attacker's last name; his name was Pierce Bolton. I willingly cooperated by giving the name to security. I couldn't wait for him to be caught so he could pay for his act.

I didn't know at the time that the USA had a different brand of justice for those deemed to be special on account of some mental or physical handicap—authentic or contrived. The guilty student was never charged. For me the whole situation was nightmarish. I kept seeing the wounded child sitting there on the exam table, and I kept wondering if the guilty student knew I was the one who fingered him.

The day after the incident Nellyann sent out this letter:

March 26, 1993

Dear students, faculty, staff, parents:

I regret to inform you that a horrible incident occurred in our school yesterday.

At about 12:45 P.M. a 14-year-old student sustained injuries in an altercation in room 313 of our school. The student received puncture wounds in the front and back. EMS was called immediately. At this point the police have informed me that he is in stable condition in the hospital. The police department is investigating the matter. So far the weapon is unidentified and the police speculate that it was the point of a pair of compasses or a pair of scissors.

As a result of this incident we are reviewing internal security procedures and practices. We will implement changes as needed. I want to thank our security team headed by Mr. Pulsar, Assistant Principal, for their prompt and efficient assistance and investigation. They were able to identify the other student and appropriate action will be taken.

We learn from this that the price of liberty is external vigilance, to paraphrase Daniel Webster, 19th century American statesman. We cannot search and check everyone at all times and maintain our freedom. Instead, we must teach and reaffirm values, behaviors and attitudes which prevent such criminal activities. When rules and laws are broken we must deal with them swiftly, harshly and consistently so as to reaffirm our respect for the law. Each of us must take seri-

ously our roles as students, parents or staff in fulfilling our responsibilities to ourselves and to each other.

Sincerely,

Nellyann Thomson

The letter didn't state, "And by the way, no one should say anything to the press about this incident", we were told that verbally. As a result, the story that appeared in the newspaper was so erroneous, it would have been better that it not appear at all. It was all over the wire that the teacher continued to teach while the students were fighting in the classroom. I can just imagine how Mr. Stone must have felt reading such a tall tale while having his injuries treated in the hospital.

I inquired, and found out that Dalton was at Stromberg Hospital. I went out, bought a comic for him to read, and a card, which I had all his classmates sign. It was one of the only times I can recall seeing students express remorse. They were genuinely concerned about Dalton's well being, and they kept asking me if he was going to be okay. I took my gift to the Hospital, but I was too late, Dalton had already been discharged. I called his home, and made arrangements to go and visit him. I told Ms. Hardy, and she decided to accompany me.

The apartment where Dalton lived with his mother was a third floor walk up. It was located in the South Bronx, in an area festering with apartment buildings. I could never help wondering where children play when there are so many of them per square mile. [01]Case in point, based on the 2000 population census the population density of NYC is 26,430 persons per square mile, compared to the rest of New York State which has a population density of 234 persons per square mile. Brooklyn and the Bronx, with 34,723 and 31,730 persons per square mile respectively, have population densities that are much higher than the City average.

Dalton's mother addressed this. It seemed there were only 2 choices, either stay inside, or hang out on the corner with friends. She was trying to keep Dalton inside. How do you keep a teenage boy, especially one as enthusiastic about life as Dalton in the house? I didn't know the answer.

I gave Dalton his gift. He was touched by the notes his classmates wrote in the card. He was indeed staying inside, and he was being tutored while he recovered.

The information we gleaned wasn't good. The student who attacked Dalton was being let off the hook, and Dalton had been harassed by the police. The police had insisted on questioning him while he was in his hospital bed. They claimed he stole a radio, which was why he was attacked. It turned out that the radio Dalton was being accused of stealing was his own. We recommended that his mother file a lawsuit against the system. I even looked up the number of a reputable attorney, called up Dalton's mother and gave it to her.

Needless to say, the lawsuit was never filed. When Dalton tried to return to school, the school administration gave him hell. The student who stabbed him was obviously well protected by the powers that be. He apparently had lawyers working hard on his side. I don't know the ultimate outcome; maybe Dalton's mother did manage to move out of the South Bronx, as she had expressed her intent to do when we visited her. This could only have been for the better.

There was another case of violence that touched me deeply. In my first semester at Berger I had to spend 1 period each day doing 'administrative duty'. This administrative duty was eliminated by the last teacher contract, thereby giving teachers more time to spend planning their lessons. Anyway, my administrative duty was to call up parents of students who were excessively absent. I called up a mother who told me that her son was jumped the first day of school by students who wanted to steal his sneakers. She said her son ran home via the train tracks in one foot of sneaker. The poor woman was hysterical as she told me the story. I told her how sorry I was to hear such a thing. I really was too. I had horrible visions of the terrified child running home on the tracks in one foot of sneaker, more fearful of his attackers than of an oncoming train.

Throughout my years of teaching I always stuck to the only important lesson I ever learnt from Talbot—don't make it personal. I would avoid learning anything about my students on a personal level. I just didn't want to know. Having taught in some depressed areas, I knew my students had lots of horror stories to tell. As an example, how do you relate to a student when you know he or she is homeless? Another example, how do you prevent yourself from being influenced by the fact that a student has been in and out of prison? I prefer not to know.

When I taught at Cooper High School I once overheard a student telling her friends of her childhood experiences. They were so horrifying that I tried to get them out of my mind as soon as possible. However, what I do recall is that when she was a young child her mother who was a drug addict would leave her alone in the home for days at a time.

Ms. Hardy had her tires slashed. She was sure she knew the student who did it, but nothing came of that. In an unrelated incident prior a student spat in her face. I can't imagine what I would do to a student who spits in my face. I just know that I would be beyond enraged

Mr. Talbot was prime target. It was common practice for students to say "Fuck you Talbot" to his face. I heard about an incident in which students broke the window of the door to his classroom. Being the intelligent man that he was, he went to look through the newly formed hole in the door. He was grabbed by his tie, and pulled through the opening, such that his neck was a mere fraction of an inch above shattered glass. I still haven't come to grips with that story.

This next story I accept, only because the student in question came to my classroom, and acted out the incident a number of times, much to the delight of the class. 2 students were fighting in Mr. Talbot's class. He got in the middle to part the fight. Frankly, I would think he of all persons would have known to call security, considering the lack of respect the students had for him. He was punched in the stomach. According to the student's dramatization, Talbot held his midsection, and fell on the floor. Of course nothing happened to the student, except for a few days suspension, which he no doubt welcomed. It amazes me that the system still has suspensions in place, and uses it on students who commit violent acts. It's like treating a hemorrhage with a band-aid.

Mr. Warner had the worst of the worst. Students seemed to enjoy beating him up. At one stage he had scratches on his face where a group of girls had beaten him up. There was an alleged incident in which he was held by his feet out of a third floor classroom window. No wonder he had many nervous breakdowns. Warner, clearly a victim, of what I'm not sure, reached a stage where he just didn't teach anymore. At his last period of the day the students would come in, he would take their attendance, and then they were allowed to leave. Principal Thomson got wind of this, and decided to put her foot down on him. She went to sit in the class, and watched to see what would happen. A few students showed up. Warner just sat there, perched on top of a stool behind his desk. There they were, Mr. Warner, Ms. Thomson, and the students. Warner must have been at the start of one of his nervous trips, because he just sat there staring into space, nodding off every now and then.

I personally observed Warner on one of his trips. I was in the science office one afternoon. Warner came in. Totally oblivious of my presence, he walked over to the copy machine. He reached up to the shelf above the copy machine for copy paper. His arm stopped in mid air, and he just stood there staring into space for what seemed an eternity. It was as if he had fallen asleep. Then he started falling. Seconds before he would have crashed into me, he caught himself. In a robotic motion he grabbed the paper he came for, and walked out of the room as though still in a trance.

Believe it or not Warner had once asked me out on a date, which I graciously declined. He seemed to fit the serial killer description that I keep in the back of my mind. The only other time I ever spoke to Warner was on an occasion when he told me Berger students were inferior, which, in his opinion, was why they didn't do well on Regents science exams. I told him I had trouble with some of the questions on the science Regents. He said, "Well, maybe you shouldn't be here".

My guess is that attitudes like his is one of the major problems with the school system—anyone who can't conform to the status quo is just plain inferior and don't belong here with the rest of us. It's hard to believe that in a city as ethnically diverse as NYC this sort of attitude is commonplace. I once attended a Board of Education public meeting and heard an Asian woman remarking to the Board that they should fire uncertified teachers who can't pass the teacher exam.

I am no expert, but I have taken tons of exams, I have never failed an exam, and I have taught students exam techniques that have gotten even my weakest students to pass the Regents exams. I can safely say that the majority of exams have a high degree of bias. I have seen this bias in Regents exams, the Graduate Record Exam (GRE), the Scholastic Aptitude Test (SAT)—which is not an aptitude test, but that's a different story, the National Teacher Exam, and the NYC police officer's exam.

I believe it's impossible to make an exam that is completely unbiased, but I also feel that the level of bias that I have seen in exams that New Yorkers have to take is unacceptable considering the diversity of the NYC population. Besides, bias is a bad thing, it assures that either you fail the exam, or you get a grade that is lower than you would have gotten with less bias.

There was one teacher I met in one of those teacher-training sessions who commented that the reason the students destroyed school property was because they didn't have nice things at home, hence they hated to see nice things at school. Obviously this guy was in the wrong teacher workshop. What he was in need of was sensitivity training. With all this talk about cultural sensitivity in health care, I am surprised no one has seen it fit to state that maybe teachers should be treated to training to make them more culturally sensitive. I don't know that sensitivity training can make people more culturally sensitive, but at least it will make it so they are not totally unaware when they think do or say the wrong thing culturally. At the very least the educational system will know that the teachers know better, even if they don't do better.

You may wonder why Warner was never dragged from the building on charges that he was unfit to remain in the school as a teacher. As rumor had it,

Warner was well connected. Warner ultimately did himself and the system a favor when he took early retirement. I'm not sure how he managed early retirement, since he was quite a young man, but as I said before he did have connections. In the NYC School System connections is everything and skills mean nothing.

I have often wondered what became of Warner after he retired. From experience I know the possibilities are endless—he could have returned to normalcy or died.

I had confrontations and threats, all verbal of course. I told the students that I had ten brothers. Knowing that I am from Barmenia, I think they took it to mean that I had ten big bad Rastafarians with automatic weapons watching over me. After all that's what the movies told them, and students do watch a lot of movies, more so than they watch educational programs. There were 2 Berger High School students, Lawrence Bonns, and Marie Baker, who on separate occasions got all loud about their grades. I merely told them to get the hell out of my face, of course not with that language or tone.

I did wonder about Lawrence. He was a strange child. He had poor hand writing, a patch in his head that seemed to have resulted from some sort of injury, and he often seemed a bit out of touch. I suspected he was learning disabled at the very least, though it could have been that he was a special education student who had been mainstreamed (placed in regular education classes).

Baker, on the other hand was quite another story. The first time she came to class was in my first week of teaching. She came in late with walkman on singing, *Murder She Wrote*, a song by Jamaican artists Shaka Demus and Pliers. "Are you Barmenian?" she asked on hearing my accent. When I answered affirmatively, she said, "Touch me", and shoved me a fist. I 'touched' her. She was quite a disturbing influence in what had formerly been a moderately well behaved class. She was extremely loud, and vulgar. I did not have to wonder if she was from Bonnstown, Barmenia. Bonnstonians tend not to be representative of Barmenians, like New Yorkers from the city are not representative of the entire State.

I was at home once, and heard myself singing *Murder She Wrote*, and it hit me that Baker had been singing the song in class almost every day. We did manage to sort out our differences, and one day I was surprise when she came to thank me for her being on the honor roll. I was proud of her, but I didn't share her enthusiasm, I knew she was getting over. The thing that bothered me about her was that I felt sure she could do a lot better if she put the effort in instead of taking the easy road.

Baker wasn't the only one taking the easy road; I would say most of the students at Berger High School were. I recall overhearing students proclaiming how much they liked certain teachers who gave them passing grades no matter what. I heard comments like: "I didn't even go to the class, and I passed"; "I just told Mr. X to hook me up and he gave me an 80". Students had come to expect that they would get an easy test at the end of the semester, and that test would determine their grade. I assumed they got that impression because a lot of teachers did use that method of assigning grades. Students were forever asking, "So if we pass this test, do we pass the class?" My answer was always a resounding "NO"; at which point I would remind them about that grading policy that they got at the start of the semester.

Students never got over on me. Bad enough I had to drop my standards, I certainly wasn't going to compromise my integrity so I could 'look good', and students could get misleading information about their academic progress. I was known for giving 64% on exams, including the Regents. Students would ask, "So can't you give me one point so I can pass". My response in all such cases was that I had no token points to give away, they had to earn it. I was also known for averaging students' grades as per the grading policy. I had a spreadsheet on my computer with formulas for calculating students' grades. When students came to complain about their grade, I would get out my grade book and calculator, and average their grades in their presence.

I developed a reputation. During the first couple days in a semester, a lot of students who were originally on my class lists would have their class changed. I didn't mind, since those who stayed with me did well. For the most part they not only did well in my class, they also did well on the Regents exam; which was the real test of the pudding.

There was one student whose name evades me now; he really stabbed the knife of fear into my heart. He was absent 6 times; I made a mistake, counted 7 absences, and gave him a failing grade. His mother came in on open school night, and I told her I didn't know him. On the Monday following, the student came in and laid down his subtle threat. Without his saying anything to me the deal was made, he would be present and do his work, and I would give him a passing grade; and so it came to pass.

I kept thinking every time I saw him that he had a gun under his coat, and any minute he would just start firing in the classroom. The presence of metal detectors in the school never gave me any sense of security, especially after hearing students relate how they had managed to bring guns into the school. A student at Berger, George Nueva, told me that he was angry with his good friend Leonard

Reyes. When I asked him why, he explained that Leonard told the dean, Mr. Pulsar, that he (George) brought a gun into the school through the side door. On quizzing George further, he confessed that he did bring a gun into the school through the side door. He was angry with Leonard for telling on him, he felt Leonard, as his friend should have had his back; in other words Leonard should have lied for him.

To my understanding, this Leonard was no saint. He had been to prison more than once. The last time he went (as per the rumor I picked up on) it was for trying to steal a part off someone's car. Leonard had a car, he needed a part for the car, he saw a car like his, and he simply proceeded to remove the part from the car. When the owner came along and saw him removing the part from his car, Leonard continued with his theft; maybe he was giving the police a head start. He got caught and was sent to prison. I don't know how true the rumor was, but it truly saddened my heart when I heard it. He was such a sweet child, and he had one of the best penmanship I ever came across. Nevertheless I believed the rumor. A number of Berger students had spent time with the department of corrections and a lot of them had fathers and uncles who had done time.

Every now and then one of my students would be absent for a while. On returning to class the student would tell me he was on vacation Upstate. I believed the students went away with family, but later someone informed me that when the students said they were on vacation Upstate, what they actually meant was that they were in prison in Upstate New York.

There was an incident wherein a security guard put his life on the line to wrestle a gun away from a student. The student, one Steven Hunt, was either Barmenian or of Barmenian parentage. I found that rather disturbing, especially considering the kind of school system that I had growing up in Barmenia. Steven was certainly a victim of the system. For many Barmenian students whose parents can't afford to send them to private school, the school system is just a big joke. Steven was in my class; intermittently he would show up, yet if ever he was present when I gave a test he always got the highest grade. He never scored under 80%. As though a perfectionist, he spent a lot of time on his test, not wanting to hand in his paper until he was completely satisfied with his answers. There were many occasions when I had to wait for his test after the bell rang, which was long after everyone else had handed in their papers.

Rumor had it that Bill Hanson, who was principal of Berger before Nellyann, was a short white man who was terrified of the students. He had a shrill voice, almost like a crude bellow, and there used to be frequent shrieking matches between him and Talbot. I believed the 'shrieking matches' part of the rumor, because I knew Talbot to be quite a 'shrieker'. The most fascinating part of the rumor is that Bill used to walk around with an attaché case in which he carried a revolver—oooh scary.

Mrs. Davenport, a teacher at Langley, recounted her experience to us in one of those sessions teachers commonly have wherein experiences are shared. She was a new teacher in a bad school with the school's worst class. Other teachers would come around to peer into her class to see how she was doing, but never to assist. This scenario is called 'paying your dues', and probably the only minority teachers in NYC who can't identify with this situation are ones who are well connected. In my years of teaching in NYC, there was only one occasion wherein I wasn't given the worst of the worst. This was also one of the few occasions wherein I taught in my license area (chemistry) for a full year. Even so I have never taught even a single school year wherein I taught only in my license area. I fail to understand why administrators can't see the great disservice they afford both students and staff when they have teachers teach outside their license area.

Mrs. Davenport said that she managed to gain control of the class. She was able to get along with all but one of the students in the class. This girl just wouldn't cooperate with her, and one day boldly told her, "I'll see you after school!" Showing mucho gusto, and not a hint of fear, Davenport said she told the student, "I'll be waiting. I'm from Brooklyn, I'm not afraid of you." After school Davenport was waiting, fear-stricken and all, but the student didn't show up. Thereafter Mrs. Davenport and the student became the best of friends.

Boys are usually mischievous, but controllable so, but when girls are bad they are truly demons. When I taught at Hedley High School in Cleveland I witnessed a commotion one day. There were police cars and a crowd outside the school. It turned out that a group of girls from the school jumped a police officer and beat him up, or should I say beat him down.

I have to say that a lot of the children who come into the lives of us teachers have not been taught a very basic socialization skill—how to effectively handle anger. Parents need to teach their children how to express anger verbally rather than physically. Fact is, the children who express anger physically have parents who express anger in the same manner. It's important to get to a point where you can admit that you are not handling anger in the most effective way, and then endeavor to work on your anger management.

Talk about handling anger physically, and expressing anger verbally. This was a trademark of PS 999 in Brooklyn—the last school where I taught in NYC before deciding it was time to get out of the game. I recall one teacher, a substitute, who would sit in the lunchroom and relate all these horror stories of how students would threaten her. She related that one boy, a 5th grader I believe it was, made good on his threat by punching her in the stomach. I believe she was pregnant at the time.

One of the things I have always maintained is not to allow students to think it is okay to raise their voices at me, or openly disrespect me. When students raise their voices at me, I usually quite calmly let them know that that's a signal for the end of our conversation, because I don't talk with students who are raising their voices. As a result, no matter how angry a student gets, regardless of how loud they were before, once they approached me their voices automatically lowered.

I recall one student at Cooper High School in Brooklyn who entered my classroom at the end of the period before I dismissed my class. When I asked why she was in the room, she quite brazenly told me, "It's the end of the period; don't you have a watch!" I knew the student's name, because she was in my chemistry lab class. I think she figured because I taught so many students between lab classes and chemistry lectures I would not recall her name. During the next period when I had my lunch break, I went to the office and got her parent's telephone number. I called her mother, reported what the student had done, expressed how upset I was about being disrespected like that in front of my students, and express that I did not want to have such an event take place ever again. Thereafter I got a lot of nasty looks from the student, but she never openly disrespected me again.

There's a saying, *give them an inch, and they take a mile*; this saying applies quite well to a lot of students. Hence, I don't give students an inch; I am always very strict, I don't let anything slide, and I know all the tricks in the book.

Then there was the 5th grade teacher who taught in the classroom across the hall from me at PS 999. She was always screaming at the students. I don't know how she managed to keep her voice, with all that screaming day after day. Her students, like most of the students at PS 999, were unruly from 8:15 am when they got on line to go to class, until 2:30 pm when they got on line to leave the building. I was expecting my second child when I taught at PS 999. You would not believe the number of threats that were issued for my unborn child, not to mention all the ill wishes for his future.

STRESS

We fight to open doors while others sit back and watch and wait. The minute the doors open just a crack, they push us out of the way, jump inside and close the door behind them before we can even get to stick a toe in. The powers that be have no problem with this because they didn't want us in the room to begin with.

A lot of stress could be relieved if we all followed a basic rule—live and let live.

STRESS

Several studies have shown that stress affects the body's ability to fight disease. Stress has been shown to raise blood pressure by causing the production of chemicals that tighten blood vessels. It's important to appreciate the relationship between stress and illness as a means of improving the well being of students and staff, as well as decreasing their absences. There's a relationship between stress management and parent involvement. Numerous studies have shown that students who have strong parent/guardian support and involvement at home tend to do well in school. This is true even for children whose parents abuse drugs and alcohol during pregnancy.

It was hard to imagine anyone doing worst than NYC's South Bronx. The South Bronx was a very depressed, AIDS infested neighborhood.

Berger High School was located in the middle of the South Bronx, amidst too much industrialization. There was a pesticide plant located behind the school. A shoe manufacturer, which was basically an immigrant sweatshop, was located to the left. To the right was low-income housing, which no doubt housed some of the students and their families. Almost in front of the building was a plastics manufacturer.

I never felt comfortable about my health while I worked at Berger, especially when every time I exited the building I smelled the sick sweet odor emanating from the pesticide plant. I was almost obsessed by it. I went by once and read the information on the awning. It was a division of Wayne Chemical Company, manufacturer of Black Flag. When I realized that it didn't look likely that I would be able to get a teaching position elsewhere in the Bronx, I decided to check out the pesticide plant myself. I took action; I got an employee to call the Occupational Safety and Health Administration (OSHA) and report poor working conditions at the company. The employee was sent a report by OSHA that proclaimed that the establishment was not in the business of pesticide manufacture, but was merely a storage facility for the pesticide company. I didn't believe the report, since I had eyewitnesses who claimed they saw workers mixing chemicals in the building. OSHA did charge the company for some minor violations, mainly having to do with labeling and handling of the pesticide during storage.

Most times teachers treat students in a manner less than satisfactory because of the teacher's ill feelings and lack of comfort with the school climate. Once, a Berger student wanted to go to the bathroom. Apparently my bathroom pass must have been missing at the time because I took a sheet of paper to write a pass. Instead of writing PASS, as I intended, I wrote BOOM. I have no idea how my fingers could transform PASS to BOOM, but that was what came out on the paper. "What is this?" the student asked. Only then did I actually realize what was written on the paper.

There was another incident, this time at Langley. I was teaching an earth science lesson. My most disruptive student, Sheldon Spear, kept talking and talking, deliberately ignoring the fact that I was teaching. Suddenly, before I realized what was happening, the chalk flew out of my hand, and went straight for his head. It hit him smack in the forehead. I was a bit flustered, because I knew that nasty child could get me into trouble over the incident. The entire class had a fit of laughter, and Mr. Troublemaker hung his head in shame, and remained quiet for the rest of the period. I never heard anything of the incident. I did have Sheldon's mother come in to school and sit in the back of the class one day. It was the only day that Sheldon behaved the entire semester. Later in a meeting between his mother, the AP and I, Sheldon astonished us by disrespecting his mother in front of us. We were so used to students who stood quietly during such meetings, only speaking when they were spoken to. Sheldon on the other hand would unceremoniously interrupt his mother in order to make whatever point he felt he needed to make.

Let's get back to the South Bronx's Berger High School. I had several reasons not to feel healthy working at Berger High School—some of which I will list here.

Mr. Lyons, AP of administration, a quiet gentle man with gray hair. He was not a very good administrator, this Principal Thomson often said, but never to his face as was usual for her. I got the impression that he would have made a great departmental AP; he was just not a good paper pusher. He had a heart attack. He didn't even know he had it; he came to school and had to leave from there to the hospital. He had been under far too much stress. The fact that Principal Thomson didn't like him, and wanted him out of the school was by far the major factor.

When Mr. Lyons recovered from his heart attack, he was told by the Superintendent to call Ms. Thomson to ascertain the status of his position. Ms. Thomson told him it was okay for him to come back. After hanging up the phone she expressed her disgust at Mr. Lyons' groveling to return to his position.

Lyons' position was being covered by Edna Kramer, who Thomson felt was doing a good job. Edna Kramer was as fat as she was ill tempered. She had on more than one occasion been a pain in my ass. Kramer was Attendance Coordinator. Quite frankly, the only thing she really coordinated was how many cigarettes to smoke in the rest room. There were only 2 rest rooms in the building for female teachers, and one was assigned to smokers by default—the stench of stale tobacco in the room was so strong that only a smoker with compromised sense of smell could tolerate it.

Vernella Wilber had breast cancer. She was Mr. Lyons' secretary. She had undergone surgery, and was getting chemotherapy. She fortunately had recovered quite nicely. It amazed me that someone so pleasant could have such a chronic illness, but then cancer has never had much respect for personalities.

Alice Cougar went on sabbatical (a break teachers take to catch up on their studies, after they have done a certain number of years of service), and was found dead in her apartment. It seemed she died of a heart attack. Must have been quite a thrombosis, Cougar weighed at least 300 pounds. She was a very miserable woman, which was not good considering her obesity. On top of everything, it seemed she lived alone. I think all these were risk factors, but still..... .

The Spanish teacher, Jesus Benito, told me the depressing news. At that time I had just managed to get out of Berger, and was teaching at Langley. Jesus said that a student delivered the news with a smile; more like a wide grin I am willing to bet. The students didn't like Cougar. She was rather strict and grumpy, to say the least. Even with all that, how heartless for a student to deliver news of a teacher's death with a grin, like it was the best news he had heard all year.

Shortly after I started teaching at Hedley High School in Cleveland they lost one of their teachers. He was a huge jolly man, who seemed not to have any concern for the fact that he was at least 200 pounds overweight. I always felt sorry for him just from the knowledge that it can't possibly be healthy to carry around that much weight. [01]According to one recent study, obesity has now replaced smoking as the leading preventable cause of death in the USA.

Anyway, back to my Berger case. Mr. Goldmark had numerous heart attacks. He was in the Electronics Department. He had been a teacher under the department AP, Mr. Ericsson, when I started work at Berger. Apparently Mr. Ericsson wasn't performing in Ms. Thomson's opinion. She endeavored to rid the school of him. She applied pressure, and not being as resilient as the others, Ericsson got the message and left. Mr. Goldmark took over, he became acting AP. He couldn't be AP because he didn't have the required license. He wasn't in a very stressful environment. He drank a lot, and that may have been part of the problem.

Mr. Talbot also had his share of heart attacks. There was one incident when I went to the teachers' cafeteria, and there he was lying on one of the tables. I though he was being melodramatic about his job stress, as usual. Rumor had it he was popping stress tablets like Tic-tacs. I didn't realize what was happening until the EMS team came and took him away. Even my cafeteria sanctuary was being desecrated. The story that came back wasn't that of a heart attack. Mr. Talbot was away for a while, nevertheless. The department ran so well in his absent, I started wondering if he really served any purpose. When he came back, it was obvious from his darkened skin tone that he had taken the opportunity to go on vacation.

There's a limit to which you can attribute the behaviors of educators to stress. Some educators are just plain whacko; they would have behaved like nuts regardless of what profession they had. I think Talbot was one such educator.

Sherice Steuben was by far my major reason. She was quite young, yet she had cancer. The chemotherapy had devastating effects on her. I couldn't look at her without feeling a bit numb. She was one of the main contenders in the very subtle fight against the pesticide company. She like Vernella was very mild mannered, though unlike Vernella she was rather slender.

Rumor had it that Mr. Ransome had a heart attack though he denied it when I asked him. He was around my age, and that bothered me. It also bothered me that he denied the rumor although I had gotten it from 2 independent sources. Mr. Ransome was a tall slender black man who was always very aggressively pro-black. In the classic clinical heart disease study, he would definitely be considered a type A personality, but still he had a heart attack at age 24. That was scary.

Mr. Gonzales got a really bad deal at Berger. He was a bilingual science teacher who only lasted one semester. This was rather unusual since after his departure the school employed another bilingual science teacher 2 semesters later. Mr. Talbot constantly complained that Mr. Gonzales was not very good at controlling his classes. There were claims of graffiti on the wall, and general chaos. The problem I found with Talbot's allegation was that Talbot was sharing classroom with Mr. Gonzales. I knew from experience that Talbot, despite being AP, was no better at controlling a class than a chimpanzee with a sense of humor. Mr. Gonzales explained that the chaos was really a result of Talbot's use of the room. Of course he was fighting an uphill battle. After all, Talbot was the departmental AP, and also a white man from Long Island. Needless to say, the only reason he lived in Long Island and worked in the South Bronx was because he was as ineffective a teacher as he was an AP.

Mr. Gonzales was transferred to Hilliard, the worst high school in the Bronx, probably the worst in NYC. No need to wonder if Mr. Gonzales had a rough time at Hilliard. It culminated in his having a heart attack on the job. He died.

The head of the Academic Department, Kevin Nolte, along with his entire Department had grudges against my mentor and friend, Ms Hardy. Part of it stemmed from her taking over the position of Coordinator of Student Activities (COSA). I think the way she got the job was probably at the root of the grudges. The position was held by a member of Nolte's department, one Vince Larget, who had been COSA for many years. Vince held on to the position by constantly threatening the principal that he would quit. Then when the position was advertised, he would survey the staff to see if anyone had an interest in applying. For the most part, he did such a good job convincing everyone he was the one for the job that no one wanted to unseat him. In the end no one would apply for the position, and he would be 'forced' to remain COSA. In truth he loved being COSA, he taught only 2 classes per day, and he got to go on lots of trips with the senior class. Plus the senior class was always very small, and made up of some of the school's best students. This was the South Bronx where the not so good students either ended up in the penal system, or dropped out of school by some other method.

Then along came Hardy with the knowledge that she could do a better job, while benefiting from a reduction in her teaching load. So Hardy decided to apply for the position. She let me in on the secret way in advance. Hardy also knew that the COSA office had its own phone line—it was the only non-administrative office with such a privilege. Hardy told me that Vince asked her if she planned to apply for the position, and she told him something like, "look at me (showing him her gray hair), do you think I am trying to get more stress in my life." So Vince went merrily on his way thinking his position was safe for yet another year.

Hardy not only applied for the position of COSA, she explained to Nellyann how Vince had been pulling the wool over her eyes so he could remain COSA indefinitely. I think Hardy's explanation must have riled Nellyann who was a very vengeful woman who did not believe in leaving any deed unpunished.

Hardy became COSA, much to the shock of the Academic Department, actually I would think to the shock of the entire school.

On becoming COSA Hardy saw the other side of Nellyann, and she quickly fell out of favor with her. Initially, Hardy was almost a confidante for Nellyann.

After all, it was Hardy who made me aware of Nellyann's secret machine. She had a telecom system in her office (I later ran into this system at Langley, but it was linked to the main office, and was set up for two-way communication). The system at Berger allowed Nellyann to listen in on any class she chose with the simple flip of a switch.

Anyway, one of the big contentions was the fact that students would conduct fundraising activities, usually candy sale, and the school was usually unable to account for the money. Rumor had it that the money from candy sale was used to refurbish Nellyann's office. Other times students would raise money for an activity, such as a trip, and the school would use the money for something else, like equipment for the gymnasium.

When Hardy became COSA, she almost immediately cancelled the Academic Department's telephone privileges. Apparently the staff of the Academic Department all had access to the telephone in the COSA office. They ran a line from that telephone to Nolte's office so that if the COSA office was closed they could still have access to the telephone line. So now they had 3 reasons for despising Hardy—she was a black bilingual woman, she had gotten the position of COSA by outsmarting them all, and she had cancelled the telephone privileges they had for many years. At the time the only 2 persons in the Academic Department who weren't white were the Spanish teacher, who was Puerto Rican, and one of the English teachers, a Jamaican man named Mr. Nascent.

Hardy added insult to injury by throwing the best darn graduation the school had seen in years. I think they must have been gearing up to torture her the following school year; she demolished them again by not even showing up.

Then there was Mr. Kalimah, he was an alcoholic and a smoker, and he always smelled of either tobacco or alcohol. I felt sure that most of the times he was drunk while on the job. I don't remember much else about him except that I always wondered how he could teach in his state.

Some teachers become burnt out from years of stress without recourse. One such teacher was Mr. Foster. When he attempted to teach chemistry labs, the students started a fire in the lab, on another occasion they blocked the sink and left a tap running so that the lab flooded. Eventually foster gave up, and Berger students had no more labs until I restarted them.

When I came across Foster he had gotten to the point where he no longer taught. He would get in early in the morning, and fill the huge chalkboard in his classroom with notes. His first class would come in and they would ask, "so what we doin' today Foster?" and he would tell them to copy the notes on the board. I could be wrong, but I think he did that for all his classes, and he probably did it every day. As far as I can recall, the chalkboard in his room was always loaded with notes. At the rate at which those students copied, I don't think there was enough time in a 40-minute period for them to copy that much notes, and have time remaining for him to teach.

Part of the problem with that picture was the total lack of respect on the part of the students. I was always Ms. Moline to my students. I was certainly never called Moline; a few students were brave enough to try calling me Maxine, but after a little threat of having to use my red pen, they quickly switched back to Ms. Moline.

My red pen was truly mightier than the sword. I had students so afraid of my red pen that all I had to do to quiet a class was raise my red pen and open my Delaney book. You see lifting my pen meant either the student would be getting a demerit, or I would be speaking to the student's parents later that day.

This teacher I heard about because she gave up on Berger before I got there. Her name was Marcia Waters, and she was one of the best biology teachers Berger had ever seen. As usual when she got her excellent Regents results there were those who had all sorts of criticisms, they claimed she helped her students cheat, much like they claimed my students cheated on the Chemistry Regents. One day Marcia had a heart attack in the classroom, she fell on the floor and the students stood over her and just laughed. They didn't even try to get help. After that experience Marcia decided that it was time to retire.

One thing that goes on in teaching that is definitely a source of stress for teachers is double standard. I have worked in schools where teachers had their time cards pulled and letters placed in their files if they were even 3 minutes late. While other teachers in the same school would come in up to half an hour late on a regular basis and nothing was done. Nellyann was forever defending a teacher who was always late; she excused him because he lived upstate New York. He would be over half an hour late, and it was okay. Quite frankly I could have lived in Timbuktu, I don't think Nellyann would have excused any lateness on my part. Those sorts of privileges were reserved for certain people.

Then there's racial prejudice, which is rampant in the school system. White teachers think black and Hispanic teachers are not as smart as they are, and hence can't get students to do well academically. When this proves not to be the case, as it is time and time again, they launch criticisms and accuse teachers of helping students to cheat. I met a mathematics teacher at Cooper High School in Brooklyn whose mathematics Regents exam results were reviewed by the Regents. Apparently too many of his students had passed the Regents exam.

Then there's prejudice between black teachers who are US-born, and those of us who are not. Then there are those black administrators who favor white teachers over black and Hispanic teachers. I have seen a situation where a student physically attacked a teacher, tried to rape another teacher, and cursed at several teachers and no disciplinary action was taken. Then the same student talked back to a white teacher and was suspended.

The situation transcends down to the black students who have little self worth because they are black. One black boy at Berger told me he couldn't do well in science because he wasn't smart. He was trying to forecast that he would not do well on the test that was scheduled for the following day. He then baffled me by stating, "Only white people are smart." I found this so very upsetting, not to mention the fact that I was quite offended. I'm a pretty smart person, and I'm not white. I sat that child down and had a nice long talk with him. He came in the next day and aced the test; he got over 90%, which was the highest grade in the class.

As can be expected, staff morale is usually very low in poorly run school, especially if they are in poor neighborhoods. There were quite a few discontented staff members at Berger. To make matters worst, staff members didn't like each other. There were a number of staff members who didn't like me. I heard rumors that the only reason my students did so well on the Regents chemistry exam was because they cheated. What was amazing about that was that the students' grades for the Regents parallel what they got for the class, with the exception of one student who failed the class and passed the Regents. The student who scored a 93 on the Regents scored above 90 on every chemistry test I gave, and was the school's top 11th grade student. The student who got an 85 on the Regents also got an 85 for the class, and so on and so forth.

Principal Thomson was most often the subject of the gossiping and ridicule. She was famous for sending memos to the APs. I can't tell you how many trees died expressing Nellyann's displeasure at one thing or another. The memos came to be known as 'Nellygrams'. The first thing the APs would do on getting a memo was exclaim, "Oh another Nellygram." Then they would proceed to find all the grammatical errors they could and circle them; it was just a real sad game. One of the big items of gossip was the hairpiece Nellyann always wore. She wore her hair in a bun, but the entire bun was made of fake hair. I always assumed it was her hair; it never occurred to me that someone of her stature could be so simple. I was to find out that the fake hair was just the tip of the iceberg.

All the administrators at Hoffman Evening School claimed a particular teacher had no classroom management skills. I didn't realize how bad until I saw her standing in a room full of people just staring into space and rocking back and forth as though catatonic. It is quite frightening the number of teachers in the NYC School System who are missing some of their marbles.

I must say I didn't gain much stress from teaching. I insisted that I could give students more stress than they could give me, and I wasn't bothered too much by the antics of other teachers and school administrators. I was convinced the majority of the administrators in the poorly run schools where I taught were knuckleheads, and a lot of the teachers were losers whom I would not consider associating with under normal conditions.

I was known for calling students' homes the first week of school. I would call students' parents if I saw the student in my class during a period other than the period they were assigned to be there.

I once overheard 2 Berger High School students talking about my class in the hallway. One student said that he didn't like me because I was known for failing students, the other student defended me saying that all one had to do to pass my class was do as I requested.

My other answer to teacher stress was humor. I managed to diffuse tension and stress in my classroom by using humor. I got to the point wherein I would have my students roaring with laughter when conducting simple activities:

Taking attendance—I once called a student's name, William Torpe III. William was absent, but I knew he was fat, sloppy, and a real nuisance to other students. I said, "Can you imagine that there are 2 others like him out there!" My students were fit to be tied they were laughing so much.

Routinely—I used students' colloquial expressions. When playing Jeopardy with my students in Cleveland I would write on the board "Bout It Biology Jeopardy." A student would do something nice for me, and I would respond, "Good looking out."

Grades—Students would ask, "are you going to pass me Ms. Moline?" or "did you pass me Ms. Moline?" and I would respond, "yeah, in the hallway."

Answering personal question about me: How old are you? "40". Are you an only child? "No, I have 10 brothers." Do you have any children? "Yes, I have 10 children." For some strange reason my answer was always 10 or a multiple of 10. After a while I got tired of the ridiculous fabrication, so I changed my response. Students would ask, "What are you doing this weekend, Ms. Moline?" I would tell them, "I will be home minding my own business." After a while they would get the idea that my personal life is just that—personal.

A student once asked me, "Ms. Moline, what is the name of your school?" I didn't understand so he explained, "with 10 children you must have a school at home."

Humor was definitely my drug of choice for job stress while teaching. I was in the cafeteria at Berger one day and remarked that the one good thing about teaching is that you get some really great jokes. I made the statement in all seriousness, but the minute the words were out my mouth the entire room erupted into laughter; all the teachers were nodding their assent amidst their laughter.

[07]I was trying to inspire my chemistry students at Northeastern to think positively about their ability to do well on the Regents. They wanted me to understand how little I understood their reality. One girl said, "My father told me that I will be lucky if I made it into college." Another girl agreed and said that her mother told her she would not amount to anything. The most disruptive boy in the class said, "My father said I won't make it to tomorrow." When the laughter calmed down, I asked him if he was going to prove his father wrong.

One of the things that can definitely stress a teacher out is theft. You have enough to worry about without having to worry about your property turning up missing.

My wallet was stolen in my second year at Berger. I made it known that I would give a $10 reward for its return, no questions asked. A student 'found' my wallet, returned it to me, and I paid him $10, no questions asked. I figured that the documents I had in my wallet were worth the $10, just to avoid the hassles of having to get them all back.

In retrospect I think I made a mistake in giving the $10 reward. Later that same school year my bag was stolen. I had a very nice leather bag, with a leather-bound planner in it. There wasn't much else in my bag at the time. I declined to offer a reward for the return of my bag. I didn't get the bag back, but I somehow managed not to have my bag or wallet stolen again.

Theft by teachers was quite a big problem at Berger. It seemed some teachers and administrators at the school felt the school and everything in it belonged to them. It was always the poorest schools that would have the greatest amount of theft. At Berger the Mathematics/Science Department was given a new computer and printer. When the computer was installed, it was an old beat up computer. Rumor had it that Talbot had taken the computer and printer home, and brought in his old computer and dot matrix printer from home. There was also a missing photocopier that was rumored to be at Talbot's house. I guess if you were conniving enough you could furnish an entire home office through supplies earmarked for public education.

I remember reading about the educational system in East Saint Louis, Illinois in Jonathan Kozol's book, *Savage Inequalities*. Then I went to the Internet and ran a search, and I came up with a number of articles on school personnel who were caught stealing from East St. Louis schools. East Saint Louis has to be one of the poorest educational systems in the country, yet school personnel can find it in their heart to steal from it.

There's a high school in Brooklyn where several lap top computers disappeared from a locked store room.

You want to hear the worst type of theft—food. There's always someone at each school who makes it a habit to steal food from the refrigerator in the teachers' lounge. I am sure this is not unique to teachers' lounge refrigerators. When Ms. Hardy was COSA at Berger she would go to BJ wholesale in New Jersey, and buy pastries to be eaten during student activities. There was one incident in which a large cake was stolen from the refrigerator in the COSA office. I had my guesses as to the responsible parties—that they all belonged to the Academic Department is a no-brainer.

In NYC teachers were given a small amount of funds to purchase teaching supplies. This money was referred to as Teachers' Choice. In my first year at Berger I used my Teacher's Choice to buy calculators that I could give to my students to use during exams. Ms. Hardy used her funds to purchase pens and pencils that she could give to students when they needed them. Students in NYC public schools seem to be eternally without writing utensils. In September when Ms. Hardy and I returned the supplies that we left in our classrooms were gone. The sad thing about that theft is that the supplies were left in locked drawers, and only 2 other people had keys to the drawers—Talbot and one of the other science teachers. Actually, the really sad thing about it was that the supplies were purchased for use by our students. It's amazing how little students figure in the events that take place in education; though without students there would be no need for an educational system.

At Berger I heard the story of a student who stole a teacher's car, went for a joy ride, and ended up crashing the car. When the police caught up to the student, he proclaimed his innocent. During questioning one of the police officers criticized the student's driving. The student jumped to his defense, and essentially confessed before he fully realized what was happening.

You know what I think the solution is? Whenever there is a theft in a school, it should be a requirement that the police be called in, and a full investigation launched. Think about it, if you left thousands of dollars worth of supplies in your office, and you came back the next day, and half your supplies were missing, you would want the police involved so you could at least file an insurance claim. In NYC public schools, by conservative estimates, thousands of dollars of supplies turn up missing each year, and nothing is done about it.

Supplies have to be constantly locked up. What business could possibly function if all supplies and equipment had to be locked up the minute you are through using them? Copiers are usually housed in the AP's office, and you are out of luck if you need to make copies at a time when the AP is not in his office. Of course the more organized schools have copy center, where teachers drop off materials to be copied, and pick them up on the date on their requisition.

THE RUBBER ROOM

The Rubber Room was the name given to the room at the superintendent's office where teachers who had allegations pending against them went to await trial. In some cases teachers stayed in the Rubber Room for years; the prime contender being a former Berger teacher, Mr. Sanabria.

Berger High School had managed to get several teachers into the rubber room. There were 2 teachers that I knew of, who went there as a result of confrontations with students.

The first Berger teacher I observed making it to the Rubber Room was Mr. Carothers, a special education teacher, who everyone maintained was homeless, because he went everywhere with a rather large bad. It is more likely that he also taught night school, and carried around papers to be graded.

The story that floated around the school, which principal Thomson and her cronies found rather amusing went something like this. In a special education classroom, a special education student sat at Mr. Carothers' desk ripping pages from one of Mr. Carothers' notebooks, and throwing them on the floor. Mr. Carothers sent for security. Unfazed, the student continued on his destructive path. Carothers tried to get the student away from his desk, the chair toppled over, and they fell in a heap on the floor. The police came, and I winced as I watched them take Carothers out of the school in handcuffs. The allegation was child abuse. To the Rubber Room he went to await trial.

Then there was Mr. Bell, who was rather vocal, and unafraid to speak his mind, a trait Thomson didn't find accommodating in anyone but herself. Needless to say, Thomson hated Bell. This is the story as I heard it. Mr. Bell was teaching his class. A student who felt that he was on par with Mr. Bell (students who feel that they are on par with teachers are very common in the NYC School system) went up to his desk and punched him in his stomach. Bell pushed the student, and he crashed into the wall, and supposedly got hurt. Thomson met with the parent of the student, and advised same of her right to press charges against Mr. Bell. Mr. Bell went to the Rubber Room. Testament to the strength of the powers that be, Mr. Bell was a UFT representative at the time of the incident.

Confrontations with students weren't the only excuse the system had for sending teachers to the Rubber Room. Quite frankly, if a tenured teacher who is sick of teaching (like a lot are) wanted to get paid for doing nothing, all he or she had to do was be a bit abusive, or act crazy, and he or she would probably end up in the Rubber Room. One could do a doctoral degree while sitting in that room with nothing to do but play all day.

Mr. Morton was sent there on allegation of sexual harassment of a student, a rather easy allegation to make up. Rumors of intimacy between female students and teachers as well as other school staff are rather common. How much is consensual, and how much is not is anyone's guess. This incident took place before Thomson became principal, and long before I went to Berger. Like Mr. Bell, Mr. Morton was confrontational, and not particularly liked by the powers that be. As I learned, he wasn't even liked by fellow teachers because he insulted students, and tried to boss teachers around.

Mr. Sanabria was another teacher accused of sexual harassment, and sent to the Rubber Room. The story was he fondled the breast of a student while they were in the book room together. No one knows the truth of that matter. As far as I saw, the student in question had breast so enormous, it was hard to come in contact with her without infringing on them. For at least 4 years Mr. Sanabria pined away in the Rubber room.

Nevertheless, based on the horrendous stories I have heard about Berger, I am willing to believe just about anything. I heard stories of teachers who would sleep with the students in return for passing grades, and stories of girls giving boys blowjobs in the stairwells.

Years after I left Berger I ran into a student I used to teach there. She had grown up, gotten married, had a daughter, and was working as a medical technician in Manhattan. She lived on Staten Island, and I ran into her a few mornings on the Staten Island Ferry. On one of these Ferry meetings she told me that she had to file charges of sexual harassment on a number of Berger teachers. I found this so unbelievable because at the time she was at Berger she was in the ninth grade and could not have been more than 16 years old.

Mr. Fisher went to the Rubber Room because he was found too dangerous to be in school. It was the most amazing crack-up I ever saw. One day he was respectable, the next he was just plain nutty. Maybe he arranged it all so he could get out of Berger. In which case I wouldn't blame him too much, considering what the working conditions were at the time.

A student, one of the School's brightest, got into a motor vehicle accident shortly before graduation. Most teachers who knew the student were distraught, but when the news was released in the auditorium, Mr. Fisher started crying. He cried so loud all the teachers heard, and wondered what the hell was wrong with him. I must have been absent that day; I seem to miss all the good ones.

He made a big thing because a student while playing in the school yard threw a ball that landed sufficiently far from him that it could not have been intended to hurt him. Then he kept getting into verbal fights with people in his department. The last straw was when he started fighting with the union chapter leader, Gerald Canaan. He was unceremoniously taken from the school. TO THE RUBBER ROOM WITH HIM.

Unlike the other Rubber Room inhabitants from Berger, Mr. Fisher didn't sit still and collect his paycheck, instead he filed lawsuits. I don't know what the results of his lawsuits were, but he was reassigned to a teaching position in another school.

Maybe for the first couple of months in the Rubber Room when you get that paycheck, and know you didn't go through the nightmare that is teaching, you are bound to feel good. Surely, though, it's bound to get boring, even unnerving, after a while. Especially having to wake up early to be on time for a job, that is not a real job.

In the NYC school system never think anything is impossible when it comes to bad behavior. I heard that some years ago a New York City newspaper did an article about the 10 worst teachers in NYC. Number 1 on the list was a Stuben High School teacher who would fondle himself under his coat while he was teaching, and number 2 on the list was a past Langley High School teacher who was always sloppily dressed and smelling of chicken. One day he hit a student whose father was a police officer, and that was it for him.

PRINCIPAL'S REVENGE

One of the best things to happen to me in my teaching career was my being assigned a mentor. It happened in my second semester at Berger High School, when I was holding on simply because I needed the money.

My Mentor, Ms. Hardy, was a pillar of strength and a fountain of ideas. She was responsible for providing me with the kind of mentoring that helped me through many tough times. Mentoring is a wonderful thing if you get the right mentor. I knew a teacher at Cooper High School who was always complaining about her mentor. She insisted she did not want him as her mentor, she complained constantly, yet he remained her mentor for the entire year. She said he would tell her about his personal relationship with his girlfriend (her mentor was a retired chemistry teacher who had to be over 50 years old) though she had no desire to hear it. He was a disruptive influence in her class. In addition he would go to the AP and tell him negative things about her. This mentor was not only a nuisance to the teacher he was assigned to mentor, but to other teachers, including me. He kept insisting he wanted to sit in on my Chemistry class, though I told him "NO" several times.

My being mentored was the reason for my being able to return to Berger High School as a substitute teacher for a second year (because I did not have New York State certification, I was considered a long term substitute); this to everyone's shock, and to the dismay of many. It was highly unusual for a black female teacher to last more than a semester in the Mathematics/science Department at Berger High School.

In September of 1994, I went back to Berger for a third straight year. I was really making school history. Boy was I ready to go. My head was teeming with ideas I picked up over the summer. I felt confident that things would be the same or even better, was I in for a shock.

The first thunderbolt hit when I found out my mentor had decided not to return to Berger High School. When I looked back at the events prior to summer I understood why.

The second thunderbolt hit when I saw the class schedule. I was scheduled to conduct physics and chemistry labs, 5 days per week at 7:15 am. My chemistry class would be a single period per day. My other 3 classes were biology recitation classes. Remember I am a chemistry teacher. In June the counselors indicated to me that there would be several chemistry classes. There was only one.

The third bolt of thunder came shattering in later when I met the students to whom I was supposed to teach Regents level biology. It was an amazing downturn from the previous year's ninth graders. On a given day my ears would hurt from the amount of foul language that was being constantly thrown across the room in loud shrieks. It was so bad that I spent most of the time sighing and wishing the annoying children would crawl back under the rocks from whence they came. All the exhaustion and frustration that had built up over the years came tumbling down on me.

What I did in response to the ridiculous, inconsiderate schedule is what I felt led to my being excessed in January 1995, which indirectly led to my getting a position at Langley High School.

Simply put, I took a stand. I told Mr. Talbot, "I can't do zero period (7:15 am)." He explained there was nothing he could do. He said, "Go tell the principal." He then added, "I wanted to do the zero period myself, since I get here at that time anyway, but she doesn't want that (by 'she' he meant Principal Thomson)." I went to Ms. Thomson. Sitting smugly behind her extra large desk in her smug office, she asked me, "Did you talk to Mr. Talbot about this?" I told her I had spoken to Mr. Talbot and he said he could do nothing about it. She said, "Well, there is nothing I can do about it." She looked me dead in the eye when she said this. Right away I knew she was lying. Initially I did not believed Talbot when he said it was her doing. Past experiences had taught me to be very wary of anything that Talbot said.

I felt Nellyann was just being pigheaded, insisting on having things her way; it was always her way or the highway. Talbot told me that he told Nellyann about my being disgruntled with zero period and her comment was, "If she doesn't like it she can get another job." I didn't know if she actually said it, as always anything Talbot said had to be taken with a cup of salt. Nevertheless, I was unnerved and hurt. But then I could be just as pigheaded. I continued to insist on not doing zero period.

The semester started. I didn't get to zero period, but neither did the students. Ultimately, I went to my union representative. He asked, "Did you request zero period?" I told him that I didn't. "Then you don't have to do it," he confirmed, "your official work hours are 8:55 to 2:15." He scheduled a meeting with the Principal.

On the morning of September 13, 1994, we all gathered in Ms. Thomson's office. Mr. Talbot, Gerald Canaan, Ms. Thomson and myself. I stated my point about having personal responsibilities that precluded my getting to Berger at 7:15 am. At the time I had a 2 year old son who I had to take to the babysitter before going to work. Also, I was afraid of taking public transportation to the South Bronx that early in the morning. It would mean being on the train at 6 am in the morning.

It was crazy of the Principal to just suddenly tell all her science teachers to show up at 7:15 am every morning with no consideration for whether or not they are able to make it. Worst, the students weren't happy with it either. From the look of things, Ms. Thomson was the only one down with the zero period. I also knew that I would end up working 9 periods most days because of all the things that would come up after 7th period; especially preparing for the next morning's lab.

Mr. Talbot again stated his willingness to do the zero period. It was obvious to everyone there that Ms. Thomson was just being pigheaded. Gerald Canaan stated that my work hours were 7:55 to 2:15, and unless I requested otherwise, I didn't have any obligation to do any other schedule. Ms. Thomson conceded, and I received a letter to that effect.

As I understand, Ms. Thomson was in quite a huff after the meeting. She said of me, "Well, she better get here at 7:55." How bitchy can you get? Gerald Canaan was amazed that I was the only science teacher to complain; he commended me for doing so. Little did I know that the compliment was empty and insincere.

I may have won the battle, but the war had just started. I became a new target for Nellyann's power parades. For 3 semesters I taught in room 212 and I never saw her anywhere near my room. Suddenly she started frequenting the area. I would be standing at my door letting students into my classroom, and she would be standing there watching. Students claimed to have seen her peeping into my room. One of the few friends I had at Berger told me, "She's after you." Talbot told me it would be in my best interest to find another job because Ms. Thomson wanted to get rid of me. I was really shocked that she could be that petty.

Anyone reading this would be convinced I must have done more than just file a grievance regarding teaching zero period, which was well within my rights. Also bear in mind that I did talk to both the Principal and the AP about being uncomfortable with zero period before filing the grievance.

On Monday September 24, 1994, during my 4th period Biology class Ms. Thomson walked in at the beginning of the second period of a double period class, and sat down to observe my teaching. I had an inkling of what was being staged. After all, in my prior 2 years at Berger High School she had never been to my classroom.

By fall of 1994 I was quite comfortable with classroom observations. Actually there's a story behind my developing confidence regarding my classroom teaching. Something my mentor did in the spring of 1993 had a lasting impression on my feelings about my classroom performance. My mentor arranged for me to observe Talbot's physical science class. What she did was to tell Talbot that he should allow me to visit his class so I could see the right way to conduct a lesson.

When my mentor and I entered the room and sat down in the back we could tell Talbot had an excellent lesson planned. However, planning a good lesson is no indication of one's ability to teach a good lesson. Talbot spent the entire period trying to work on a single sentence on the board, which was apparently his motivation for the lesson that never came. The students were not at all motivated, and they were not paying attention to what he was saying.

A couple of students kept turning to us and exclaiming "He can't teach!" Then someone would call out, "Okay set it off." This was apparently a cue to alert everyone it was time to start a racket. The students started stomping on the floor, banging on the desks, and making animal sounds. Talbot prevailed to the end through the racket and the interruptions. Every now and then he would call out almost in a shriek, "Young man do you want me to call your parents?"

There isn't a shred of doubt in my mind that if he observed me conducting a lesson like the one he did that day, he would have given me an unsatisfactory rating.

In our post-observation conference with Talbot, Hardy told Talbot how impressed she was with the lesson. She said she was particularly impressed by the fact that he did not allow the students' interruptions to spoil his lesson. Ms. Hardy would look across to me for confirmation and I would nod in agreement; I knew the game she was playing and I was only too happy to play along. After the meeting Ms. Hardy and I went back to her classroom and we had quite a laugh at Talbot's expense. Henceforth I was never uncomfortable about being observed.

So when Ms. Thomson walked in that day to observe me I continued on confidently with my lesson. It was a great lesson; actually a follow-up lesson from the previous period. Recall that Nellyann came in during the second half of the class.

I started out with concept mapping. I had all the life functions listed on the board; I had the students tell me words that came to mind when they heard each of the listed term. Then I went through the students' list of words and pointed out key words that they should associate with the life process for Regents exam purposes. For example, one key word for the life process *respiration* was *energy*.

Having completed the concept mapping I proceeded to use a projection microscope to project the image of a hydra onto a screen (the projection microscope was one of the relics I found when I cleaned up the store room). I knew how impressed my students were with that particular image. I challenged students to indicate how they felt the different life processes were carried out by the hydra. They did an excellent job. My class went out of their way to impress the Principal with their class participation. It was one of the best lessons I ever taught at Berger.

Ms. Thomson requested that I meet with her later that day for a post-observation conference. I went and sat across from her at the huge conference table in her office.

One of the reasons I have never allowed my sons to sell candy for their schools was what I learnt at Berger. It was rumored that some of the furniture in Ms. Thomson's office was bought using funds raised for student activities by candy sale. When the students were ready to use the money for the purpose they intended it, the school administration was unable to produce it.

Nellyann asked if I had a pen and paper to take notes. I told her I was fine. Did I mention that Nellyann was a typing teacher before becoming principal? Remember what I said before—in the NYC public school system connections is everything and skills mean nothing. Ms. Thomson proceeded to tear a page from her notebook, which she pushed across the table to me along with a pencil.

She could find nothing good to say about the lesson. Students were always complimenting me on my classroom. They insisted I had the nicest classroom in the school. They were right too. I had one of the biggest classrooms in the school, and I made good use of all that space. I always made sure the desks were all neatly aligned, and the students kept it that way. My classroom was also very clean, because absolutely no eating was allowed. I had relevant posters on the wall, and students' assignments (mainly research papers) were displayed on bulletin boards around the room. Ms. Thomson didn't even comment on my classroom. She ranted and raved about what she wanted to see happen in the classroom. She spoke of how poorly students were doing in science. As though to site an appropriate example she said, "Do you know what the Regents chemistry results were last year?" I indicated to her that I assisted in the grading of the papers so I was quite aware of the results.

She said, "Only 16% of the students who took the chemistry Regents passed." I told her that maybe she had chemistry confused with physics because 16% was the result for physics. The chemistry result was actually 50%, and this was with all the students from the class taking the Regents and 2 students scoring 64. She got into quite a huff insisting that she was right. As though to prove her point she went to her file cabinet to get the data, and came back without it. Apparently she checked and realized I was right.

She came back to the table and continued with her tirade without even a hint at an apology. At that instant I knew I could do no right at that school. To make matters worst I hadn't taken any notes. I left the pencil and paper sitting in the same spot where she placed them.

That day when I went home I called up a friend of mine who was a junior high school AP at the time. He told me in no uncertain manner, "That principal is out to get you; you need to get out of there." He was nice enough to set up an interview for me with Mr. Don Seeley of Coolidge High School.

I went to Coolidge High School to meet with Mr. Seeley. He ran into me on my way to his office for my interview. He exclaimed, "You are Ms. Moline?" When I indicated that I was, he said, "I saw you teach night school at Bissell. You want the job, it's yours." So I was hired, and we skipped the interview and begun discussing schedules, textbooks, and lab assignments.

I met the principal and he started making plans to have me transferred over. When Ms. Thomson was contacted by Coolidge regarding releasing me, she had a serious problem with it. She said she had no one to replace me so she was not willing to release me. She asked me why I didn't talk to her about it before I went ahead and made plans to transfer. This from the same woman who made it her job to terrorize me, and went around the school telling people how weak a teacher I was, and how much she wanted to get rid of me. I had my reliable sources in the school who kept me informed about who was saying what about me.

Nellyann told me she had no intention of releasing me. It was up to me, I could quit and go to Coolidge or I could stay. It was quite a drag. I spoke to Mr. Seeley, and we concurred that I should stay for the rest of the semester and then leave. He was sure to warn me that he couldn't guarantee his school would still have a position in the spring.

About 2 weeks after she conducted the classroom observation, and a few days after refusing to sign my release, Principal Thomson wrote me up an unsatisfactory observation report. I wrote a rebuttal but didn't bother to attach it to the report. I just signed the extra thick report and gave it back to the poor secretary who must have spent an entire day typing it on her word processor. Here's a part of that observation report:

As I entered the room you were going over your Do Now. I noticed that written on the board were your name, Regents Biology, the date and the aim ("What are Cells?"), Do Now—Write Words Associated With the Following: nutrition, excretion, synthesis, reproduction, regulation, transport
Also, displayed in the classroom were the following words:
  kingdom, phylum, order, family, genus, species
  2. polisis, protozoa, algae
  3. plant trachepy
After completing the Do Now you began to review a previous test. Some questions you posed were: How do you get energy? How do you get nutrition? You read each one the questions which you had written for the test and you wrote each answer on the board. Toward the end of this you called on two students to read the questions from the test. At this point you asked the students if there were any questions on the test. The students answered in unison "no". You stated that the students should make sure they copied the test answers from the board. You then introduced a large version of a microscope displayed in the front of the classroom. You wanted to show what a hydra looks like through a large microscope. You stated that this is a organism that lives in water. You showed where the cells are. You then went into an amoeba but the slides did not properly display the amoeba. At this point the bell rang and the class left.

During the post observation conference we discussed the following:
Commendations

1. *Your room is nicely decorated with words relating to biology, i.e. phylum, synthesis, etc.*

2. *Also, you had written on the board your name, subject, date, aim, and do now.*

This was followed by almost 2 pages of recommendations, then:
I have suggested to your assistant principal that you meet with him n a scheduled weekly basis to work on enhancement. In view of all the recommendations listed above this lesson was unsatisfactory.

I wrote this rebuttal to the observation, but I didn't bother to attach it.

October 19, 1994

I was extremely perturbed today by the occurrence of the following episode. Mr. Talbot and Mr. Lyons entered my classroom, and handed me two copies of an observation report for my signature. When I proceeded to examine the report, I was told, "you don't need to read it, just sign it". I refused to sign the report simply due to the fact that the situation seemed highly unusual. There are a number of things that bear mention:

1. *The observation and post-observation conference were done on September 26th, which meant the written report was being issued over 3 weeks thereafter.*

2. *The rating on the report was "unsatisfactory", even though there was no indication of this in the post-observation conference. It's rather unusual that a lesson that was unsatisfactory was deemed so over 3 weeks after the fact.*

3. *The only recommendation that was made at the post-observation conference was that I use more visual aids. I have tried my best to meet this objective, which I happen to share. There are constraints—the lack of textbooks for student use, lack of photocopying facilities, and lack of suitable teaching aids.*

4. *The actual observation report itself is erroneous. For instance, I would never ask the question, "How do you get nutrition?" since nutrition is a process and not a thing.*

5. *In reading the observation, my only conclusion is that the unsatisfactory rating was a result of my teaching technique deviating from what is expected. I am not a biologist, and I was never trained as a teacher of science. I have always worked in industry where workers met the demands of training that I offered. In my two years of teaching I have relied mostly on my own creativity, mainly a result of the limited support I received at Berger. My technique has at least had marginal success (70% pass—RCT science; 50% pass Regents chemistry).*

6. *I don't recall indicating that the students are weak. I usually have very high expectations for students; sometimes I think I believe in them more than they believe in themselves. I had a recent incidence where a student told me he felt he was dumb. After spending a half an hour convincing the student otherwise, I loaned him my textbook, told him what section to study, and he scored over 90% on the test the following day. Also, more than 70% of the class passed the test, due in part to my stressing the need to prepare for the test.*

On one of the copies of the report Talbot scribbled
On 10/19/94 teacher refused to sign this observation report.
   Talbot
   Lyons—Witnessed by

I didn't bother to include Nellyann's page and a half of recommendations, which only further highlighted her ignorance. I will just make some quick comments; I just read this report again after all these years, and it got me quite angry. 1) Nellyann came in during the second half of a double period biology class, and the majority of the observation report was focused on the few minutes I spent at the end of the class going over a test that the students took the Friday before. If this were an observation aimed at helping me to improve my teaching skills, then Nellyann would have consulted me before coming in, or at the very least consult my schedule and come into my class at the beginning of the lesson instead of near the end. 2) I am embarrassed to know that I was employed by a school with a principal with such poor grammar. I know most of it had to do with her lack of knowledge when it comes to science, but still 'polisis', plant 'trachepy'; I couldn't even find those words in any dictionary or glossary. 3) Just about every satisfactory observation I received while teaching mentioned the fact that I had excellent classroom control, Nellyann didn't even mentioned that in passing. 4) According to Nellyann I should have a lesson plan displayed on my desk. I usually have a lesson plan on my desk but it's for my benefit only.

My lesson plan is usually very detail to ensure I have enough activities to capture students attention for the entire period. Actually I did not develop this skill until I taught at Langley High School, after leaving Berger. Of course as far as I knew a written lesson plan was not required. The agreement between the UFT and the Board was that the teacher's lesson should show evidence of planning. 5) The most amazing part of the report was where she stated that she wanted me to meet with Talbot on a weekly basis to work on enhancement. The entire report highlighted one major fact—Nellyann was completely oblivious to what was going on in the school she was supposed to be in charge of.

In true persecution style Talbot came in to observe my biology class, and guess what he gave me. Right oh—an observation report that said my lesson was unsatisfactory. Regardless of the fact that the lesson he observed me teaching was better then the one I observed him teaching by a long shot.

I went and had a talk with Mr. Canaan about the grand conspiracy that was unfolding. I did not know then that Mr. Canaan was one of the actors in the drama. I can't stop wondering if a few teeth cleanings and a couple of cheap lens is worth the over $4,000 I have paid the UFT over the years. I have yet to receive any other benefit from the UFT. Union representatives always seem to have closer ties with school administration than they do with teachers, though they collect dues from our salary with the pretense of representing us.

I taught in Cleveland, Ohio for a year. I did not join the teachers' union there yet I had just as much benefit as in New York, and a lot more comforts. The only difference was I got more money per month because my salary was spread over 10 months instead of 12. Though I made more money per pay period (2 weeks) I paid less in State taxes than I did in New York, the high tax state of the union, but that's another matter.

Mr. Canaan assured me that since both observations were for biology, and my license area was chemistry then those observations could not be used to give me an unsatisfactory at the end of the school year.

As though to make up for the discrepancy, Talbot came in to observe the only Chemistry class I had. Again I did what I felt was an excellent lesson, yet once again I was given an observation report that said my lesson was unsatisfactory. Let me just say that in all honesty Talbot observed me teaching lessons that I considered less than satisfactory, yet I was given a satisfactory rating. Essentially what they were saying was that after 2 years of getting all satisfactory ratings observation after observation (Talbot had given me 12 satisfactory observations in the past 2 school years), suddenly I could not teach a satisfactory lesson to save my life. At the last post-observation conference I asked Talbot the rhetorical question, "is this a conspiracy?" He put on his high beam when he answered "no", so I could see just how much he was enjoying my persecution.

At the end of the semester I was excessed. Talbot was assigned the only chemistry class so they had no need for a chemistry teacher. It didn't seem to matter that only one science teacher in the building was there longer than I was. The UFT did nothing. I later heard that Mr. Canaan went around telling people that I could have avoided being excessed, but I couldn't make up my mind if I wanted to stay or not.

I was assigned to sit in the class of an unlicensed teacher to enable him to teach. So for about a week I sat in this teacher's class and worked on my crossword puzzles or read a book while he taught.

In that week I got a call from the then science AP at Langley High School in Queens, Mr. Egan. I went in for an interview, and was offered a position. It turned out that on realizing he wouldn't have a position for me for that spring Mr. Seeley had gone ahead and referred me to Mr. Egan, who had a position available.

The following week while Langley High School was working on my transfer I was given a letter requesting that I attend a hiring fair in Manhattan. While I was at the hiring fair trying to dodge the alternative high schools that were trying desperately to hire me, a secretary told me that I had a call from Langley High School. The message said it was an emergency. When I called Langley they told me to come over right away.

The secretary at the hiring hall thought the emergency had to do with a child I had at Langley. I played along so I could get out of there without any problems. I was informed prior to the fair that if offered a position by one of the alternative high schools I would have to accept it. Mr. Egan has often told the amusing story of how he rescued me from the alternative high schools that day.

MY CLEVELAND EXPERIENCES
Hedley High School, Cleveland Ohio (August 1996 to May, 1997)

Students long to belong. They realize too late from behind bars that the land of the free is not free for all.

MY CLEVELAND EXPERIENCES
Hedley High School, Cleveland Ohio (August 1996 to May, 1997)

The community in which Hedley High School was located was in all likelihood the most depressed area in Cleveland. Most times I was depressed from walking through the neighborhood.

What did amaze me was that so many of the students were able to rise above the despair. Others became victims of it. Most of the victims seemed to have been grouped together as my 6th period class.

Teaching in Cleveland made NYC schools seem like paradise, and that's not an understatement.

On my first day in my classroom without students I thought it was heaven. It wasn't until about the second week that I realized it was just hell in disguise.

It was easy for me to be fooled. The classroom was beautiful compared to what I was used to in NYC. There was a television mounted on the wall at the back of the room. Yes a television, and it wasn't just my classroom either, most of the classrooms in the building were like that. The television was turned on throughout the building during the homeroom period. I got a computer for my room. Yes my very own computer for school use, it had, would you believe, a Pentium chip, and the latest version of Microsoft Works.

It was a lab and classroom in one. There were about thirty swivel chairs. There were 2 black lab counters that spanned about two third the length of the room. The lab counter at the teacher's desk was green and quite large. The counters were equipped with electrical sockets to plug microscopes; there were also sinks, and gas lines. There were 2 storerooms at the back of the room. There were also 3 storage cabinets, a teacher's desk and a filing cabinet. Just about all the things I always wanted all to myself when I was in NYC.

We were issued office supplies, and paper to decorate our bulletin boards. Again my surprise—pens, pencils, markers, highlighters, stapler, staple remover, paper clips, chalk, index cards, tape, tape dispenser, and file folders. I was not only given a key to my room but also keys to the science supply rooms. Yes, I could go in and get what I needed.

Then reality set in. I found out early that the school's administration was weak, and the students wouldn't know respect if it walked up to them and slapped their ignorant faces. To top things off the principal's name was Billy Jean, the name alone was reason for the students to mock him. The strongest administrators were 2 women, one ran the 11th grade unit office, and the other ran the 12th grade unit office. Based on grade level, students at Hedley were assigned to unit offices which handled guidance and discipline. The person in charge of the unit office was like a guidance counselor and dean of discipline combined.

My year at Hedley High School in Cleveland was a futile waste of time.

Surprisingly, of all the schools I have taught in, the only one that seemed to have had strong administration was Langley High School. As a result, Langley was the school I found with the least number of serious disciplinary problems.

I have decided to talk about my classes period by period, omitting those students who were no shows. I must first say that up until the end of the first semester new students kept coming into my class, up until the middle of the semester students were being transferred out. The only problem this gave was my needing to add and remove names from my roster, in the broader scheme of things it didn't matter because about two thirds of my classes didn't bother to show up.

At Hedley I decided I would make a serious effort to make a difference with my absentees. So every morning I would spend about half an hour calling students' homes. If I didn't have any luck in the morning, I would try again in the afternoon (the last period of the day was a preparatory period for me). I dare say I was making an average of about 20 calls per day every day; included in this amount were calls I made for students who were disciplinary problems. I had a folder in which I kept a log of all the calls I made and the results of those calls.

The section that follows was written during the 1996–7 school year while I was still teaching at Hedley, and hence some of it is written in the present tense.

First Period (biology)

This is the class I am supposed to teach about DNA replication and transcription, yeah right. This is not to say that it is impossible, I do have about half a dozen students who come every day and do well enough to get a B or higher.

I don't know where this falls in the scheme of things, but most of my students have expressed dislike of their fathers. Some have even expressed dislike of their mothers. It seems the fathers are a poor influence in their lives.

Larry Cooper showed up a couple of times, faked interest and tried to conceive ways of getting out of coming to class. Whenever I called his home all I got was an answering machine. I referred it to his unit office, and they sent the referral back with the same number I had been calling in vain. I took that as my cue to leave it alone.

Ben Delaney is a sweet child. He is a ninth grader who is almost always present and never late. As good as his attendance is his classroom attitude is almost opposite. He and I have had to fight and fight to bring his grade up to passing, not because he is weak on the intellect side but because he spends far too much time talking when he should be working. He once told me his parents don't like me, so they don't care what I say. He expressed that he felt it was in my best interest to stop calling his house. He went on to tell me, "You don't know how crazy my mother is." If he wasn't such a small child who I couldn't attach any cruel intentions to, I would have called his home to have things sorted out.

Alice Duncan and Lavern Ebersole I placed together because I was never able to distinguish between them initially. They both came to me to try to talk me into giving them passing grades. I told them if they were present from that time to the end of the semester then I would see what I could do. I believe they were both absent the next day. I gave them an extensive amount of make-up work to do and hand in; I am still waiting. One of them came to me to ask that I let her sit in another teacher's class and then she would bring me the grade from the other teacher, I said I didn't work like that. I have never seen 2 students try in so many ways just to get over. The energy they spent trying to get over they could have used to pass the class and then some. Then talk about attitude, they will curse me out if only I will let them.

I went through a lot of changes with Alice; I recorded speaking to her father, her mother and twice to her uncle, plus writing her a referral, all for poor attendance. I am pleased to say Alice is no longer an absentee, and Lavern is no longer in the class. Lavern came up with her father, and I told her if she didn't like the class I was in agreement with her changing, and she did. I found out Alice is pregnant. I spoke for many days with her mother, and she came back to class, made an A for the first marking period of the semester, and has been doing well ever since. One day poor Alice threw up in the hallway. I guess she was having a bad bout of morning sickness. I felt so bad. You know what though, she never stopped coming to class.

Dean Eason is the cookie kid, he carries cookies and cake to school to sell; I tasted a sample and told him it was good. I guess he expected me to buy some, but I figure I make better pastries myself. His grade started falling after that or is it just my imagination. Then he hooked up with this Willie Winkleman; I don't think I have ever seen 2 boys talk that much to each other. What do they find to talk about?

Sara Fogg is a really sweet child. She joined the class in the second semester, stayed a while, did excellent work, and then never came back. I called her number and found out she is a foster child, who has decided to leave her guardian's care.

Jenny George and Denise Williams—'batty (behind) and bench' as we say in the Caribbean. It was rare for me to see one without the other. I must say they did work fairly well together.

Bret Greco is late for class a lot and always talking. I recorded speaking to his mother about both, but neither improved.

Roy Hood is another talker. I had him suspended, spoke to his Junior Reserve Officer's Training Corps (JROTC) sergeant, spoke to his grandparents (he got a kick out of that one), still he talks on. At least his grades have continually improved.

Tom Holley just refuses to come to class. The number I had for him turned out to be incorrect. I called and was told, "There is no one here by that name, and I have been living here for the last 2 years." He gave me the right number but continued to cut class. I had him suspended 8 days total to no avail.

Tammy Hasara is a cute little girl. She has been doing pretty well, because I am quick to call and reach her mother, and her mother apparently quick to discipline.

Betty Jenkins is the little fighter. If there is a fight she might be in it. Hard to believe she is a 9th grader. She does really good work, and she is very responsible about making up work after her suspensions. In other words she is always making up work. We made a deal that I would sign for her to be a cheerleader if she agreed not to fight again for the rest of the school year. She talked me into excluding the last day of school.

Gary Johnson is a truly disturbed child. On the rare occasions when he did come to class, he came early took one of the chairs and sat outside the door even after the bell rang. If I gave a lab assignment he would destroy the things he is supposed to be working with. There was one stage when he did settle down and do work. Surprisingly it was the time I accused him of stealing my keys. I still feel he did it. He is no longer in the school.

Marion Logan was often absent or late for 1st period. I kept calling his father. He told me his father said I should stop calling his house. I spoke to his father; he claimed he said he wished I wouldn't have to call. Then he went on to give me the name and number of Marion's parole officer. That's when I decided not to call anymore.

Martin Malle is basically a good kid, so childish though. I got his grades up, but he still talks and laughs too much. He once gave me candy—2 packs of twisters, I felt that was so sweet.

I called Sally McDonald's mother over and over again. She can't seem to control her daughter, and certainly couldn't get her to come to 1st period. Had her suspended for 8 days, still nothing. I got the feeling her mother was tired of my calling, so I said fuck them and the horse they rode in on, and I stopped calling.

Lelieth Taylor is absent a lot, but I don't think she misses anything since when she is present she does very little work.

Fred Taylor always comes out of dress code because he wants me to send him out; I always keep him in class, and refuse to give him a pass to the bathroom, which was always his plan B. Such a listless child; his mother said he got good grades when he was in junior high. Spoke to his mother over and over, also spoke to the unit office; no one seems to be able to get through to him.

David Turner is definitely destined for good things. He is a very responsible 9th grader who has been student of the month every month, and has maintained an 'A' for the entire year. While at Hedley, I made it a policy to award 2 certificates per month per class—*student of the month*, and *most improved student*.

Walsh Williams does more talking than anything else. He just got expelled, it turns out my class was the only one he was attending, and lots of times he was late.

Debra Waters comes to class, feigns interest, gets all her makeup work, then disappear for a month or 2, or is it a semester or 2.

Dinah Washington is a really sweet child who is very dedicated to doing her work and talking at the same time.

Third Period (biology)

Sara Adams, like David Turner of first period, is destined for great things. She reminds me of me when I was in high school. She thinks writing is in her future and I think she has the confidence to make it happen. She never cuts, is always serious and very responsible. If she were the only student present in a class she would sit down and get to work, business as usual.

Delta Carr showed up a few times, got make up work and then disappeared. She is in the process of being expelled for absences.

I will definitely miss Toni Cassidy. She is such a sweetheart—witty, intelligent, and shows clear evidence of advance thinking.

I don't know what kind a game Naomi Capshaw and her mother are playing. She has been having trouble with her schedule from she started school until now. I just leave it alone. I figure if her mother is her partner in crime, then I am west and I need not be in that mess.

Jeffrey Clay's parents were upset with his grade; he has been improving, but he is nowhere near what he is capable of.

I Spoke to Kenneth Cole's mother a number of times, and she seems as lost as I am. I think he might be in rehabilitation, because the few times I have seen him, he was intoxicated.

I don't think I know Richard DeVito, but the last I heard he was going to boot camp, which could be a good thing.

Jimmy Duddman is just dazed and confused. He is a good kid, but I think he may have skipped junior high school. He reminds me of kids I have taught for whom English was their 2nd language.

Mark Farvin is a trip. He talks back, is disruptive, always out of his seat, always out of dress code, and does little or no work. I have written a lot of referrals on him, which resulted in suspensions and Saturday schools. Usually when I write a referral for 3rd period it's on Mark, everybody else behaves and does their work. In case you are wondering, this is the same Mark Farvin that was in a fight with the teacher.

Hannah Frank started in the 2nd semester. I started out staying on his case by calling his parents and grandparents, until I realized that by having him in class Mark had a partner in crime, that's when I decided to leave it alone. I would rather have 1 student lose out, than have that one student cause my entire class to lose out.

Harry Khan drops in every once in a while.

Nancy Harriman was a really sweet girl when she did come to class. Nevertheless she has been expelled for non attendance.

Arlene Hall is in the process of being expelled for absences.

Katherine Hall—same as Arlene, except I have seen her far more times than I have seen Arlene.

Marlene Hilman is a very sweet girl, except for that time she raised her voice at me for not showing her her grades right away.

Tornthon Holms has been having 'scheduling problems' all year.

I tried to get Morris Munroe to do better, instead he just stopped coming to class. I don't think he missed much since he had gotten to the point where all he did was draw in class. Maybe he'll become a famous artist one day because I allowed him to draw in biology class, and didn't insist he learn biology.

For a long time I thought Carlene Penn was pregnant; she was always so bored, serious and 'pouty'. I think it may be that she is being abused mentally at home. She is fairly consistent in her work and attendance, and for that I am happy.

Jackie Portman's dad is a lawyer. According to his grandfather, his parents are both busy doing their thing. His grandfather has been sitting on his case. I don't even think he is smoking anymore. Turns out he is a very sharp child mentally.

Milton Robinson drops by every now and then to complain and give the many excuses why he hasn't been coming to class.

Pauline Todds is a chubby 9th grader, and one of the few students who have bothered to act their age. She has been absent a lot because one of her other teachers decided to sign her up for conflict management. Maybe she needs to learn to handle conflict more than she needs to learn her subject matter, I don't know.

Lerlene Yates decided not to return to Shaw after some nasty girl said nasty things about her in the cafeteria, I don't blame her.

Fourth Period (general science)

Warren Bingham is a very bright child, but extremely rude and disgusting, especially with his bad breath. I have had to write him up a number of times for insubordination.

I thought Daniel Butts was slow, until I failed him, and saw him turn his grades around. He is extremely quiet and respectful.

I always have to remind myself that Allan Barkley is in the 11th grade. He is so childish, and tempest. I had to write him up about dress code and insubordination.

I think I have seen Sally Benjamin once. She is in the process of being expelled for absences.

Nilsa Cummings left for another school, and boy was I happy to see her go. She was loud and insubordinate. Her ambition was to outdo Jerrie Dinkins as the fight starter. Once I gave her a referral and the office gave her 'office detention'. I decided either I could question what the fuck that was, and burst a blood vessel, or I could just ignore it.

Frank Cutler is very childish; I guess you could say he is just acting his age. Apparently he is a foster child, and his foster parent has a lot of them. The foster parent told me that she's doing the best she can.

Reyann Custuss—Boy what it takes to be a cheerleader these days; it seems my most boisterous students are the ones signing up for cheerleading. She is disruptive, writes on the board, and exposes her body parts and talks about them. I Called her home many times, and then she disappeared. I gave her a low grade, so she has to come to class and behave in order to be a cheerleader and play sports.

Jerrie Dinkins is the fight starter himself. The only fight I ever had was one he started with Vince Gottard. When I call his mother it spells only temporary relief. I am always writing him up for insubordination (talking back to me), and being disruptive.

The students in the class tease Roy Edmunds about his clothes. One day he spent the entire period trying to convince the class he doesn't wear cheap clothes, how pathetic. His mother keeps calling and missing me. I hope she continues to miss me until Thursday when I leave, because Roy has been cutting and I haven't had time to call as I promised I would.

Vince Gottard is a huge boy who spends the entire period trying to draw attention to himself. I have written him up for being disruptive, called his parent about his singing in class, and wrote him up for sticking a metal object into the electrical socket.

Jarrett Gentile is a very quiet student who rarely comes to class.

Nereen Hunter once threatened to hit me in the face. Now we are communicating well, she does my attendance, and brings my mail sometimes.

Lorna Iseman used to talk a lot when she came to class. I saw her the other day, said she is dropping out of school to work.

I don't know Tonya Jordan, but I gather she has a child.

Ilizabet Kurl is a real good student. Her grade and attendance has been falling off lately.

I Hardly see Dennis Marzon. When he does come, he spends the period complaining that I don't teach him anything. Last time I spoke to him, he told me he had to go to court.

Denville Masters is a quiet child. He used to cut a lot. Now he has a leg injury so he comes to class just about every day. The nasty children hide his crutches.

Albert Morgan was a headache and a half. He was also a senior. He would sing, bang on the desk, get all the other students into it, and essentially prevent me from teaching. I once said to him, "I can't believe that you are a senior." His response was, "I can't believe that you are a teacher." I saw him at graduation, said he already got his high school diploma, and got accepted to college. May the Lord have mercy on him, and whoever he gets as instructors when he gets to college.

Ray Peyton was doing poorly, and then I spoke to his mother and told her just how much better he could do, so he improved.

Kyle Prince is in the 11th grade. I get the feeling he should be in the 12th. He comes to class sometimes, claims he can't stand me, maybe I require too much of him.

Tammy Sheldon was in my class for a semester. She came to class when she felt like it, spent the period talking about who is 'getting paid'. She failed the class and came crying to me to change her grade so she could graduate. I refused to change it. I saw her at graduation, I have no idea how she pulled that, and I don't care.

Jamine Wilton is a 9th grader who I had to write up the first week of school. He has been kicked out of Hedley.

The Sixth Period Nightmare (general science)

I guess there's hardly a high school teacher who has not had the sixth period from hell. If you have no sixth period class, the nightmare usually shifts to fifth or seventh period.

Some say, "It's all that sugar they get at lunch time." or "They're already hyper, feeding them at lunch time with all that sugar just makes things worst." Yes I know, it sounds like precautions for the care of gremlins.

One of the worst 6th period classes I ever had was at Hedley High School. They were so disgusting that at times I would write 4 to 6 referrals, and have someone from my 7th period class take them down. When they came the next day, I would tell them, "You have an outstanding referral so you can't come in." Most times they would disrespectfully push pass me, and I would have to resort to having them removed by security. Usually they would get a Saturday detention and return so we can start the cycle all over again.

In my years of teaching I have found that these disruptive children are usually the ones with the strictest parents, these children are barely able to utter a foul word at home without reprise. These parents clearly institute the wrong kind of discipline. The children think, "Oh I'm gonna do it all right, I'll just make sure I don't get caught, and if I do get caught, I'll just lie like a rug."

Most of my sixth period nightmares had a ninth grade homeroom. They weren't really supposed to be in the ninth grade. They were there because, though they were age-appropriate for the 10th grade, they hadn't made the grade to move up. Most of them were excessively absent, and a lot of them were on parole. I found out about their parole situation from a set of referrals I wrote. I wrote referrals on a number of my sixth period nightmares. Below the description of their offense I expressed that I was constantly being harassed by the student, had written several referrals to no avail, and if no action was taken I would take the matter up with the Cleveland police. Apparently the troublemakers got wind of my threat because they behaved in class for a change, and even attempted to do work. Later they expressed that I was trying to get them in trouble with their parole officers. I did not even try to find out why they were on parole.

I later found out that for most of my sixth period nightmares, my class was the only one they attended; I guess tormenting me became a favorite hobby. The bulk of the referrals that I wrote were for this sixth period class, yet they had the worst attendance of all my classes. I guess I was quite lucky, I can't imagine what my situation would have been like if they had good attendance. [07]I taught general science at Northeastern High school and got to find out what it's like when you have a class full of extremely disruptive students with good attendance, but that's a later chapter.

In May of 1997, for personal reasons, I decided to leave Cleveland and return to NYC. About a week before I left I told all my classes, actually all except the sixth and seventh periods; they got the news before I was able to deliver it myself. I meant to tell all but my sixth period class. When my students got the news, their first response was disbelief. I think most of them had plans of me teaching them chemistry the following year. After the realization set in, they all gave me the silent treatment; all but sixth period. My 6th period nightmares were very vocal, and very angry at me for leaving. They expressed that I didn't care about them, because if I did I wouldn't leave. They accused me of merely pretending to care about them. I felt they were upset because they would no longer have me to torment. Someone once told me that maybe I was actually making a difference in their lives, and that they were actually sorry to see me leave. Yeah right!

Just to show you how filthy the minds of these children were, one day I wrote some of the classroom rules on the chalkboard. I also wrote "Problems—see me 5th period." Someone erased 'period' and wrote 'Ave'. On another occasion I told them I am allergic to cursing so they should try not to do it so much. I told them instead of saying fuck they should say fuji. So someone blurted out, "fuji you Ms. Moline." At least he addressed me as Ms. Moline, and not plain Moline, or worst bitch.

Andrew Bolton was one of the most amazing success stories I ever came across, he went from being the most out of control student in the class, to being the most studious. Andrew was a problem from the very start. It got to a point where I would write his referral during 5th period, so all I had to do at 6th period was fill in the offense.

A look at Andrew gave no inkling of the amount of anger and mischief that lay below the surface. He was a relatively small skinny boy with a very pleasant face—the kind you would associate with a pleasant personality. After seeing his turn around, I have come to conclude that he had 2 equally strong opposing forces tugging at his consciousness, and he had been responding well to the one propelling him to do wrong.

During the first week of school, I wrote him up for using foul language, getting out of his seat without permission, and throwing a pen across the room. He got Saturday detention. As you will come to realize, at Hedley High School detention was the punishment, regardless of the crime.

Later that month I wrote him up for running around the classroom, leaving the classroom without permission, and fighting with Eve Edwards. From all indication he and Eve had a thing going on. I wasn't sure what the exact nature of their thing was, but she seemed to like hanging on to his coattail, and he seemed to enjoy beating her up.

Eve's mother was not aware of this relationship, so I took the liberty of filling her in, much to Eve's dismay. It wasn't long after that that Eve changed schools. I may have been wrong, but I felt that if I had a teenage daughter who was in an abusive relationship, I would want to know about it.

The day after the referral for fighting with Eve, I wrote a referral that said Andrew was rapping in class, wearing a hat, refused to do his work, and prevented me from teaching.

In October he was treated to Saturday detention because he was banging the door, running in the classroom, wearing headphones, left the classroom without permission before the end of the period, and was in the hallway making noise. I also wrote him up a second time that month for disrupting the class and leaving the class before the end of the period. The Office claimed to have called his mother. Of course the next day I had to write him up again, this time for being out of his seat, playing around in class, and throwing papers. I also wrote on the referral, "Don't have correct phone number for student. (He is) usually inattentive and out of (his) seat a lot." The 11th grade AP, Ms. Martin, gave him Saturday detention. Ms. Martin was a petite black woman whom all the students had reverent fear of.

Next he got Saturday detention for wearing his coat in class. I also wrote a general referral to go with that dress code referral—"Extremely insubordinate, constantly leaving room without permission, extremely disruptive." Below that I wrote, "I want to see his parent or parole officer before he returns to class." He got Saturday detention for that referral too. Less than a week later he was running in the hallway and making noise. Again he got Saturday detention. The following day his referral said, "Left the class without permission, insubordinate, disturbing the class, walking around room." Then, "I have had enough nonsense dealing with this student. I think someone needs to do something about him. He is totally uncontrollable." The result, you guessed it—Saturday detention.

The next year started the same way the old one ended. In the first week of January he was wearing headphones and goggles and refused to take them off, he was also disrespectful and disruptive. The following day I wrote, "Cursing and arguing in class with Andrew Bolton (I don't know what I was thinking here since I was writing about Andrew Bolton), left room without permission, lying on desk, out in hall screaming, swinging on the door." He got office detention, which meant that the next day during 6th period he stayed in the 9th grade unit office instead of coming to my class.

He gained 3 Saturday detentions (to be served consecutively I assumed) for cursing in class, being out of his seat without permission, leaving the classroom without permission, and for being half hour late to class without a pass. Later I got a note from Ms. Martin saying he had early dismissal. Near the end of January I wrote that I called his grandmother, and also wrote that his behavior improved.

After this point I wrote no more referrals. It was around this point that Andrew made his remarkable turnaround. Apparently he tried out for baseball, and found out that he was pretty good. In order to be on the baseball team, he had to pass all his classes, including mine. Hence, while all my other nightmares continued to wreck havoc in the classroom, Andrew would sit down and concentrate on his work all period. The others tried everything in their power to get him to join in their disruption, but Andrew refused to budge. A couple of months later, Andrew changed residence, and as a result had to change school. Had this change happened at the start of the school year, I would have gone home, pop back a few beers and had a party. However, Andrew had become one of the best students in the class; he had even gotten certificates for most improved student and student of the month. I was really sorry to see him leave.

I was never quite able to figure James Childs out. I think somewhere deep down inside him was a good child who was trapped in a child who wanted more than ever to belong in bad company. Nevertheless, James irritated me, from the retarded manner in which he called my name—Ms Mooooline, to the manner in which he would slither around the room with his shirt out of his pants.

In October I wrote him up for disrupting the class and leaving the classroom before the end of the period. Then I got a welcome break because he was suspended for 3 days. The following Monday he was back to business—cursing in class, he was suspended for 2 days. In January I wrote him a referral because he was extremely disruptive, cursing, and he left the classroom without permission 3 times. On this referral I included a note "James curses constantly without regard. This student is a constant problem. He is always late, comes without notebook and pen, and does no work."

The following day his referral said, "Playing around in class when he should be working. Left classroom without permission. Student is usually disruptive, insubordinate, does very little work, and wearing jacket with shirt out of pants." He was suspended for 2 days. The following week I wrote that he was playing around, throwing objects, and left the classroom without permission. The following week he was cursing in class, refused to change his seat as I instructed, refused to leave the room, and kept cursing. His referral said, "Class disruption. Refuses to pay attention." I called his house and left a message regarding his behavior. It didn't seem to do much good because he continued to curse in class, play around in the hallway, and as usual he did no work.

I spoke to his mother about his behavior. Then the next day I left a message about his behavior. In February he got a referral from the substitute because he was *"disruptive—talking loudly to other students + refused to be quiet and do work. Excessive horseplay, swearing."*

March Monday Madness: Monday March 3, 1997 found him cursing in class, talking dirty, out of his seat without permission, and climbing over the desk. The following Monday, March 10th, he was disrupting the class, talking loudly, and playing around. Then on Monday March 17th he was cursing in class and disruptive as usual. To top things off, on Monday March 24th his referral said, "grabbed referral from me, cursing in class, talking dirty, cursing at me, left room and came back with referral he claimed Mr. Walton signed, harassing me constantly, continued to disturb the class after I told him to leave". I added at the end—"These problems have been ongoing—if nothing is done I will file charges on my own regarding this harassment." He was suspended from March 25–27.

He started April with a bang, "cursing, out of seat without permission, disruptive, playing around, disrespectful". I wrote on his referral, "James is always insubordinate and disruptive; his mother promised to come sit in on the class but never came." Then where it says corrective effort I wrote "none taken—came back to class the next day with the same behavior."

At times I felt bad about giving James so many suspensions and detentions, but it was always a momentary regret. After all, James didn't even try to accomplish something when he was present. The only thing he was successful at was driving me up the wall.

Near the end of September I wrote a referral on Eve Edwards because she was outside in the hallway without permission screaming and fighting with Andrew Bolton. As I said before she was always fighting with Andrew Bolton. Later that month she was cursing in class and confronting other students. In December I wrote her up because she was wearing headphones which she refused to take off. In January she was cursing in class with Andrew Bolton, I wrote a referral, and she got office detention. Eve was eventually expelled for fighting a teacher. This actually happened in my class, and she behaved like a true knucklehead.

Jerry Fitts: This child was a chronic absentee, but every now and then he would come to school, and attend only my class. Normally when he did come to class he would make my day by leaving before the bell rang. He would say something like, "time to bounce", or he would look at his partners in crime (or his 'road dogs'), Ronny Boors and Elton Wards, and say, "let's bounce". I would watch them leave and think something on the order of "good riddance to bad rubbish".

Also I don't remember him ever coming to class and not being out of dress code. The first week of December I wrote him a dress code referral for wearing his coat in class, and I wrote him a regular referral for being extremely disrespectful, disruptive, constantly out of his seat, and leaving the class without permission. Also I wrote—"unable to teach class with student there, I want to see his parents before he returns to class." He got a Saturday detention; I never met his parents. Around the middle of January I wrote a referral because he left the class without permission and came back 10 minutes before the bell without a pass, he got a Saturday detention. The first week of February he was disrespecting me, telling me I smell like chronic because I spoke to him about his smoking.

Smoking was a huge problem for this 6th period class. Sometimes the students came to class with cigarette or marijuana smell so pungent on their breath and clothing that I had to hold my breath when they were near me. Somehow they had gotten wind of the fact that I was from Barmenia, and they insisted that I had access to marijuana, and was able to supply them with 'bud' or 'chronic' as they affectionately called it.

In truth I had never come across students with such wanton disregard for their own lives. They drank, they smoked, and they just didn't give a fuck. I couldn't for the life of me figure out how to reach them, or how to get them to care about themselves. Their parents had given up hope a long time ago, and they were not exactly priorities of their parole officers. Even my telling them that I got paid whether they learnt or not didn't seem to have any impact. I guess the only thing I ever did that seemed to have impacted them was my leaving to return to NYC.

The first week of February I wrote Jerry a referral because he left class before the bell with his friends, he got 2 consecutive Saturday detentions. The following day he was out of dress code, and left the class without permission; I wrote him a referral for his deeds and he was suspended for 3 days.

Altamont Frazer was the student from down South whom I truly believe I hated. He was just obnoxious, plain and simple; his upbringing had not instilled even an ounce of decency. It was apparent he had a rough life down South. He had this extremely sinister way about him; and it didn't help that he always regarded me with contempt.

In October I wrote him a referral for disrupting class and leaving the classroom without permission, he got Saturday detention. Later that same month he was cursing in class, and had confrontations with other students. In February I spoke to his mother about his attitude. Later that month I wrote a referral for his leaving the classroom without permission, he got Saturday detention.

Like March Mondays was James' day, it seem Tuesday was Altamont's day. I got lucky with him one Tuesday in March when I caught him in a curse; he Said, "I'll fuck you up." I wrote this on his referral, I also wrote that he was disrespecting me before and after he got the referral. He got 5 days suspension—YES.

Somewhere along the way someone told me not to just put down that the child was cursing in class, but to also write down the child's exact words. After all, writing that the child said, "I'll fuck you up", is more expressive than writing that the child cursed at me in class; it's also more likely to lead to suspension or detention.

My relief over Altamont's suspension was short-lived, near the end of March he was back cursing, and engaged in a confrontation with Sheryll Lanks. This Sheryll Lanks was quite a character as you will find out later. In April I wrote a referral on him because he climbed over a desk, played around, and talked back to me, he got 5 days suspension. I'm not sure how that 5 days suspension went because the next day I recorded, "Called me niggar, harassed me, grabbed the referral I wrote from me, and told me I was half way dumb. He refused to do his work, said his mother didn't buy any notebook, out of his seat and climbing over the desk."

I truly believed in Benny Gitano until I found out about a horrendous referral that a substitute teacher wrote about him. He denied it emphatically, to the extent I started believing the teacher had indeed confused him with someone else. I believe he must have known how disappointed I would have been to find he was the one.

In September I wrote that he was wearing his hat in class, rapping, and refused to do his work. Actually wearing a hat and goggles, rapping and refusing to do any work was really Benny's trademark. In November he got a referral for fighting in class, he got 3 days suspension. In January he got a dress code referral for wearing goggles and headphones in class, and refusing to take them off. Near the end of January I made contact with his mother who said she was trying to resolve the problem. The next day came the referral I spoke about—"*Came to class but did no work. Not doing work, swearing at another student. I told him to stop it or leave. He said he wasn't leaving, and began cursing me out. "Fuck you, you'd better recognize this E.C., bitch we hoodrats. Don't be telling me what to do, this ain't Shaker Heights or wherever the fuck you from. That's why you get dogged comin down here trying to hate on a niggar. You can't make me leave, this is my class. Fuck around and get slapped." Gave a sarcastic 'apology' a few minutes later. Left class without permission at 2:00 pm.*"

When I read the referral it sounded more like Altamont Frazer. I could close my eyes and picture those words coming from his mouth in a deep southern drawl. The apology definitely made me think it was Benny. The other students bold enough to talk like that to a grown up were also insolent enough not to even consider an apology, let along utter one. Altamont definitely would not have apologized he would more likely have followed up on his threat and slapped the teacher.

Again at the end of February he got a referral for being out of dress code, wearing headphones and goggles which he refused to take off, out of his seat, writing on the board, and refusing to take referral to the office. He got 5 days suspension.

Montel Hamm was as fat and sloppy as he was insolent, and I could never determine which bothered me more, the fact that he was fat and sloppy and made a mockery of the school uniform, or that he was so very insolent. On the odd occasion when he did come to class, he would wobble his way into the class, and plant his massive behind on the window sill, this was the indication that he was there to institute confusion rather than learn.

In September I wrote "Sitting on window sill with body outside, disrespecting teacher." In October I wrote "Montel Hamm grabbed student's pen and threw it out the window, tore up referral and didn't report to the unit office." He got 2 days in-school suspension. Later that month I recorded that he was cursing in class, and generally disruptive. I wrote him a referral to take to his unit office. Later that day I went down and asked Ms. Martin about the referral, and was informed that she never got it.

In January he was rewarded with 3 days in-school suspension for wearing a hat in class. Later that month I wrote him a referral that said, "Climbing on window, playing around in class, playing with blinds, constantly out of seat." Then "Montel is usually disruptive." He got 1 day in-school suspension. At the end of the month his mother called and left a message for me to call her. I called her back and left a message. The first week of February I wrote "Talking too much, insubordinate, told me he doesn't care, said his mother is dead, said he is on welfare and can't afford book, out of seat, playing around, shouting, jumping up and kicking." The following day I wrote that he was disturbing my 1st period class—"came in shouting and disrespecting me". This was written by a substitute who substituted for me in my absence, "left class without permission had also been talking out of turn and not doing work—very obnoxious".

It seemed Montel wasn't content with molesting me during his assigned period; for the second time in February he came in to disturb my class—this time my third period class. I wrote that he was rude and insubordinate and that he tore up the referral I wrote on him. He got 3 days suspension.

I found that the 'tearing up the referral' bit worked wonders for getting disrupters suspended. I would write a referral, give it to the student, and say something like, "Here's your referral, go, take it to your unit office." By this time I had come to learn that certain students were known for 'losing' the referral, others who were bold enough would tear up the referral in my presence. Either way, during the subsequent period, I would write another referral, and have one of my better students take it to the unit office. If the student had torn up the previous referral, I would make sure to write that on the referral.

In March Montel was out of his seat, disruptive, and being very rude and insubordinate to me, as usual. He got in school suspension from Ms. Martin for his evil deeds. In early April came the straw that broke that bull dog's back. He threw a chair out the window. They did a mini-investigation on him—his 7th period teacher wrote "*Not in class, I have not seen him all semester, I have only seen him maybe 10 times the whole year.*" Not too long after that I got a note from his unit office "*10 days suspension, with recommendation for expulsion. Paged mother but did not return page. Ms. Martin spoke with grandmother.*"

Kyle Levin was my worst sixth period nightmare because he was almost always present. In September during the first week of classes I wrote that he was constantly disrupting class, and left the room without permission. About 2 weeks later I wrote a referral for his destruction of school property, being out of his seat, playing around in class, and throwing papers. Near the end of September he was wearing his hat, rapping in class, and refused to do the class assignment. In early October I gave him a dress code referral for wearing his hat and coat. Later that month he got a referral for destroying school property, disrupting class, running around the room, and leaving class without permission before the bell. He got 1 week of cafeteria duty, in other words he got a chance to play around some more. If it's fun for the child it's not punishment. It's like equipping a child's room with a Play Station and cable television, and then sending the child to his room as a means of punishment.

In December I wrote that he was extremely insubordinate and disruptive. Would you believe this child's father was a retired police officer who sometimes worked as a substitute at Hedley?

Near the end of January I spoke to his father, so he cut class for a few days. Then I spoke to his mother a few days later and found her quite disillusioned. I could tell from my conversation with his mother that she had spoilt him, and pretty much allowed him to have his own way. I didn't get the sense he was subjected to any level of discipline at home. How then was he supposed to learn about limits and consequences in school? That's probably why he couldn't seem to appreciate that there was a limit to what behaviors would be tolerated, and that there were consequences for his actions.

The first week of February he got a referral for being out of his seat without permission, destroying school property, and playing around in class. He got Saturday detention.

Sheryll Lanks was a transfer student who joined the class late in the school year. She started out quite good. Then the boy developed a liking for her, or was it the other way around? Nevertheless, the result was their constant harassment of her. She was younger than they were, and not as worldly, but she had a short fuse, and little or no self control. What was also interesting was if ever I paid any level of attention to Sheryll the boys would get upset. On a number of occasions they accused me of being racist, and giving her special attention because she was white. Of course Sheryll did not think she was white, and it all just came out as a big confusion, that resulted in more shouting matches between Sheryll and the boys.

As you will see Sheryll was rather constant, her offenses were almost always 'talking loudly and involved in confrontations'. February—"disturbing class, talking very loudly, playing around, refused to change seat." March—"engaged in a confrontation with Altamont Frazer, cursing and screaming"; for this she was suspended for 3 days. April—involved in a confrontation, cursing—"I don't give a fuck", and calling student "ho ass bitch". The next day I gave her a dress code referral for her shoes, she got Saturday school; I also wrote her a referral for disrespecting me, refusing to change her seat, horse-playing, cursing and screaming, and involved in a confrontation with Ronny Boors, Elton Wards, and James Childs. The AP for the 9th grade Unit Office, Mr. Walton, had a conference with her parents, and she was suspended for 2 days.

I don't think there was ever a day at Hedley wherein I didn't have cause to write a dress code referral. Most times I would talk to the student about the offense. If the student was rude, refused to correct the offense, or disrespected me, then I would write a referral. For the most part students from the other classes would apologize, explain the reason for the offense, and even go to the bathroom and change. My 6th period on the other hand always had at least one student who was out of dress code. With the exception of a few students, all of my sixth period nightmares had the new Michael Jordan sneakers that retailed for over a hundred dollars. I knew the price because the students were always valuing their attire. When they did come to school in something resembling the school uniform, they wore Tommy Hilfigher pants and shirt, some even wore Hilfigher coats.

I guess the Tommy Hilfigher clothing line had tapped into quite a market, because the colors of their clothing line matched that of Hedley High's uniform, and of course most schools that opt for uniform opt for blue and white.

In January I wrote Elton Wards a referral for cursing in class and refusing to change his seat. Below that I wrote "Elton is always loud, disruptive, and insubordinate." He got 3 days suspension. In February he was playing around in class, talking back to me, and left the room without permission. I wrote on the referral that I wanted his mother or grandmother to be called. He was given 3 days suspension by Ms. Martin. Later that month he had a dress code referral for wearing the new Jordan sneaker, he was suspended. When he came back he continued to wear the sneakers every day.

In March I wrote him a referral for being out of dress code, and leaving class without permission. He got Saturday detention. Later that month I wrote "Cursing in class. Insubordinate and obscene. Destroying school property. Hitting other student with paper. Said, "I don't give a fuck." Threw book on floor. Throwing objects in class—one almost hit me. Left room without permission. Elton is always disruptive, obscene and insubordinate." Again in March I wrote, "Elton was out of his seat, cursing in class. Cursing at me, and pointing his finger in my face. Threw a student's work into the garbage." Below that in the space indicated I wrote, "Elton is usually insubordinate, disruptive, and inattentive. Usually talks back to me, does no work, is constantly out of dress code, and playing walkman." He was sent home with 3 days suspension.

In April I gave him a referral for cursing in class—"I don't give a fuck", etc. Later that month I gave him a referral that told it all, "Playing walkman, out of seat, dancing, cursing, horsing around, out of dress code, talking back to me, left room without permission." Below that where it said 'previous incidents involving student', I wrote "This student is always disruptive and insubordinate." Then where it says 'corrective efforts', I wrote "None taken—came back the next day with the same behavior." He was given 5 days suspension. I don't know what kind of suspension that was since he was in my class again the very next day.

In December I wrote a referral for Wesley Yates for the usual "Extremely disrespectful and disruptive, and refusing to take his coat off." I also wrote him a dress code referral for the coat. In January I wrote him a referral, and he told me to take it myself. Later that month I wrote him a referral for leaving class without permission before the bell. I spoke to his father the first week of February, and he promised to take care of the problem. I saw his mother in April, during parent-teacher conference.

There were 21 other students on my sixth period roster. 2 were good students who were there almost everyday, and didn't give me any problems. One of the 2,

Devon Morris, was the top student in the class; the other, Renny Berns, seemed to be extremely illiterate. There were 18 students who were excessively absent; some of them I didn't see the entire year; and there was Doris Daye. Until Sheryll came along, most of the times Doris was the only girl in a class full of bad boys. I think some of their badness rubbed off on her, because she used to curse pretty harshly in class.

I once called Doris' mother about her cursing, and her mother remarked, "Doris doesn't curse." This was the first time that a parent questioned what I said about her child, it was certainly not to be the last. I went back and looked at my records, because I felt sure the mistake was mine. The next day I went to class, and there was Doris 'sailorly' cursing nice and loud. I looked at her in shock, "And your mother says you don't curse!" I exclaimed. She clammed up, but she didn't give up the cursing.

She once brought in a picture of her when she was a little girl. I can't imagine what would provoke her to bring in such a picture to show her knuckle-headed male classmates. Anyway, I confiscated the picture, and would you believe I still have it. I placed it along with the records I kept of her. It was at Hedley High School that I learnt to keep notes on students. I was told it comes in handy if the student has a suspension hearing. I kept a binder in which I kept records of what I wrote about students when their classroom behavior was less than satisfactory. I also kept copies of all other documents that related to discipline such as referrals, meetings with parents, suspension notices etc.

At this point you must be thinking why did she write so many referrals on these students, and get them suspended so many times. Here's the truth. This was my worst class. Actually this was the only class in which I wasn't carrying out the instruction I wanted. I was unable to teach because of the disruptive knuckle-heads. 50% of the time they were either suspended, or they were in school and didn't bother to show up. At least 25% of the time they were just absent from school. The few times they did show up for class they made it impossible for the few good students in that class to learn. Despite their absenteeism, or maybe due to an ingenious plot on their part, there was almost always one or more of them in attendance during sixth period.

The bottom line, teaching was my livelihood, and I was merely protecting my livelihood. I made myself a pledge that I would harass students far more than they could ever harass me. If they came to class, and followed my directions, then we had a great year in which they accomplished a lot. If on the other hand they tried to test me, then I would go out of my way to make life quite miserable for them, and you better believe I was quite successful at making life difficult for them. The students who were on my shit list were always jealous when they saw how I related to the students who were on my 'good' list.

Also I knew there was a chance that if these students were always getting detention and suspensions from messing around in my class then they would be in my class less often, because they were either suspended or didn't want to get another suspension or detention. This is in fact what happened, so I was quite pleased with the results of my effort.

Probably the most interesting thing about the students in that class was the fact that the majority of them did not bother to come to school. The ones who did come would cut all their other classes and attend mine. There are indeed 2 schools of thoughts here, either they felt as they indicated when I resigned that I really cared about them, or they relished the torment which they afforded me with their presence. I guess that will just be one of those unsolved mysteries.

Seventh Period (general science)
Seventh period was always a relief after dealing with sixth period, plus it was a rather small class because most of the students on the roster were chronic absentees.

Taisha Belmont stopped by a few times.

Manuel Benz is a very bright child, who I haven't seen in a while, I think he is playing the fool and messing around with dropping out.

Cordelia Boggurt is a really sweet girl. I had her for a semester; she did very well, and moved on.

Tounsend Bowman is a bench warmer with good attendance. He is 18 years old, and still in the 10th grade. The students tease him that his children are going to graduate before him. Personally I think Tounsend has some sort of emotional problem.

Razor Copps—I don't know him; but I hear he is in jail.

To make a long story short, Braid Elsford cut all of last semester, and the first part of this semester. His baseball coach, his counselor, and his learning community teacher all wanted me to give him a passing grade, while he fooled around, and pretended to try. I declined. I think they are all mad at me but they dare not say it. Hedley has what are called learning communities, where all the teachers in a learning community collaborate on teaching the subject matter and on discipline. I am not part of any of their learning communities, so I can't judge their effectiveness.

Rashaw Fossett—I saw him and his parole officer for a while, then I saw neither.

Arthur Guardner is new for this semester. The student with the crush; he wants me to take him to Barmenia. He seems to think he will be able to get lots of marijuana there.

Sheryl Harvey says she can't stand her mother, not much hope there. She doesn't come to class too often; too much of a headache when she comes.

David Louis is a good child, but he just craves attention, and thinks he is a comedian which he is not. I had to write him up for fighting with Jashua Maldonex. He has been expelled.

At first Jashua Maldonex was funny, now he just gets on my nerves. I have to keep writing him up for being stupid, and he never seems to learn. I think he spends more time in the in-school suspension room than he does in class. I know this because he is always coming to me for work to do in in-school suspension (most of these suspensions came from referrals from other teachers).

Lance Marsh is the New Yorker with the jade thick-lensed glasses. He dropped my class for study hall. He wasn't doing so well—extremely slow.

Fran Moline (no relation to author) used to come to class, ask for a pass and stay out the entire period. Eventually she got tired of that and just stopped coming all together.

Stephanie Moxley is a very sweet girl. She does very well, always complains that she is going to fail tests then gets the highest grade in the class. She is very active in school extra-curricular activities.

Miggy Pearson's probation officer makes sure he comes to class. The poor guy is tired of checking up on Miggy. Whenever I give a test Miggy always looks around for the answer key so he can copy.

Tamara Petron rarely does any work and seems to be very spoilt.

Alecia Rosen is always student of the month. She does really well, and has pretty good attendance. I see her waiting for her teacher every morning, almost.

Karen Shraw is a very petite child. She drops in for class every now and then. She was transferred from another science class.

Marlon Weeler—A good child going bad.

THE TURNING POINT
Cooper High School, Brooklyn (September 1998–June 1999)

It is the silence of the good people that let tyrants get away with murder.

THE TURNING POINT
Cooper High School, Brooklyn
(September 1998–June 1999)

In September of 1998 I went to teach at Cooper High School in Brooklyn. I had spent a year doing cancer research, wherein I found out that cancer research had more to do with advancing people's careers than it did with finding cures or treatments. It was a horrifying revelation for me. In the research lab where I worked there was constant bickering amongst the staff. There were times when I went home and cried because I knew it was that sort of selfishness that contributed to the death of my friend Kay Samuels who died of breast cancer at the age of 30. I decided that I had a far greater chance of making a difference if I taught than if I joined the rat race that was cancer research.

I called up a few schools, and I spoke to one AP who told me to attend a hiring fair in Brooklyn. I was on line at the hiring fair when this man pulled me out of the line, had me fill out a paper and told me to report to his school the following Monday. I assumed that based on the manner in which I was pulled off the line that the person I conversed with was the same person I had spoken to the day before. It was such a chaotic event that by the time I realized that the man who pulled me off the line was a complete stranger, and the school he was hiring me to teach in was one I had never heard of, I decided I was just happy not to have to keep searching for a job.

When I went back into teaching, I went back with a much subtler approach. I was not so much the mean teacher who never smiled anymore. I even went as far as to let the students make up the classroom rules. I had everyone submit rules that they felt would make their learning experience better, after removing duplicates I came up with 33 classroom rules from the submissions of my 9 classes (I had 4 recitation classes and 5 lab classes). Actually they weren't rules they were just what the students felt constituted appropriate classroom behavior: Respect each other. Don't talk while someone else is talking. One person speaks at a time. Listen to each other. Be quiet in class. Sit in your seat. Be on your best behavior in class. Do onto others as you would have them do onto you. Do not laugh at another's mistake. Everyone should pay attention. Don't leave your seat without permission. Don't talk while the teacher is talking. No chewing of gum. No littering. Don't call out answers. Don't move the chairs or tables. Be nice to each other. Try to learn the work. Sit in rows. Speak only when chosen by the teacher. Be on time for class. Always be prepared for class. Raise your hand when you have a question. Have assigned seats. Five to ten points should be deducted from your grade if you talk without the teacher's permission. Students should be punished for disrespecting the teacher. Respect school property. Keep track of your belongings, and put things back where you found them. Clean up your area after work. Don't disrupt the class. No stealing. Hand in your work on time. Teacher should give 1 week notice for an exam.

I did get some odd responses, such as "there should be no homework", but I dare say the students had it all covered. Whenever students broke any of the rules I would remind them that they were the ones who made up the classroom rules. Students who were demons in other classes were angels in my class.

Anyway it didn't take long for me to realize that Cooper was a very troubled school, this was exemplified when about half a dozen new teachers left at the end of the first semester. I guess I should start off by saying that there were about 16 new teachers who started with me in September. An additional 5 new teachers came in February and 2 older teachers left; marking the greatest teacher turnover I ever saw. Mathematics, which was the area where the school performed the best, was shattered by the departure of one of the mathematics teachers. Thus the second semester was done with 3 new mathematics teachers and one older mathematics teacher. As a result the Regents exam results were disastrous. Next year promises more of the same; most of the new teachers who remained for the second semester had plans of leaving at the end of the school year.

I took 2 school administration courses while I was at Cooper. As an assignment for one of the courses I wrote this analysis of Cooper High School:

The vision

- Greater personalization.
- No more than 700 students at a time.
- Provide strong academic college preparatory education.
- Focus on developing skills in mathematics, science and technology.

The reality

- Teachers are too overworked to provide personalization.

- There are less than 700 students, but the desire to be selective is absent.

- There are no advanced placement classes.

- Mathematics and science scores are very low relative to other subjects. Use of technology is limited.

School features

- Use of Morsley College science and computer labs, gymnasium, auditorium, research library, and exchange of cultural programs with Morsley.

- Visiting speakers from Morsley.

- Liberty Partnership Program which offers academic and recreational enrichment.

- Parental support—Parent Teachers Association (PTA) scholarship, Recognition Day for teachers, fundraising, and volunteering to accompany students and teachers on trips.

- School support for parents—parenting workshops and conferences.

- Partnership with City University of New York and Morsley College, and support from the New York State mentoring program.

Reality

- There is currently no structure in place to realize students' use of the College's science or computer labs. Use of the College's gymnasium and auditorium is limited. Students can use the research library, however many students are not aware of this, and a considerable number don't understand how to. In addition, students are not allowed to borrow books from the library to take home. I am not aware of any cultural exchange between the High School and the College.

- I am not aware of any structured inter-visitation between High School and College educators.

- The Liberty Partnership Program does offer recreational enrichment, but the academic enrichment is severely deficient. The deficiency stems from the small payment for tutoring services—$15/hour—for which qualified teachers are unwilling to work. The program seems to rely for the most part on student tutors from the College who are paid $10/hour. Then there's conflict with after school tutoring, which is offered by the School, and pays $31.40/hour.

- The school's PTA seems to be very strong. I attended one PTA meeting where I was a little disturbed to see that it was dominated by the School's principal. The Teacher Recognition Day was not held last year, and it is questionable whether or not it will be held this year. Teachers seemed shocked when I mentioned the statement about parents volunteering to accompany teachers and students on trips. Clearly, there's no structure in place to facilitate this.

- Parenting workshops and conferences may have been held as part of PTA meetings, but I am not at liberty to state since I have been to only one PTA meeting. I am somewhat concerned that my students claim that their parents don't attend the PTA meetings.

- I am not aware of any partnership in reality, so it must all be on paper.

Teachers

The school is populated by new teachers (new to the School and new to the school system). Teacher morale is extremely low, with a corresponding high absenteeism. A number of teachers are concerned that the building does not have adequate ventilation, and as a result is making them sick. Many teachers have expressed the desire to leave the teaching profession—2 of the teachers left the profession in January. This feeling of exasperation was heightened at the beginning of the second semester when teachers were denied paper for the copy machine. Everyone knew there were at least 50 boxes of paper locked away in a store room for which only the principal had the keys.

Students

The majority of the students are black, with about a 50:50 gender split. About a third of the students are foreigners, mainly from the English speaking Caribbean. An even larger number are from foreign born parents. Student attendance is over 90% on average. The percent of students receiving free lunch dropped from 64.1% in 1995 to 24.9% in 1997. It's unlikely this drop represents that significant an improvement in income levels.

Discipline

The number of incidences for this school parallels that of NYC, but there are fewer suspensions. There is a general attitude among students that they can do almost anything and get away with it. There is a tendency by the School's administration to accept the student's word over that of a teacher.

In essence there were 3 problems with Cooper High School 1) poor management 2) lack of discipline and 3) too many people willing to engage in social promotion even if it meant helping students to cheat.

Management

The principal, Lee Minott, was the worst administrator I had ever come across, exclusive of Talbot of Berger High School (first prize for worst administrator will always belong to Talbot, at least I sincerely hope so).

Minott had done quite a job on the parents of Cooper High School students. He would charm them, feed them and buy into their every wish. That way they adored him, and never bothered to question his management of the school, or question the quality of the education their children got at Cooper.

I once called a parent of one of my students who told me she called the Principal, the APs, and the guidance counselors about her child. When I asked her why she didn't call me, she had no answer. The 'call the principal' mentality was so ingrained in the parents that even when logic demanded them to do so, they couldn't break away from it. I was given a parent's number by the guidance counselor. When I called the parent she told me she called the Principal, the APs, and the guidance counselor. When I asked her why she didn't contact me, she told me about hearing that I was being 'taken care of' (this was at around the time when Minott started his campaign to relieve me of my livelihood).

The school had tons of supplies they were just not for teachers. For a period of about 2 months teachers were denied copy paper though there were 2 storerooms next to the Chemistry lab/classroom/storeroom filled from floor to ceiling with paper. The reason the classroom was also serving as a storeroom was due to the fact that the rooms that should have been used for storing science supplies were being used to store paper. While teachers were going off to Office Max and Staples to make copies, I observed strangers making trip after trip to remove paper from the storerooms. I couldn't help wondering what that was all about.

It wasn't just paper, lots of other supplies would turn up missing, things like computer and video equipment that must have cost the Board a pretty penny would vanish from the store rooms to which only school administrators had the keys. Here's the topper, Cooper High School did not have a band. If my memory serves me correctly, they didn't even have a music teacher. Yet, the school had quite an extensive supply of musical instruments—drums, guitars, etc. These musical instruments would gradually disappear from the storeroom. Teachers were not allowed access to the storerooms.

At around the time when we were getting ready for Regents exams the duplicating machine broke, and was not fixed because the bill for service was delinquent. Some teachers found out about a copy machine on the ground floor. They would sneak into the room to make copies for their classes. One teacher reported that while making copies in the room a school secretary came in and screamed at her to get out.

Minott was having an affair with one of the APs, actually rumor had it that she was his girlfriend. One night they apparently had a dispute which resulted in physical violence on his part. She called the police and reported this act of domestic violence.

Indeed Minott was a very unusual principal. During the year I spent there, the staff Christmas party was held at a nightclub. Most of us who were at the party had to hold our breaths in fear, Minott was getting on so bad on the dance floor we felt that at any moment he would strip down to his underwear.

Of course, as is usual with weak administration, there were inappropriate teaching assignments, and teachers who were having difficulties got no help from the school's administrators. After the school's experienced mathematics teacher left to work in a field other than teaching (I guess he got tired of the madness that is not teaching), the School hired a Russian woman to teach mathematics. This teacher's classes are so out of control it is clear to everyone the students are in control. Needless to say she gets no classroom management assistance from the School's administration.

There's a mathematics teacher, and a gymnastics teacher teaching global studies, both of whom have to be taught the subject matter by other teachers before they go to the classroom to teach.

Social Promotion

Cooper High School's motto was *where excellence is the norm*, but in fact the motto should have been *where social promotion is the norm*. There were so many cases of cheating and social promotion, all occurring at a time when the Chancellor was expressing that he planned to put an end to social promotion. Stories of students' Regents answers being changed were rampant.

One teacher Mr. Brinks was told by a school administrator to give failing students reports to write so they could pass for the year. Another teacher, Mr. Santana, was asked to allow a student who was excessively absent all year to write a paper as a way of passing his class. Many of the teachers who have been at the school for more than a year have made it the norm to have students who don't attend class just write a paper at the end of the year as a way of passing. There are a number of English, Global Studies and U.S. History teachers who give passing grades to students who have been absent all year if they simply hand in a paper at the end of the year.

One of the English teachers, Ms. Tomkins, gave a passing grade to a senior who was in her 9th grade English class, and did little or no work. She did it because she felt she needed a satisfactory rating, and if that's what it would take then she was willing to just give the student a 65.

One day a student came to my class fuming, crying and complaining about a grade she received in mathematics. She vowed that she was going to have her mother call the school and see to it that the mathematics teacher, Ms. Falcon, change the grade. I dismissed the student's rambling as her being her usual spoilt self. Later that week I heard Ms. Falcon complaining about how she had to change the student's grade. I was quite shocked to know that it was that easy for a student to get a teacher to change her grade. I have had a few occasions over the years in which I changed students' grades, in all cases it was because I realized that I made an error in calculating the students' grades; otherwise my grades were always final.

There's the report of a teacher who had all her grades changed by the school administration. I can almost guarantee that most, if not all my grades have been changed. I met this teacher when I taught summer school the summer after I left Cooper. She explained to me that it was the norm for things like that to happen. The administration would try to get the teacher out of the School so the teacher doesn't learn of the fact that the school has changed all of the teacher's grades.

Students claimed that Ms. Villane and Ms. Patricks gave them answers on the biology and mathematics Regents respectively. This story was repeated by a number of students from different classes. Trust me, if a student admits that a teacher helped him or her to cheat 9 out of 10 times it's the truth; and that 9 out of 10 is probably an underestimate. This year Ms. Villane went into the biology Regents exam room and told students answers to questions on the exam.

A student told me that Ms. Patricks told her an answer on the mathematics Regents. According to the student, Ms. Patricks pointed at a particular question on her paper and shook her head. When she looked at Ms. Patricks inquiringly, Ms. Patricks said, "I'll SEE you later", and then walked away. The student told me that she interpreted Ms. Patricks' action to mean the answer to the question was 'C'.

There are also stories of teachers staying until late in the night to "grade" papers, resulting in extraordinarily high grades for otherwise failing students.

I taught chemistry lab at 7:30 am. The chemistry students were assigned to lab once per week. I had the lab assignments set up so that if a student was absent, all the student had to do was come to the lab session another day of the week. In addition I allowed students to do more than one lab assignments in a lab session if they were falling behind. Even with all that there were only a handful of students who completed the required number of lab hours by the end of the lab sessions. In order to give the students additional leeway, I received a letter requiring that I give students even more opportunities to make up lab assignments.

To: *Science Lab Teachers*

From: *Genard Rizzo, Assistant Principal*

Subject: *Make-up Labs*

Date: *May 26, 1999*

According to Board of Education's regulations, all students must be given the opportunity to make up work/labs that have been missed.

You need to provide that opportunity to fulfill our responsibilities to the students.

Please speak to Mr. Felder and me to work out the necessary strategies.

Thank you.

c: Lee Minott

Thomas Felder

Rizzo was not the only one writing me letters. These are letters that I got from students at Cooper who wanted explanations for the grades they got in my chemistry lab classes. For most of these students I can't imagine why they were questioning their grades. I was being confronted on a regular basis by students who found themselves in danger of not being able to take the chemistry Regents because most of them couldn't be bothered to get up early in the morning to attend the lab classes. Not having the patience to deal with these students' demand for an explanation, I told them all to ask me in writing, which to my surprise they did. The requirement is a mere 30 labs for the school year. To complete the 30 labs the students were required to attend <u>one</u> lab class each week at 7:30 am.

Dear Ms. Moline,

My name is Daphney Sparks I have lab on Tuesday. I told you that I only missed one lab and that the reason that I did not do the project was because I was in Canada when you gave it out.

Dear Ms. Moline,

I am not satisfied with my grade because I've worked very hard on the ten (10) labs for this marking period. This is the first that I have completed so much lab work. I was hoping for at least a satisfactory grade.

Your Student

Janet Bent

From: Nicole Wilson

Dear Ms. Moline,

I received my report card and I am dissapointed in my grade that you gave me. You gave me a "U" which is unsatisfactory and also a 55.

I've been to class every day <u>early</u> and the 1st one there. I did my report I did my labs and written them out and gave you my folder neatly. I never disrespected you or anything so maybe there was a mistake in your behalf or in my behalf but please check it out for me thank you.

Nicole Wilson

PS. I would like to sit and discuss this with you. It's Important!!!

Lab Student

Wednesdays

Ms. Moline

I think I've shouldn't have gotten a U because I did all my lab and came every Friday. I hope it was a mistake on the computer.

Christian Grant

This student came so infrequently I hardly remembered him.

Wendy Anson
Thursday Lab
Dear Ms. Moline,

I think I deserve better than a U. I did all the labs except for 2 plus I did your project. When you have time can you please sit down with me and tell me why you gave me a U because I know that I did not deserve that grade.

2/2/98 (should be 99)

Dear Ms. Moline,

On my report card for the 3rd marking period, I received a grade of a "U". I honestly believe that I deserved at least an "S". The reasons why I think I deserve an "S" are listed below:

- *I report to lab every Tuesday.*

- *I completed my project with my partner Linda Carson and both of our names are on the project.*

- *I handed in all my completed labs.*

- *I passed the 1st and 2nd marking periods and I don't think that I could fail the semester if I passed the first two marking periods.*

I will also like to know how you did our grades. I will like to know if a person did all 30 labs and fails, could they still take the Regents. If I know I didn't do my work and I didn't go to lab, then I wouldn't be complaining, but I know I do my work and I show up every week and I am concerned about my grade. Thank you.

Yours Truly,

Alison Ford

Wednesday LAB

I DO NOT UNDERSTAND MY CHEM LAB GRADE!!

Antoine Barr

To Whom It May Concern.

Good morning Ms. Moline,

I don't think that I deserve this grade for lab because I did all my labs and I turned them in, and I did the project, a U is not acceptable for all the work I did and a U means I didn't do anything. I think my grade should be changed.

Yours truly.

Melinda Accent

Dear Ms. Moline

This is Albert I have lab with you on Wednesday and I forgot to give you my lab book. I was looking for you today 12//98 and I didn't find you. Can you please grade my lab book even though the grades are due Friday. Please do this for me.

Sincerely: Albert

Dear Ms. Moline. My daughter Francesca had you For two or 3 cycle and every time you have failed her I know the type of Person Francesca is you Can Check Her Report Card. She Assured me She Completed your Assignment I ask her many a times if she did. I hope to make a trip to the school to discuss this Problem. I also worked in the school system, I really find this unbelievable Can you Please look into this Problem.

Sincerely,

Gloria Paterson

P.s. My number at home is (718) 111–1111

I was smart enough not to hold my breath waiting for this parent to show up because she never did. The answer to the problem was staring her in her face, but she refused to acknowledge it—her daughter lied to her. The student in question rarely came to the lab classes.

Dear Ms. Moline,

On receiving my son Alvin Spence's report card, I saw that he got a U in your class. He was very disappointed and thought that he did better and was undersving of such a grade. Could you please explain to me why he got a U. You could reply to me in writing or call me at home # 000–1111. (after 6pm) looking forward to hearing from you.

Yours Sincerely

Ms Alice Girth

2/1/99

Glenda Ortega
Chemistry Lab
Ms. Moline

Why did I get a N when I did all my labs, the project and I even came an extra day?

2/1/99

To Whom It May Concern:

I am writing you this letter to inform you that I am aware of the grade that you gave my daughter Glenda Ortega. My daughter assures me that she did all her work (labs; project). If she did all her work she deserves a grade better than a "N". If you do not have the grade changed by Tuesday (2/2/99), I will go to the school to speak with Mrs. Rizzo (the supervisor) and with Mr. Minott (the principal).

Sincerely,

Helena Ortega

The letter was apparently written by Glenda and signed by her mother.

7th Period

Mark Scott
Dear Ms. Moline

My name is Mark Scott and I am in your 7th period class. On my last card I received a 55 in your class and a 55 in your lab. I feel that I deserve at least a seventy in your class because I attended your tutoring which gave me extra points towards my participation grade and that should boost my grade. Another reason why I feel my grade should be changed is because I do all your homework and get good grades on test and I participate. In regards to my lab grade I feel I should have received a seventy five because I have completed all your labs except for one and my partner Melinda can verify it.

Thanking You in Advance

Sincerely

Mark Scott
H. Peters (his parent, I assume)
2–1-99

This child was quite delusional as you can tell.

Dear Ms. Moline,

I feel that I do not deserve my Chemistry Grade because I am only missing 2–3 homeworks. I have passed three tests. One student in your class did no homework + passed 2 Exams and got a 70. Can we please have a conference discussing my grade. I would really appreciate it.

Thank You,

Mindy graf Pd. 3

Jill Forbes
2/1/99

Ms. Moline,

I don't believe that I should have deserved a 70 in Chemistry class. I believe that I should have received a 80 in this class. I passed all of the test for this marking period with an 80 or better. I passed all of the test. I also did all my homework for this marking period.

In the area of Chemistry lab, I don't believe that I should have received a U. I did all of my labs, but the only problem was I wasn't able to give you my lab book. I will still give you my lab book so that I get a grade that goes towards the next marking period.

Jill Forbes

Period 3

Finally a student taking the blame for her actions. Students seem to always have such selective memories; to them passing one test out of 6 means they are doing well in the class.

Jill was right, she should have gotten an 80 in the class. She had the potential to get a grade of 80% or higher, but the effort she put in was only deserving of a 70; such sad commentary. While at Cooper I was always reminiscing about the students I had at Berger. The students at Berger did not have the academic abilities of the students at Cooper, yet they achieved so much more because they were willing to work for it. The interesting difference was the Berger students believed in me and I believed in them, and most important, they believed in themselves. Students at Cooper had the abilities but they did not believe in themselves, somehow it was as if they felt they had to get a helping hand in order to make it.

Dear Ms. Moline,

I don't understand how I failed your class last marking period. I know I didn't do all of my homework but I passed all of my tests. All this extra credit towards the test, where does it go? I don't understand how I could get a fifty five. And for my lab how could I get a U when last semester I never gave you my lab and everything else. I would like you to look back at your grade book and show me why I failed.

Respectively + Sincerely
Yours truly,

Sidney Barnes
2nd Pd

The interesting thing was that I did not get any letters from the students who came to the lab classes and did the required number of lab assignments. Of course the other thing is that these students made up their own letter writing rules, and the grammatical errors are not typos.

Even more interesting were the correspondences from the parents. The parents and students of Cooper High School had learnt one thing really well—if they didn't like the grade they got from a teacher, all they had to do was complained to the school's administrators, and the grade would eventually be changed. I have taught at several schools as you saw from the earlier chapter **Around the System and Back Again**. Cooper High School was the only school where several parents question the grades I gave their children. This is not to say that I resent parents asking questions about the grades their children get. What bothered me was that these are parents who I never met at parent teacher conferences or otherwise.

I think if these students and their parents exerted as much time and effort into learning as they did in trying to get over those students could have accomplished a lot. The students at Cooper had more potential than students that I have taught in other places. However these potentials were never realized, it was a sad waste of talent. Those children could have been so much more if their parents and the school administration hadn't trapped them in a pit of decadence.

I did give students every opportunity to make up lab assignments as Ms. Rizzo implored. Needless to say, only a handful of students showed up for the additional lab session I held to give them an opportunity to make up the work. Out of spite I made those additional lab assignments extremely difficult in comparison to the regular lab assignments. I actually got the work from my chemistry textbook that I used when I did chemistry in Barmenia. The problems were far more challenging. Say what you want, but I don't think those students deserved any less.

After succumbing to excessive pressure I gave Rizzo a list of chemistry students with a yes beside the names of 92 out of 169 students (approximately 54%). I accompanied the list with this note:

A yes beside the names of students with less than 25 labs is not an indication that I support the taking of the Regents by students who are ineligible. I firmly believe that students who have not met their lab requirement should not be allowed to take the Regents.

If you have gotten the hang of how things worked at Cooper you are probably guessing that many of the students who had a 'no' next to their names took the Regents anyway. Such a guess is right on point. Of course many of these students who did not meet the Regents lab requirement but took the chemistry Regents anyway failed.

Discipline

I could describe discipline at Cooper with one word—absent. Students did what they wanted, when they wanted, and however they wanted. I recall maybe one suspension the entire time I was there. A female teacher was harassed by a male student. The teacher's husband was a police officer, and he insisted that she not returned to Cooper; I believe the student involved was suspended, but I could be wrong.

I wrote this concerning discipline at Cooper High School:

Discipline at the school seems to be constantly eroding. Part of the problem is inadequate space, such that even if the school wanted to have in-school suspension for cutting class, there was no place to house students. The space crisis is a result of District 250's occupancy of the first floor. District 250 recently moved, and it will be interesting to see how that space is utilized. Another major part of the problem is lack of access to telephone services for teachers. Teachers have to call down to the secretary, and give the secretary the number to be dialed. That sort of thing can quell a teacher's desire to call the home of a misbehaving student real fast. The other major factor, which stems from a lack of enforcement of the Board's *Code of Conduct*, is that there is no penalty for acts of indiscipline.

As a result of the total lack of discipline, teachers suffered at the hands of students. Ms. Tomkins had a truly interesting year. She found a student in her class with a razor blade in his mouth. No action was taken because when the school administrators questioned the students in the class they did not corroborate her story. She found a student in her class flicking on a lighter. No action was taken. When she questioned how such action can be allowed to go unpunished, the principal told her in the midst of a staff meeting that she should shut up and stop making trouble or else she would get burned. A student from her class cursed the Dean in the presence of other students. No action was taken. A student in her class bashed another student in the head with a padlock. The floor was flooded with blood, police officers were called in. The student responsible was in school the next day boasting about what she had done. The incident was probably not officially written up.

Principal's Revenge 2

I made the mistake of applying for a UFT grant to establish a chemistry lab program. I was just very inspired, but very misguided. The grant was not well written, and was thus not funded. Minott saw my proposal because he had to sign off on it before it could be sent out. He was impressed, and he stopped me in the hallway and spoke to me about how impressed he was. Then I had a guess from the United Nations come in to speak to my class, and Minott was privy to that too. He decided that he wanted me to prepare the students for Salomon Smith Barney's proposal writing competition. When I contacted the Smith Barney program they told me that we were about 4 months behind schedule. I passed this on to Minott but he felt the students should be involved anyway. I guess this involvement confirmed to me that he was not a straight thinker.

One day Minott stopped me in the hallway and asked, "how would you like to go to Africa all expenses paid?" I thought it would be nice, but of course I am always wary of such extravagance. Now in retrospect, I believe the offer of the trip to Africa was probably a lure to coax me into joining Cooper High School's 'Social Promotion Society'. I guess someone should have schooled him about who he was dealing with. I am never for sale, hence I can't be bought.

In my second semester at Cooper I was given a class of 12th graders. I was charged with teaching them health. I had never even heard of such a science course until then. Health classes were normally taught by physical education teachers and focused on personal hygiene. Many of the seniors were illiterate, and at least a third of them had been held back the previous year. I stood between them and graduation, because they needed the credit for the class to fulfill their science requirement for graduation. I think Minott intended that I would give passing grades to all the 12th graders in that class in return for a trip to Africa. The thing that was wrong with that picture was those students didn't even try, they came to class, kicked back in their chairs, chatted and laughed with their friends and completely ignored me.

At the end of the first frustrating marking period all but 3 students had failing grades. The parent teacher conference that took place in March of 1999 was quite interesting. Parents who I contacted but got no response from over the 6 weeks of the marking period crawled out of the woodwork all set to beat me down. One day a stranger stopped me on the street, and told me he heard about what I was going on with me at Cooper. He went on to threaten me about passing students.

Less than a week later I was given a letter stating that I should meet with Ms. Rizzo to discuss my grades.

March 26, 1999

TO: *Maxine Moline,*
          Teacher
FROM: *Lee Minott,*
          Principal
SUBJECT: *Complaints from students and parents*

Because of the large number of complaints that I have received from students and parents about their grades in your Health Class I am directing you to meet with Ms. Genard Rizzo, (your supervisor) to review your grades.

Please provide to her a copy of your grading policy, test grades, homework grades, and any projects that were used to determine students' grades.

Ms. Rizzo will contact you today, to schedule a meeting in regards to this matter. This review must be completed by Tuesday, March 30, 1999.

Right away I had a sense that this was meant to be my induction into the School's Social Promotion Society. I had no desire to be a member of the Society so I asked Ms. Harold, who was the UFT representative at the school to accompany me to the meeting. We went, met with Ms. Rizzo, and discussed my grades. During the meeting Minott called Rizzo, when he found out that Harold was present for the meeting he told Rizzo to stop the meeting.

The following Monday while I was teaching my class, Minott walked in and handed me an envelope. After my class I opened the envelope, it had a letter that said that I should meet with Ms. Rizzo that period.

March 29, 1999

TO: *Maxine Moline,*
          Teacher
FROM: *Lee Minott,*
          Principal

You are hereby directed to meet with your supervisor, Genard Rizzo, today at 10:45 A.M., in her office.

Failure to do so will constitute insubordination.

I went up to meet with Rizzo, and found her in the process of leaving her office. I showed her the letter, and she told me that she did not know that we were supposed to meet that period. She then said, "but you are still not comfortable meeting without your Union representative present?" I can't remember my exact words, but I indicated that I did not feel comfortable meeting with her without UFT presence. I told her that had it been just a casual meeting it would have been fine, but I received a letter requesting the meeting, which made it formal. Later that day, I received a letter stating that I should meet with Minott that coming Wednesday.

March 29, 1999

TO: *Maxine Moline,*
            Teacher
FROM: *Lee Minott,*
            Principal

Please report to my office on Wednesday, March 31, 1999 at 8:20 A.M. You may bring your UFT representative with you.

I went to the meeting, which was more like a lynch trial. On April 21, 1999 I received a letter stating that I had been terminated for insubordination.

April 21, 1999

Maxine Moline,
Teacher

Dear Ms. Moline:

On Wednesday, March 31, 1999 you, Carol Harold—UFT Chapter Chairperson, and I met to discuss your refusal to meet with Ms. Genard Rizzo, your supervisor, to discuss your grading policies and procedures, due to the large number of complaints that I had received from parents and students.

In my memo to you dated March 29, 1999 I directed you to meet with your supervisor to discuss your grading policies (note, the letter did not say why I was meeting with Ms. Rizzo, and when I spoke to Rizzo she had no idea I was supposed to meet with her). *The memo, also, stated that "failure to do so will constitute insubordination. "*

During the course of the meeting, your chapter chairperson stated that you had been advised not to meet with Ms. Rizzo unless your union representative was present (lie—no one told me that, I merely stated that I felt more comfortable with her there—I just wanted there to be a credible witness). I, then, informed you that the meeting was not a disciplinary meeting, therefore, you were not entitled to have your union representative present.

Due to your failure to meet with your supervisor, as directed, I have no choice but to terminate your employment at Cooper High School effective, close of business, Monday, June 28, 1999 for insubordination.

Lee Minott,

Principal

I have received a copy of this letter and

Know that it is being placed in my file:

Then there was space for my signature and the date.

The interesting thing was that the termination letter came the day after I attended my first school leadership meeting. My peers had selected me to represent teachers on the school leadership team. School leadership teams were created to give parents a greater say in their children's education. Of course in a school like Cooper, parents didn't even attend the PTA meetings or the biannual parent-teacher conferences. When I went to the meeting what I found was that the parents on the leadership team were the same ones who ran the PTA, and of course as was the case with the PTA meetings, Minott was the chair.

You would think that if the intent was to give the parents more say, then it would have been mandated that the chair be a parent. Having the principal of the school as chair represented a serious conflict of interest. Minott was not just the chair of the team, he was the head honcho, and he made the decisions and everyone just agreed. I had some issues with some of the things, so I was the one odd vote on a number of issues.

While we are on this trend, here's another interesting tidbit. I volunteered to be on the committee to select an AP for the school. When I went to the candidates' interviews, I was given a document from the superintendent's office that had a list of suggested questions for the candidates. Guess who was the lead actor? Correct, Minott. Guess who were the supporting cast? Right again—the same group of people from the PTA, namely the president and vice president. I of course asked a couple of questions of the applicant, none of my questions were on the list. Later I spoke with the only other teacher on the committee, and he told me that what we went through was just for show. Minott had no intention of hiring another AP, but by law he had to interview the qualified candidates. This is not to say that there were any candidates that seemed to be up to the job.

Let's get back to Minott's revenge. I had only gotten one classroom observation, which was satisfactory:

January 6, 1999

Maxine Moline,
Teacher

Dear Ms. Moline:

Ms. Rizzo, Assistant Principal, and I briefly visited your second period Chemistry 1 class on Wednesday, January 6, 1999. Our visit was towards the end of the period. You and the students were involved with equations and the process of balancing equations. After working on one example, you instructed the students to complete the handout for homework.

We notices that even to the very end of the period, the students were still quite attentive and involved with the task at hand. You were quite professional in your manner of teaching.

The lesson at that juncture was satisfactory.

It was a pleasure to visit your class. Ms. Rizzo and I concurred when we reflect back to the day we met you at the "hiring hall", that you are a definite asset to Cooper High School.

Regards,

Lee Minott,
Principal
I have received a copy of this letter and
Know that it is being placed in my file:

As always there was space for my signature and the date.

So on January 6, 1999 Minott stated that I was an asset to Cooper High School, 3 months later I was being charged with insubordination. In any case I called up the Brooklyn UFT representative who told me I should not worry because all it meant was he didn't want me at Cooper High School in September 1999. He told me that it would become a whole different issue if he gave me an unsatisfactory rating for the year. Of course the representative felt that that scenario was quite unlikely—Minott couldn't be that crazy! Little did he know.

I decided to interview for another teaching position in Brooklyn, and I was offered a position by the first principal that interviewed me. I finished the semester at Cooper without much mishap. I even managed to turn around the health class; I got the majority of the students to get down to serious work. I was impressed by their abilities. They told me, in a rare moment of contrition, that my failing them was a good thing, and it marked a turning point in their lives. Indeed I only got to see their true capability because they came to realize that I was not going to be intimidated by their parents or the school's administration. They correctly concluded that if they wanted to pass my class and move on to college they were going to have to work for the grade. The only ones who did not get a passing grade were the ones who were performing at an elementary school level.

When the semester ended I kept asking for my annual evaluation because all my colleagues had gotten theirs, I was told mine wasn't ready yet. On the evening of my last day at Cooper, Ms. Rizzo called me at home to ask me to change the grade of a senior who was excessively late to class, performed poorly all year, and failed the chemistry Regents. I told her I could not change the grade, especially in light of the 53 she got on the Regents. Ms. Rizzo then said in a threatening manner, "so is this information I can pass on to Mr. Minott?" I didn't justify the threat with a reply.

I went on vacation and came back to find a message from the principal that wanted to hire me. When I called her she told me that I had been given an unsatisfactory rating. She was surprised that I didn't know about the rating, and that I had not been given a copy of my evaluation. She indicated that I should have gotten it about 2 weeks before the end of the semester.

Later that month (July, 1999) the Board returned my license application with a stick-on note that said "Unable to renew. Employee's service was rated unsatisfactory by principal". I called up the UFT to find out that the Brooklyn representative was on vacation. I made several calls to Cooper High School to get a copy of my evaluation. Note, as a result of the unsatisfactory rating, I am unable to renew my license, thereby eliminating my only source of income, yet I have not seen my evaluation.

Amidst the frustration, I wrote a letter to Chancellor Coley, and he sent me a very prompt reply:

July 12, 1999

Ms. Maxine Moline
My address

Dear Ms. Moline:

I regret that I will not be able to accommodate your request for a meeting. Since all appeals of "U" ratings and/or discontinuances come to me for final determination after due process hearings, it is inappropriate for me to meet with individuals outside of that process.

However, I have referred your letter to Dr. Maren Harris, Chief Executive for School Programs and Support Services, for investigation into your allegations regarding pressure to change students' marks. Dr. Harris will take appropriate action based on her review of this matter.

Sincerely,

R. C. Coley
Chancellor
C. Maren Harris

Eventually the UFT resumed working, and I was able to get my appeal started by writing a letter to the Board of Education's human resources director:

(My address)
August 31, 1999

Executive Director
Division of Human Resources
Board of Education
65 Court Street
Brooklyn, NY 11201

I hereby appeal the unsatisfactory rating given me by Mr. Lee Minott, principal of Cooper High School, District 73, for the school year ending June 1999.

Sincerely,
Maxine Moline

In October I finally got a copy of my unsatisfactory evaluation because by law once I submitted an appeal of the "U" rating Minott had to submit documentation of the reason for my "U" rating to me and the Appeals Board.

Let's take some time to look at what constituted my unsatisfactory annual evaluation. I was never late, and I was absent twice. I had satisfactory for all but 5 areas:

1. Professional attitude and growth.

2. Effect on character and personality growth of pupils.

3. Maintenance of wholesome classroom atmosphere.

4. Maintenance of good relations with other teachers and with supervisors.

5. Effort to establish and maintain good relationships with parents.

The support for all of these malfeasances were the above 4 memos. My professional growth was unsatisfactory, yet that was the only time I actually took graduate education courses while I was teaching. I was taking 2 supervisory courses, because I was thinking of trying to get a supervisory license. I had unsatisfactory relationships with teachers and supervisors, yet I had been elected to serve on the school leadership team, and on the committee to select APs. My efforts to interact with parents were the same as always—I sent home progress reports, I made calls as appropriate, and I promptly return phone calls. I even had a web page established through a local non-profit organization through which students and parents were able to contact me. On the web page I had homework answers, and hints for doing the research paper, among other things. The school did not have a web site, and I was the only teacher at the school with a web page. Most of the emails I got from the web page were from students.

The most interesting one was the unsatisfactory 'effect on character and personality growth of pupils'. I guess if you insist that students achieve a certain standard of learning in order to get a passing grade, then you are having a negative impact on their personality and character. I did not maintain a wholesome classroom atmosphere. There were rarely any confrontations in my class. There were no fights, though a lot of my students were involved in fights in other classes.

Also, that was the first year I tried *secret santa* with my classes. I placed all the students' names in a container and had them pick names from the container; each student bought a gift for the student that they picked. The restriction was that the gift could not cost more than $5. Also, that year I got more Christmas cards than at any other time in my teaching career. Even though I had limited space in my classroom/lab/store room, I made use of available wall space to showcase students' work. I even gave cool prizes for students who performed really well.

The Appeals Board set up a meeting for Minott and me to meet with them in the presence of Chancellor Coley in December of 1999. I was anxious about the meeting. I could not wait to find out how Minott intended to justify what he had on my evaluation.

Here's an excerpt of the statement I prepared to use at the hearing:

I have seen events the past school year that I truly wish I had not seen. Witnessing those events however strengthened my resolve to practice standard-based learning in my classroom, wherein students must meet certain standards in order to get a passing grade.

The fact is students do not need token grades from teachers; students will achieve if they are required to do so. A recent survey of students across the country found over 75% of students saying accordingly.

Bearing all this in mind, it's not hard to see that I take my grades very seriously. I spend hours determining students' grades in a fair and objective manner. A passing grade in my class is always an indication that the student has demonstrated, at the very least, a basic understanding of the subject matter. It's no surprise that my class passing average is usually in unison with my students passing average on Regents exams.

Naturally, when on March 29, 9999 I received a letter from Mr. Minott requesting a review of my grades I was concerned. I grew even more concerned when everyone to whom I expressed such concern blatantly told me, "they are going to make you change your grades."

I feel the result of this hearing will answer the question I have been asking myself lately—"is there a place in the New York City public school system for standard-based learning, where students are required to establish that they have attained at least a basic understanding of the subject matter in order to receive a passing grade in a class."

Needless to say the meeting never took place. With the impending threat of this meeting, Minott decided to change my unsatisfactory rating to a satisfactory. The way the UFT representative explained it to me was that I would agree to certain stipulations, and Minott would change the rating. I did not like the stipulations, which made it sound as though I was guilty of some wrongdoing.

However, I agreed to them because the UFT representative explained to me that with the level of corruption on the part of the Board, there was no guarantee that they would have vindicated me.

The terms of the resolution Minott, the UFT representative and I agreed to were:

1. I would withdraw my appeal of my U-rating.

2. I would not seek employment in that Brooklyn school district.

3. Minott would reverse my overall evaluation to satisfactory.

4. I would receive a new rating sheet with an overall evaluation of satisfactory.

It's easy to understand why I made the decision that I would never teach in NYC again.

Some interesting things happened after I left Cooper. The most shocking event was that Minott became superintendent for the district. That explains why he did not want me in that school district. When Minott left to become superintendent Rizzo was made principal of Cooper. One of my former colleagues was moved up to the position of AP left vacant by Rizzo. My colleague actually called me up trying to convince me to come back into teaching so I could serve in her department. I told her in no uncertain terms that I had no interest in ever teaching in NYC again.

My colleague's success didn't last very long. Minott, from his perch as superintendent of the district, selected a principal for Cooper who replaced Rizzo. So, Rizzo was demoted back to AP, and my colleague was demoted back to science teacher. She was quite crushed by the turn of event, so much so she wanted to quit, but then bills always have to be paid, so she stayed. I don't know if she is still there.

The principal of neighboring Poceless Heights High School didn't fare any better. Minott went to a woman who was an AP in another school. "How would you like to be principal?" he asked her. Of course he also told her he needed her response in short order, as was his style. She told him yes, and he sent her to Poceless. The horrible thing about that arrangement was that Poceless had a principal at the time. The then principal of Poceless showed up one morning to find this woman in his office. When he asked her what she was doing in his office, she informed him that she was now the principal of the school. How gross is that.

[01]Probably a year or so later when NYC got a new mayor and all the city agencies started to get the shake up, I found out that Minott got fired from the posi-

tion of superintendent. Rumor had it he ended up teaching at a prison; a very fitting end for his career.

⁰¹ TIME TO GET OUT OF THE GAME

Spare the rod and spoil the child. Don't spare the rod and still spoil the child

01 TIME TO GET OUT OF THE GAME

PS 999, Brooklyn (February—June, 2000)

By the time the Union resolved my case, it was already the end of semester one, and budget cuts had already eliminated teaching positions for semester 2. I did manage to get a position in an alternative high school. The superintendent for the alternative high schools did not want the school to hire me, but insisted that they hire some other teacher that they wanted to send over. The school decided if they could not have me they would rather leave the position unfilled, which is what they did.

I never knew for sure, but I had a funny feeling Minott may have had something to do with that turn of events. Usually when a school selects a teacher the superintendent's office doesn't interfere, even when the school is going against the rules in selecting the teacher. All the high school positions were filled, so I decided to try for a junior high school, found PS 999, and did my first and only stint as a junior high school teacher. Actually a woman at the Board begged me to give PS 999 a try.

Ideally I should have just stayed out of teaching until the start of the next school year, but I had bills that needed to be paid on a monthly basis. Would I ever teach junior high school again? In a word "NO", I would rather starve. Actually, based on what I know is taking place in NYC schools, I would not want to teach in any school in NYC again.

Most of the parents of the students at PS 999 spoke French and very little English. This gave these students free reign to pull the wool over their parents' eyes. I met some of the most devilish students whose parents thought they were angels.

The biggest problem I had at PS 999 was attendance. When you have bad classes, excessive absence is your friend; when you have bad students with good attendance, you are in for a rough ride. The students at PS 999 had excellent attendance. Apparently the parents made sure their children went to school; they just didn't bother to see to it that their children were learning while they were there. I know I am preaching to the choir, we all know this is the way it is—'take my child for the day and leave me the hell alone, because I can't be bothered'.

The only discipline at PS 999 was that instituted by teachers and school administrators on an individual basis. There was no standard procedure that was followed, at least not any that I was made aware of, and believe me I was searching.

I had a 7th grade class as my official class, and I was assigned to teach them math and science. I tried to teach them math for 2 periods—1st and 2nd, 6th period I took them to lunch and picked them up from lunch at the end of the period, I tried to teach them physical science 7th period, then I had to return to dismiss them after 8th period. I had breaks 3rd and 4th periods, these were my preparation periods. 5th period I tried to teach science to another 7th grade class. Each day was usually wasted until 8th period when I taught earth science to Mrs. Neil's 8th grade class. That 8th grade class was the only one in which I actually taught. At Hedley High School I taught 5 periods, and only one was a nightmare, and it was the class with the worst attendance. At PS 999 I taught 5 periods, and only one wasn't a nightmare, plus the students at PS 999 had excellent attendance. Matter of fact attendance was the only thing my students at PS 999 could get a grade of excellent for.

PS 999 was run by a principal, Ms. Clemons, and 2 assistant principals—Mr. Duvivier and Ms. Esterman. My first day at the school was Thursday February 3, 2000. I didn't stay at the school very long because I went on maternity leave early in May, and returned the last week of the school year to wrap up my paper work.

7C: My Official Class

When I think back to this crazy period in my teaching experience, I believe those poor children were really crying out for help. There are only 2 ways to effectively handle such a situation, either you silence the cry with strict rules, or you answer it with patience and compassion. PS 999 did neither, so the children did what children do when no one addresses their cry for help—they act up.

The only think that remotely resembled discipline at PS 999 was a form that teachers would send home to let parents know what their children did in school, based on items checked off on the form:

I found out that before a student could be held back you had to have sent at least 2 such letters out to the parents. In light of that I sent letters out on February 10th, shortly after I started at PS 999, and again on May 1. These are the students for whom I was compelled to send letters home.

I sent a letter home for Stanley Armond's parents in February.

- *No homework*
- *Poorly completed class work*
- *Uncooperative*
- *Talking at inappropriate times*
- *Leave seat without permission*
- *Disruptive*
- *Other—extremely late to math class*

The day after I sent the letter I recorded that he was late to class, and that he was constantly out of his seat.

Stanley was a strange child who would stammer when he got excited. Apparently, during the lunch periods, other students from the class would tease him about his speech impediment. Stanley was also very sneaky, as soon as I turned my back he would get out of his seat and go and interfere with other students.

On Tuesday February 15, 2000 I wrote that he was talkative and did no work. The next day he was absent due to an illness. That evening after school I met with Stanley and his mother. His mother assured me that I would see some change. This did not come to pass, the next day he was out of his seat, and talking during a test. On Wednesday March 1, 2000, which was probably our first day back after the winter break, he had a confrontation with Rita Carmichael, and was taken to see the AP, Mr. Duvivier. The following day his father met with

Mr. Duvivier about Stanley, and I call his home and spoke to his maternal uncle about the fight and about Stanley's behavior in general. You may wonder why I did not just speak to his father when he met with Mr. Duvivier, fact is I did not know of the meeting until I called the child's home, such was the disorganization at PS 999.

On Friday March 10, 2000, I again wrote that Stanley was out of his seat. The following Tuesday he had a fight with Holly Cummings, I tried calling his home and found the number consistently busy. The following Tuesday he was involved in a confrontation with Rosemarie Louis, I called and set up a meeting for the following day with his mother—she did not show up for the meeting. The following Tuesday I spoke to his father about his being constantly late to class and about the confrontations he had with other students. I set up a meeting for the following day with him—his father did not show up for the meeting.

Mark Barns was the only student I taught at PS 999 who I could never accuse of disrespecting me. I got the sense a lot of Mark's woes at PS 999 were due to the fact that he was Barmenian. To make matters worst Mark was a very hot-tempered child; even the calmest of statements came out of him as a loud and confrontational assault.

On Thursday February 3, 2000 he got very fresh with one of the School's custodians, who from his accent seemed to have been Barmenian also. I called his mother about his behavior. On Tuesday February 8, 2000 I called his house and spoke to both parents, yet the following day he was doing the usual—talkative, out of his seat. That Friday the 11th, I wrote 'out of seat, throwing objects'. Monday I wrote 'shouting', Tuesday 'inattentive, shouting, out of seat, instigating fight, shouting across room, cursing'. On Thursday it was 'out of seat, eating, playing around, and distractive influence'. To top off the week on Friday he was involved in a confrontation.

If you are a teacher in NYC, one of the nice things about February is the Winter Break—an entire week off in February. I say this to let you know that when you see a break in reports during the month of February, it's not that the students suddenly became studious, but rather that I got a welcome break from them.

On Thursday March 2, I wrote 'in the hall when he should be in the auditorium, shouting across room, out of his seat'. I called his home and spoke to his mother. The reason I didn't call Mark's home more often was because he was always making verbal agreements with me. Most of these agreements meant that he would misbehave, and I would give him second and third chances. I think I went along with these agreements because it represented an attempt at improvement, which was more than I got from the majority of the other students.

On Tuesday March 28, 2000 he was chewing gum, out of his seat, calling out answers, and talkative. Again I spoke to his poor mother. I eventually met Mark's mother at parent-teacher conference. She seemed like a very nice person. Apparently Mark had been attending school in Barmenia, and had recently migrated to the United States. My guess was that Mark was having trouble adjusting to the New York school system and its many freedoms. I really felt sorry for Mark. I felt he had the potential to do a lot better than he was doing. To make matters worst he had joined company with one of the school's worst nightmares, Carl Pommels; the school's administrators were forever threatening to expel them both.

Monday February 7, 2000 I called Boris Bozzel's mother because he was doing the usual—out of his seat, and talkative. His February letter:

- *Poorly completed homework*

- *Class work not done*

- *Uncooperative*

- *Talking at inappropriate times*

- *Leave seat without permission*

- *Disruptive*

- *Other—excessively late to math class, eating in class, and playing around in class*

On Tuesday February 15th, I wrote that he was talking, out of his seat, and did no work. That Thursday he was talking during a test. Prior to teaching at PS 999 when I gave a test and told students that there should be no talking during the test my instruction was adhered to. At PS 999 I used all manner of threats, and the knuckleheaded students continued to talk.

The students at PS 999 were privy to something that I only learned near the end of my time there—they could do whatever they wanted and get away with it because there was nothing I could do to them, and if I gave them a failing grade the school's administrators would see to it that they got promoted anyway.

On Thursday March 2nd I wrote that he was in the hall when he should have been in the auditorium. Students hanging out in the halls when they should be in class was a common problem at PS 999 because there was no security in the building. There was one school safety officer, and he spent all his time in the main lobby monitoring visitors. Most times the students roaming the halls were from one of the 2 7th grade classes that I taught.

Two boys were expelled from 7C the day before I started at PS 999. Greco Jacks and Edman Perell were expelled for sexually assaulting a female student whose mother worked in the School. After the incident they had superintendent suspension (which is much more serious than a principal's suspension), then after a hearing they were transferred to other schools. Even such an extreme act didn't do anything to improve security in the building. I often saw girls and boys going into the boys' bathroom. On numerous occasions I would enter the stairwells and hear footsteps of students running, their laughter floating with them up and down the stairs.

If I found students in the hallway or stairwell near my classroom and I knew their names I would make a note of it, and then I would call or write their parents. This I did, not because I expected the parents to take any action, but because I wanted to make sure I had documented it. One of the things I learnt a long time ago is that it's important to document everything. It's called CMA (covering my ass). The very first question out of people's mouths when something happens in public school is, 'so what did the teacher do?' or 'why didn't the teacher do anything?' or 'where was the teacher when all this was happening?'

When the Berger student was stabbed in the chest by his classmate, the newspaper carried a story that claimed the teacher stood there while students from his class fought and did nothing. The same teacher the newspaper spoke about was actually in the hospital recovering from injury inflicted on him when he tried to stop the fight, and the students did not belong in his class that period. The question that should have been raised was why were students in the hallway fighting when they should have been in class?

Would you believe that PS 999 was in the school district that was most vocal about the New York Police Department (NYPD) being in public schools in NYC. They even held a poorly attended demonstration outside the Board's Livingston Street headquarters in Brooklyn. The impression the district gave was that there would be police officers with guns in the schools. It turned out that it was the same school safety officers who would be in the schools. The only difference was they would be trained by the NYPD. Please don't get the impression that I felt this training was necessarily a good thing; to the contrary, civil servants are not the brightest people. There are 2 types of people in civil service—those who couldn't cut it in the real world, and those who are there because they truly want to make a difference. Unfortunately those of us who are civil servants because of our call to advocacy are in the minority. On top of that police officers are certainly known for having IQs slightly above that of a potato wedge.

On March 2nd Boris' mother, Carlene Bozzel, paid me a visit. We spoke about assigning Boris extra work. I wasn't sure how I was going to do that since Boris wasn't keeping up with the regular work. Students and parents tend to misunderstand extra credit, thinking it's to make up for missed work when in fact it's extra work given to select students who have kept pace with the regular course work, and have demonstrated the ability to handle additional work.

Later that day the other mathematics teacher commented on the fact that Carlene came to see me. He told me that it was the norm for Carlene to visit the school, feign interest in her son then disappear never to be seen again for the rest of the year. I never saw or heard from Carlene after that day.

Maris Bruce, a petite girl who was a consistent scream for help. I have never gone back and forth so many times with a student's mother without even an ounce of improvement. On Wednesday February 3rd I called her mother because she came in late and was talking too much. Her mother told me she would speak to Maris. That Sunday I again spoke to her mother about her lateness and talking. Her mother promised to work to improve. I don't know what kind of improvement her mother had in mind because the next day, Monday February 7th, Maris refused to change her seat or her behavior. She was sitting in the back, and I felt if I moved her forward it might help. Though she would not change her seat, she was constantly leaving her seat to talk to students sitting in the front of the class. She talked constantly, and was forever getting into verbal fights with her classmates.

On Wednesday February 9th, Maris was up to her usual antics again, I called her mother about her behavior and the need to change her seat. I realized later that Maris' excuse for not wanting to change her seat was a valid one. There were only a few students with whom she could sit. It seemed she was at odds with most of her classmates, and a lot of her schoolmates. That Friday the 11th I wrote that she was late to class again, and that she refused to sit in her assigned seat, and as usual she was constantly out of her seat. Later that day I noted that she was late to the auditorium after lunch.

On days when the students didn't go outside during the lunch period they would assemble in the auditorium after lunch, and their homeroom teachers would go down and pick them up. On days when the weather was nice and they were allowed to go outside, they were to line up behind the square in which their class number was painted. On such occasions I would go outside and stand next to the square that said 7C. On seeing this, the school aid would hold up her bull horn and shout into it with a very strong Spanish accent, "7C, your teacher is here". My students would continue to run around like lunatics, pretending to be unaware of my presence. Gradually a few students would get on line, I would take them and leave, and all the others would be marked late. In addition, by the time the latecomers got to the class, their classmates would have already started on the day's science assignment. Of course it was always the knuckleheads who were late hence the minute they got to the class they would turn it upside down. At one point I tried conducting science labs with them to see if I could give them an enriched science experience. I ended up giving up after a few futile attempts. The experience was analogous to playing hopscotch in a mind field, and I think I would have had better luck in the mind field.

Maris' February letter:

- *No homework*
- *Class work not done*
- *Uncooperative*
- *Talking at inappropriate times*
- *Leave seat without permission*
- *Calling out*
- *Rude*
- *Fighting*
- *Disruptive*
- *Other—excessively late to math class, playing around in class, and inattentive*

On February 14th I wrote that she was out of her seat, talkative, fighting during mathematics class, and playing around. I sent a letter home, with conference scheduled for February 18th because of the fighting.

You may wonder why I kept such detailed motes on these students. Well, I was hoping to be asked to testify regarding my students at suspension hearings. Most other schools where I taught in the past, the things that students did at PS 999 were grounds for suspension. At PS 999 however, students did whatever they wanted without reprise. The principal seemed content with the fact that when she walked into a room the students remained quiet. Ms. Clemons was a former PS 999 teacher who got promoted to principal. Probably a lot of the students recalled her as a very strict teacher. It mattered not that when her back was turned the students would make statements like "fuck Ms. Clemons, I'm not scared of that bitch".

At first glance it might seem that all I did was sit around and make notes on students' bad behavior. On the contrary, I had a system set up so that all I had to do was mark a certain check against a student's name to indicate the type of behavior they were involved in. In so doing I ensured that my making notes on the students' behavior did not take time away from my teaching. During my preparation periods I would update the students' files and contact their parents. I did not prepare my lessons at school during my preparation periods; I planned all my lessons at home where it was peaceful and quiet. I have gotten some truly great lesson ideas while sitting in the tranquility of my home and thinking of what I want to accomplish in the classroom.

On Thursday March 2nd I wrote that Maris refused to sit in her seat, and was very disruptive. I called her mother and we set an appointment for the coming Monday at 10:30 am. Her mother came in the following day. I found out from talking to her that she didn't know how to control her daughter. The poor woman was obviously at her wits end. This is a common problem—the students with the worst behavior more often than not had parents who had no clue how to control them. They would ask me for help and I would send them to their child's guidance counselor.

Brooklyn parents, in addition to having poor control over their children, had little respect for the teachers' time. They would ignore making and keeping appointments, and instead show up at the most inopportune time. If you were unable to meet with them they would go and complain to the principal or the assistant principal. At Cooper High School a parent got upset with me because she came into my classroom while I was teaching, and I told her I would not be able to meet with her that period. Can you believe that? She expected me to stop teaching in order to have an unscheduled meeting with her about her child.

Anyway, Maris' behavior did not improve at all, if anything it got worst. I met with both her parents on March 21st to no avail. At that point in the road I decided that I had important things to occupy my time.

I think Avis Concord was the photo queen. Which is to say I think she was the one bringing pictures to class most often. On February 3rd and 4th I noted that she came late to class, was constantly talking and sharing a photo album, banging on desk, and shouting. I called her mother that Sunday to talk about her tardy, and her poor performance on the practice test I gave. Her mother told me she would talk to her.

There were certain times that I liked to call students' homes, and it was all very strategic. By far my favorite time to call was early (8 am to 10 am) on weekends. I figured it would be to my advantage if the students' parents had to wake up early on weekends to listen to me preach a sermon about their children's behavior. My other favorite time to call was Friday evenings, preferably the Friday before a long weekend; in general it's always good to call just before the holidays. When I call homes on weekends I usually get lots of rolling eyes on Mondays. I would hear the students surveying each other to find out which homes were called. Invariably there would be a student whose parents I was unable to reach for whatever reason. The students would exclaim, "how comes his/her house wasn't called?" I would take note and make sure that student's home was called; no one got away. If there was a student who gave the wrong number, I would make such a big deal about it that the student would have to give the correct number to me or the school administration.

On Monday the 7th I note that she was talking, out of her seat, and did no work. After calling Avis' mother I wrote, "Mother doesn't sound serious about resolving problem."

On February 11th I wrote that she was eating in class, asking for answers during a test, playing around, and cursing. In addition she was also late to class in the morning, and late to the auditorium at lunch. Avis had a chronic lateness problem. The most irritating part of it was that she would stroll in nonchalantly half an hour late the way one would stroll in if they were half an hour early. She constantly reminded me of the nursery rhyme:

> *A dillar a dollar a ten o'clock scholar,*
> *what made you come so soon.*
> *You used to come at 10 o'clock,*
> *but now you come at noon.*

The other irritating thing about Avis was that she never tried to do anything on her own, preferring instead to assume other students' answers were correct, and then just copy them. Maybe it was all just laziness; actually I bet it was. I dreaded the ordeal she would have with the real world of work if she didn't have an attitude adjustment soon.

On February 14th I sent a letter to her home that spelled out all her dastardly deeds:

- *No homework*

- *Class work not done*

- *Uncooperative*

- *Talking at inappropriate times*

- *Leave seat without permission*

- *Disruptive*

- *Calling out*

- *Using disrespectful language*

- *Rude*

- *Other—excessively late to math class, sharing photos during class, eating in class, banging on the desk, cheating during test, playing around during class, and late to auditorium at lunch time*

The documentation and calls home continued to no avail. On February 15th I wrote, 'out of her seat, talkative'; 2 days later, 'talking during test'; on March 10th I wrote that she was playing with a Pokemon toy; and on March 13 and 28, 'inattentive and talkative'.

When I called her home I could never be sure if I were talking to Avis' mother, or to Avis pretending to sound grownup. The person's voice sounded grownup, but the statements she made didn't sound like they were coming from a grownup.

Rita Carmichael was an intelligent girl; one of the few students in the class with computational skills. Unfortunately it was hard to deal with her because she was chunky and ill-tempered, and I think those 2 negative traits were constantly feeding on each other. From the sound of things Rita's mother wasn't afraid to drop some serious spanking on her. To avoid spanking at the hands of her mother, Rita did what most bad children do—lie. To say she lied like a rug is an understatement.

My first day with the class, Thursday February 3rd, she acted as if she wanted to fight me. I wrote, 'refused to change seat, talking, fighting, and looking at photos'. The next day I wrote, 'disrespectful, talkative, had playing cards'. I spoke to her mother that Sunday, and she had a lengthy discussion with her daughter in French about the fact that Rita did not own any playing cards. I reiterated the truth, I didn't say she owned playing cards, but I saw them in her possession.

Nevertheless that Monday, February 7th, I saw some improvement. This didn't last as long as I would have liked. On February 17th I wrote, 'continuously out of her seat, kept opening window'. Take note that it was February 17th, the middle of winter, and she was opening the window. The students would come in every morning and fling all the windows open. Then an hour later, all the skinny people in the class without coats would be shivering, and we would have to fight to get the windows closed. What I did, which was successful most of the times, was to open the windows just a crack at the top, and as soon as the students came in have them take their coats off. The only trouble I had with that measure was that, when I wasn't looking, someone (I think that it was sneaky Stanley, because I didn't see him do it) would open the back windows all the way up, and I would have to get into a huff and stomp to the back of the room to close them.

The students were really not at fault, PS 999 was just another one of the many NYC schools with an antiquated heating system. As a result it was always too hot in the building, regardless of what was happening with the external weather. The other part of the problem was that 7C had gone too long without any sustained adult supervision. Hence the students had gotten into the habit of doing things how they wanted to, and who was I to demand that they change.

Things got even worst with Rita after the winter break. Maybe she had too much time home with her parents. Recall that the worst students in class are the ones who are angels at home. The logic is they don't get to be themselves at home, so they do so at school. On March 1st Rita was involved in a fight with sneaky Stanley. The following day I met with her mother, and after the meeting I wrote, 'Met with her mother re incident. She doesn't seem to believe anything I say about her daughter. Met in presence of Mr. Duvivier. Not much resolved from the meeting'. I remembered thinking, 'it seems I have nothing better to do with my time than sit around and make up stories about Rita to tell her mother'. Her behavior—inattentive, talkative, out of her seat constantly—continued unchanged. I spoke to her mother once more then gave up.

Mild-mannered Holly Cummings was one of the few students in my classes that I actually liked. I think I liked what I sensed about her, because her behavior was as bad as most of the others.

I called her home my first 2 days in the school—Thursday February 3rd and Friday February 4th—because she was talkative, inattentive, and out of her seat. That Thursday I spoke to both her parents and they promised to discipline her, then on Friday I spoke to her mother who promised to talk to her. The next week she was just as bad.

I remember when I was growing up in Barmenia we had to deal with the 'it takes an entire village to raise a child' mentality. Hence other parents were always on the lookout for your bad deeds so they could report it to your parents, and see to it that you got a good spanking.

Most parents would treat their children to a good spanking if they heard any bad reports. My mother however was quite different, she didn't believe in spanking. When spiteful neighbors came by and reported on us (my rebel sister and I), my mom feigned anger. She would take us into the house, and we would oblige her by doing our great acting routine—my mother would hit the furniture, and we would scream and holler as if we were getting the spanking of our lives. After a few minutes of this ordeal, we would peak out the window to see the informer leaving with a satisfied look on his or her face.

I tell this story because I think this is what probably happens when I called some students' homes. This would explain why their behavior after my call home was equal or worst than before I called.

Holly's behavior deteriorated into and beyond the winter break, and her grades went downhill with her behavior. On March 2nd I called her home and the number was not in service. The next day I wrote that she was destroying school property and running around the room.

I usually say 'destroying school property' when students throw or otherwise mishandle their textbooks. I have witnessed the destruction of thousands of dollars worth of textbooks. I am always very angry when I see students destroying textbooks because I know how expensive textbooks are. If it were up to me whenever a child damages a textbook his or her parents would have to pay for it. There are those who may say the parents of children in poor schools can't afford to pay for textbooks. This is not true. I have seen students at PS 999 spend enough on food at the corner store in a week to buy the most expensive middle school textbook.

Some schools have gotten into the practice of charging students a rental fee to make sure textbooks are returned in fair condition. In Barmenia parents are issued a booklist at the start of the school year, and they are responsible for buying the books. It's not unusual for the parents of a high school student to spend the equivalent of US $1,000 for books, uniform and other school supplies in a single year. Many students in Barmenia depend on scholarships to attend high school. I once purchased a chemistry textbook for a private school student I was tutoring in NYC. With tax the price of the textbook was almost $70 (her parents refunded me, of course). I think the fact that they can get at no cost what they would have to pay thousands of dollars for back home is part of the reason Barmenian students tend to do so well in American schools.

Having Danielle Hess as a student was a truly classic experience. On Monday February 7th I noted that she was talking, out of her seat, and playing around. The following day I recorded that I called and spoke to both her parents about changing her seat. I felt if I were able to get some strategic seat assignments in that class I could change a lot of things. Case in point, I was most successful when I placed them in these groups that I designed to make sure that everyone got split up, and each group had at least one person with some knowledge of the subject matter (mathematics).

Just when this was beginning to work, they split the class between me and one of the other 7th grade mathematics teachers. He had the students self-select themselves out of the class and just about all the calm students went to him, all the ruffians insisted on staying with me. You must begin to think that bad students are attracted to me. That might be so, but it certainly is not a mutual thing. Anyway, I decided to forget about doing groups, instead I merely made sure I had lots of space between the students, and I tried to prevent more than 2 students from working together.

The unruliness of the 7th grade classes at PS 999 was the result of years of poor management of the school. The school was on to its third principal in less than 3 years, and she was recruited from the ranks of the teachers. Anyone with half a brain knows it's a bad idea to let disruptive students stay together for years on end. Indeed it's the worst form of segregation. The students at PS 999 had stayed together from kindergarten all the way through to the 7th grade, hence they all got to know each other, and they had their little groupings in the class. Don't get me wrong, I'm not saying students shouldn't stay together for years. Matter of fact I am the product of such educational segregation; in high school I spent 4 years with the same group of students. Now, 20 years later, I still maintain the friendships I developed in those merry youthful years. However, if you have a school in which students are totally out of control and no discipline is in place, then you only make things worst by blocking students and allowing them to move from year to year as a fixed group.

To get back to the story, on February 9th Danielle was eating in class, talking, and was extremely disrespectful to me. By disrespectful I mean I spoke to her and she threw back a pert retort as was the norm for her. Again I recorded talking to her parent about her behavior and about changing her seat.

That Friday the 11th I made note that she was sharing photos in class, and kept talking during a Test. Later that day I made a note that she was late to the auditorium at lunch time. That Monday February 14th I wrote, 'fighting, eating in class, talkative, disruptive, refused to change seat'.

That day I mailed a letter to her home:

- *Poorly completed homework*

- *Class work not done*

- *Uncooperative*

- *Talking at inappropriate times*

- *Leave seat without permission*

- *Disruptive*

- *Calling out*

- *Using disrespectful language*

- *Rude*

- *Other—late to auditorium at lunch time, playing around during class, eating in class, sharing photos during class*

Actually for homework I checked both none and incomplete, which meant most times she didn't do her homework, and on the few occasions when she did it, it was incomplete. I gave a lot of incomplete for homeworks in that class. I would assign homework from the textbook. Unfortunately the student edition of the text had the answers to the questions in the back. Knowing this I told the students I wanted them to show their work; I wanted to clearly see how they got their answers. This was also important because the Citywide 7th grade exam required that students show all their work in solving problems. Nevertheless the majority of my students that did homework simply copied the answers from the back of the textbook. Hence I gave incompletes, each such incomplete homework was worth half the credit of a completed homework, and that was me being too generous.

The next day I note that Danielle was playing with a toy (blowing bubbles), eating in class, and did no work. The day after that I wrote, 'Student wrote note assuring she will behave. We agree if she behaves in class and does her work I won't call or write home'.

Dear Ms. Moline,

I am really sorry for my behavior towards you since you came to the school. I am making a great promise now that you will see a big change in my behavior and classwork during school hours.

Sincerely

Your Student
Danielle Hess

Danielle seemed to like writing notes, and she wrote a number of others to me.

Dear Ms. Moline,

I apologize for being disrespectful in class but I think you should have let me go to the bathroom when I asked. I would really appreciate if you would not call my house tonight because I have enough problems at home as it is.

Thank you

Danielle Hess

That last statement was quite telling, because Danielle was always terrified of me calling her home.

Dear Ms. Moline,

Could you please stop calling my house and getting me in trouble. I really try hard to get along with you and do my work but it's not working.

Sincerely

Danielle & Nicoletta

P.S. Maybe if you stop calling my house I won't have a problem respecting you and doing my work.

Anyway, Danielle didn't abide by our agreement. The day after she wrote me the note I wrote, 'talking during test'. On March 2nd I wrote that she was extremely inattentive and playing with beads. I gave up and called her mother who said I should change her seat. The next day I wrote, 'out of seat, combing hair'.

Essentially she continued to misbehave, and I continued to call her parents. On April 5th I noted that I sent a letter home with her test that she did poorly on. I think I must have picked up the 'send the test home for the parents to see' idea from another teacher, I can't recall who though.

This Danielle was quite a feisty child. I saw her in a verbal battle with the school's French teacher in which she behaved like a regular little she devil. Sad to say the French teacher didn't behave much better. Danielle and the French teacher were engaged in a shouting match. Danielle came over to me and tried to shout an explanation to me. I told her that I could not have a conversation with her if she was shouting. She immediately lowered her voice, explained herself, then returned to her shouting match with the French teacher. It was truly a sight to behold.

I have seen a lot of teachers get into shouting matches with students, that's a no no in my book. If I want to quiet a class immediately, all I have to do is raise my voice. That's because I usually speak very softly. If I want them quiet for the entire period, then I throw a tantrum. The first time I threw a tantrum in the classroom I was teaching at Berger High School in the South Bronx. I cursed out my 8th period class, I gave them quite a verbal thrashing. I called them all sorts of names such as selfish and inconsiderate. They were truly ashamed, and they were quiet the entire period. That's how I learnt that tantrums can be effective. My Berger 8th period students grumbled that I didn't know them like that, how dare I call them selfish; that didn't matter, the important thing was that it sank in.

Nicoletta Jazze's February 10th letter:

- *No homework*
- *Class work not done*
- *Uncooperative*
- *Talking at inappropriate times*
- *Leave seat without permission*
- *Disruptive*

- *Calling out*

- *Rude*

- *Other—extremely inattentive, sharing photos during class (daily), talking during an exam, eating in class, extremely insubordinate, and showed a total lack of respect*

Her mother wrote this response under comments: *I spoke with my child about the letter. She said, 'she will try her best to change'. I will take whatever step is necessary to correct this situation.*

Nicoletta wrote me this letter:

Dear Ms. Moline,

Sorry for disturbing your class and make you mad. I thought by doing my work and homework that would be enough, but now I know you have to have manner and know how to follow rules. I just telling you that I'm sorry and for now on I would do my work <u>and</u> behave myself.

Sincerely

Your Student Nicoletta

I had to wonder what work she was attesting to doing. In any case there was a change in Nicoletta's behavior after this. I did meet Nicoletta's mother, and found her a very wonderful woman. It is so important for parents to be aware of who their children interact with in school. Bad company in school can slowly change the most angelic child to a total ruffian.

Roshart Jonel got a February 10th letter:

- *Poorly completed homework*

- *Class work poorly completed*

- *Uncooperative*

- *Talking at inappropriate times*

- *Leave seat without permission*

- *Disruptive*
- *Calling out*
- *Rude*

This student was as frisky as a fawn, and just as brainless when in the head-lights.

I send Karen Jeffreys' mother a letter on May 10th as well:

- *No homework*
- *Class work not done/poorly completed*
- *Uncooperative*
- *Talking at inappropriate times*
- *Leave seat without permission*
- *Disruptive*
- *Calling out*
- *Rude*
- *Other—late to class on 2/4, extremely inattentive, sharing photos during class (daily), and late to auditorium at lunch time*

When I spoke to her mother after this letter, she requested that I change Karen's seat. Before my arrival, the class was subjected to one substitute after another. I was the first person to stay as long as I did with the class. As a result the students had selected the seats they felt comfortable with. Meaning they had their talking partners close by. When I arrived, one of the first things I tried to do was change seats, I had a big fight, and in the end they stayed in their seats. So I was only too happy to oblige Karen's mother by changing her seat.

After the letter, the talk with Karen's mother, and the seat change, I saw a different Karen.

Ashton Juvie's February letter:

- *No homework*
- *Class work not done*
- *Uncooperative*

- *Talking at inappropriate times*
- *Leave seat without permission*
- *Disruptive*
- *Calling out*
- *Rude*
- *Other—throwing paper in class, extremely inattentive, and refused to change his seat*

The letter was returned for 'insufficient address'; probably the apartment number was missing. I spoke to another teacher who told me that Ashton's family was having a hard time financially. The least the child could do was behave in school so his parents would have one less headache in their lives. Instead he was busy being Roshart's partner in foolishness.

Paul Lamarque February letter:

- *Poorly completed homework*
- *Class work poorly completed*
- *Talking at inappropriate times*
- *Leave seat without permission*
- *Disruptive*
- *Playing with toys*
- *Rude*
- *Other—extremely inattentive*

After the letter I met Paul's father. I was called down to Miss Clemons' office, and there was this very old man sitting in the chair across from her. She introduced him as Paul's father. Shortly after I got there Paul came in; apparently Ms. Clemons had sent for him too. I spoke at length to his father about his poor classroom behavior, and how poorly he was doing academically. By the time I was finished, Paul was in tears. Miss Clemons said, "don't cry, don't cry", in the manly voice that she always seemed to use with the students when they were not behaving. This only made Paul cry more.

I thought, 'gotcha', expecting that Paul's behavior would improve. I was shit out of luck there; Paul reverted to his usual poor behavior almost immediately.

Rosemarie Louis' February letter:

- *No homework*
- *Class work not done*
- *Talking at inappropriate times*
- *Leave seat without permission*
- *Disruptive*
- *Calling out*
- *Rude*
- *Other—extremely inattentive, show total lack of respect, constantly in the hallway without a pass, absent from the auditorium at lunch time, and sharing photos during class*

Rosemarie was one of the students taken out of my class and placed in the other mathematics class. I was only too happy when she self-selected herself out of my class. However, my happiness was short-lived because the other mathematics teacher was always sending her back to me.

One day I was teaching, and I suddenly noticed that a lot of eyes were directed towards her desk. I strained to see a little furry thing in her hand. Apparently she had a hamster that had given births and she brought the babies to school. That was kind of the last straw for me. I sent for security, and insisted that she and the animals leave the classroom. She insisted she did not have any animals. The matter was taken up with the principal, and her mother was brought in. When Rosemarie and her mother met with Ms. Clemons; Rosemarie told Ms. Clemons that I merely thought that I saw hamsters in her possession.

Ms. Clemons sent for me to give my side of the story, which I did. Ms. Clemons later told me that the child had so convincingly insisted she did not have any hamsters that had I not been present she would have taken the child's tale as gospel.

Yvonne Maxwell touched my heart because she always had this sad look on her face. That did not stop me sending a February letter:

- *Poorly completed homework*
- *Class work not complete*

- *Uncooperative*
- *Talking at inappropriate times*
- *Leave seat without permission*
- *Disruptive*
- *Other—sharing photos during class, and sharing answers during a test*

Yvonne kept company with a lot of knuckleheads who always wanted her to give them answers on tests. She was not the brightest student in the class she was just the one who worked the hardest. Those who copied from her were forever mistaking diligence for intelligence. She almost always did her homework, and she would get to the classwork when it was assigned.

Fabian Petersen was the little boy with funny teeth who was always bringing chewing gum to class. I guessed his parents had a candy store because he came to school loaded with candy everyday.

He got a February letter too:

- *Poorly completed homework*
- *Class work not done/poorly completed*
- *Talking at inappropriate times*
- *Leave seat without permission*
- *Disruptive*
- *Calling out*
- *Playing with toys*
- *Fighting*
- *Other—playing around in class, and extremely inattentive*

I called Fabian's mother after I sent the letter. She said with a very strong Jamaican accent, "Me get de letter, and me ask Fabian a wha kin' a letter dat me a get from school." When I explained to her that Fabian wasn't doing very well in class, wasn't doing his homeworks, and was in danger of failing the class, she said, "Every evening homework do in a dis ya house, matter a fact, is a group a parents sitting round de table right now doin' homework." So I asked, "is Fabian doing homework?" I heard her calling, "Fabian, Fabian, come out here an' do yu homework."

Fabian, Paul, Ashton and Roshart were at least 2 grades higher than they should have been. They didn't have the skills or maturity to handle seventh grade work. They were there because they had gotten token grades from teachers who believe the rhetoric 'it's bad to give failing grades to poor students'. Many teachers seem to feel that if you fail poor students it will lower their already low self esteem. Then the answer is to dedicate more time and resources to making sure poor children do well, not give them token grades in the hope that it will bolster their self esteem. I was one teacher against the world with my belief—'give students what they earn'.

In any case, Fabian spent at least 90% of his time in school running around and playing. I don't know, maybe he missed out on pre-kindergarten and was busy trying to make up for it.

I did not like Goldy Pinto because I sensed she had a real evil streak in her that made her capable of extreme meanness. I felt the same sensation from her as I did from Altamont Frazer of Hedley High School.

Her February 10th letter told the truth about her:

- *Poorly completed homework*
- *Class work not done*
- *Uncooperative*
- *Talking at inappropriate times*
- *Leave seat without permission*
- *Disruptive*
- *Textbook damaged*
- *Rude*
- *Other—extremely inattentive, doing other work in class, playing around in class, drinking juice in class, extremely insubordinate, shows complete lack of respect, and absent from auditorium at lunch time*

Whenever I spoke to Gilda she always had a pert reply to offer, and of course she never did anything I told her to. If ever there was an ideal candidate for kids' boot camp, she was it.

Carl Pommels' February 10th letter told of his dastardly deeds:

- *Poorly completed homework*
- *Class work not done/poorly completed*
- *Uncooperative*
- *Talking at inappropriate times*
- *Leave seat without permission*
- *Calling out*
- *Disrespectful language*
- *Rude*
- *Textbook damaged*
- *Fighting*
- *Other—extremely inattentive, destroying school property, writing on board without permission, extremely insubordinate, shows complete lack of respect, and absent from auditorium at lunch time*

On February 15th I sent a letter out because he was fighting, and I scheduled a conference with his mother for February 18th. His mother didn't show up for the meeting, I didn't get a response from the letter, I was never able to reach his mother by phone, and there was no attempt on her part to contact me.

Carl felt it was a lot of fun to be mean and destructive all day long. He was a bully in the making. He enjoyed harassing other students. When I say enjoy, I do mean enjoy, he would have a look of pure joy on his face when he was in the midst of making someone quite miserable.

Kamela Rizzi was the brightest student in the class, and the only one with critical thinking skills. Nevertheless, the statement 'a mind is a terrible thing to waste' always popped into my head when I thought of her. Kamela, Carl, and Rita were way ahead of the rest of the class. I think they may have been in a higher class at some prior point, but got demoted because of poor behavior. This probably explains why they were so restless.

7C had a very bad mix of students—there were those who should not have advanced to the 7th grade, those who would have benefited from an advanced 7th grade class, and those who needed comprehensive remediation; just more symptoms of poor school management. If they paid more attention to students' real abilities, and less to assuring social promotion, the deficits would have been realized and corrected.

Her February 10th letter said:

- *No homework*
- *Class work not done*
- *Uncooperative*
- *Talking at inappropriate times*
- *Leave seat without permission*
- *Disruptive*
- *Calling out*
- *Disrespectful language*
- *Rude*
- *Textbook damaged*
- *Fighting*
- *Other—eating in class, sharing pictures during class, and destroying school property (books)*

On February 15th I sent a letter out because she was fighting, and I scheduled a conference with her father for February 18th. I met with her father who did a good job of defending himself, but did little to assure me that Kamela's behavior would improve. After the meeting I got this letter from Kamela, but I did not see much change in her behavior.

3–22–00

Dear Ms. Moline

I am sorry for interrupting the class yesterday (3–21–00). I am also sorry for talking back to you and being rude.

I will try my best to improve my attitude and my grades in math and science. I am sorry for all the trouble I cause U yesterday and any other day. I hope you except my apologie.

Maud Satchell was a regular irritant, like using the wrong soap on a daily basis because you forget your allergies at the point in time when you are taking a shower. Needless to say she got a February 10th letter:

- *Poorly completed homework*
- *Class work not done*
- *Uncooperative*
- *Talking at inappropriate times*
- *Leave seat without permission*
- *Disruptive*
- *Calling out*
- *Other—combing her hair in class, left classroom without permission, and absent from auditorium at lunch time*

Maud was a spoilt brat who reminded me of the daughter of a woman I knew. This woman made an idol of her daughter. She took her out of public school because she felt she would do better in private school. The result was her daughter ran away from home and became a prostitute.

Anderson Tomme was the little Haitian roughneck-wannabe. His February 10th letter said:

- *Poorly completed homework*
- *Class work poorly completed*
- *Uncooperative*
- *Talking at inappropriate times*
- *Leave seat without permission*
- *Disruptive*
- *Calling out*
- *Rude*
- *Fighting*
- *Other—playing around in class, extremely inattentive, chewing gum in class, and refused to take off hat*

He always wore this black knitted hat, which he would pull down over his forehead while he did his 'skanky' bad boy walk around the classroom. As I write this I have to smile at the memory of that little roughneck-wannabe who was barely 4 feet tall.

Tamara Tobbs wasn't a bad girl, she was just unfortunate enough to be in the company of all bad girls—the likes of Goldy, need I say more. Her February 10th letter said:

- *No homework*
- *Class work not done*
- *Uncooperative*
- *Talking at inappropriate times*
- *Leave seat without permission*
- *Disruptive*
- *Rude*
- *Other—absent from auditorium at lunch time, doing other assignment in class, playing around in class, and sharing photos during class*

Edwina Wilson's February 10th letter said:

- *Poorly completed homework*
- *Class work not done/poorly completed*
- *Uncooperative*
- *Talking at inappropriate times*
- *Leave seat without permission*
- *Disruptive*
- *Calling out*
- *Disrespectful language*
- *Rude*
- *Fighting*
- *Other—extremely inattentive, sharing photos during class, talking during exam, eating in class, and late to auditorium at lunch time*

I met Edwina's mother on open school night in March. She expressed concern about Edwina's performance in school. She told me that she was thinking of sitting in on Edwina's classes so she could see for herself what was going on. I told her that was a great idea. Edwina's mother came in and sat in on Edwina's English class, and was quite appalled at the behavior of the students in the class. I found out about the parent's visit from other teachers who said that the students' behavior was so bad that the parent had to comment on it. The principal called me into her office the next morning to ask if I told the parent that she could visit her daughter's classes. Ms Clemons was quite upset, and essentially told me that I should not tell parents that they can visit my class or any other class. This was a first for me—first to be told not to have parents sit in on my class, and the first I knew the principal had the right to deny parents access to the classes their children attended.

I don't doubt that all those letters I sent home generated more responses, but Brooklyn parents are famous for preferring to call principals about teachers who contacted them about their children, rather than respond directly to the teacher.

7B: Physical Science

This was the seventh grade class from South Hell that I tried in vain to teach physical science to. There were maybe 2 sane students in the class. I sent letters home at the same time I did the letters for 7C. For just about all the students I had to check off the same things—they did not complete their home and class assignments; they were extremely inattentive, spoke at inopportune times and/or found other interesting means of disrupting the class, and they constantly left their seats without permission. I will recount some of the most interesting of the lot here.

Fisher Balkan—This student did quite an amazing turnaround. It wasn't a complete turnaround because I still had to write him up once, but the turn-around was enough to impress me.

On February 14th I sent a letter to his home along with that of most of the others:

- *No homework*
- *Class work poorly completed*
- *Uncooperative*
- *Talking at inappropriate times*
- *Leave seat without permission*
- *Disruptive*

The next day I noted that he was out of his seat, and throwing objects in class. Then the following day I made a note that he was playing around, and talkative, followed the next day by, 'out of seat, uncooperative'.

The first week of March was pretty bad. On the 2nd, 'constantly out of his seat, playing around', the 3rd, 'disturbing others, eating in class, playing around, out of his seat, constantly left room without permission, standing on chair'. I left a message for his mother, then called back and was able to speak to his mother. On March 6th I wrote, 'lotioning legs in class, running around room, out of seat, disruptive'. The next day I wrote, 'out of seat, disruptive'.

It was at this point that Fisher made his turnaround. He came to me and asked if he still had a chance to pass the class, and if so, would I help him. I gave an affirmative answer on both counts, and things just improved. Even his pen-manship improved. The only other write up I did on him was on March 28th

when I wrote that he was out of his seat, threw a book, and was running around the room. I guess that must have been an off day for him.

Horace Bowers was a classic. He reminded me of Lawrence Bonns from Berger, which is to say I felt he had mental problems. Saying he was extremely unstable is an understatement.

I sent a letter to his home on February 14:

- *No homework*
- *Class work poorly completed*
- *Uncooperative*
- *Talking at inappropriate times*
- *Leave seat without permission*
- *Disruptive*
- *Calling out*
- *Rude*
- *Other—throwing objects in class, and extremely inattentive*

On May 1st I sent another letter home about his behavior. On the letter I wrote, 'Refuses to remain in classroom. Leaves the room without permission, and spends entire period in hallway. Horace cuts class on a regular basis'.

When I met Horace's mother everything became clear. He behaved normal one day, and that was the day his mother came to school. When I spoke to his mother she made every excuse in the book and then some. She insisted her son was a perfect student, and that I was the only teacher complaining about him. I thought to myself, 'clearly I have nothing better to do with my time than sit around and make up stories about this woman's son'. Anyway, to be redundant, I went around and spoke to Horace's other teachers, and I found out that they had the same complaints I did.

I think I, unlike the other teachers, believe the discipline of a child is the parent's responsibility. There were teachers who would punish students by doing things like keeping them in the classroom during lunch or after school. What that means is that the teacher is losing out on his or her time in order to punish a child when in fact the teacher is not supposed to be punishing any child. A child and his parents could quite easily file a lawsuit against a teacher who does such a thing, and I believe that the teacher would lose the case. I discipline my own children; I refuse to discipline anyone else's children.

A lot of the disciplinary actions that teachers take are simply wrong. The only legally correct action that I know of is to document the incident and forward it to the school administration and/or the child's parents. That is what the Board's *Code of conduct* states. I saw teachers hit students at PS 999; that should never happen. Last I heard spanking was illegal in public schools in the United States.

Anyway, Horace's mother proceeded to ask me questions about my classes, and to tell me what she had gathered from conversations with students in my class. She spent more time focusing on me, and my teaching, than she did focusing on her child's behavior in my class, which was the sole reason I had for meeting with her. I wanted to tell her that I have had an excellent academic experience, and my son who would put everyone in my PS 999 classes to shame had been skipped twice, and still managed to be the top student in his school. (My son was 8 years old at the time and in the 5th grade. He graduated from the fifth grade as the salutatorian, and received more awards than the school's valedictorian. [07]My son is now 16 years old and a member of Massachusetts Institute of Technology's class of 2011.)

Michel Briggs' February 10th letter:

- *No homework*
- *Class work not done*
- *Uncooperative*
- *Talking at inappropriate times*
- *Leave seat without permission*
- *Disruptive*
- *Calling out*
- *Playing with toys*
- *Disrespectful language*
- *Rude*
- Other—throwing objects in class; and disturbing other students while they work

I sent another letter on May 1:

- *No homework*
- *Class work not done*
- *Uncooperative*
- *Doesn't follow directions*
- *Talking continuously*
- *Leave seat without permission continually*
- *Disrespectful language*
- *Generally rude*
- *Other—child is extremely disrespectful, leaves room without permission, he cuts class on a regular basis, please acknowledge the seriousness of these actions*

Below that I checked that the parent should speak to the child about the letter, and make an appointment to see me.

Needless to say, I never heard from the parents. I did hear through the grapevines that Michel's parents were worst than he was. According to what I heard, the parents were known for threatening to fight teachers. That knowledge made me start hoping never to meet them.

I have to think that most parents would respond immediately on hearing that their child was not in class when he's supposed to be. I also saw Michel in the hallway during other periods, so I knew he was cutting other classes too. I didn't even get a telephone message from his parents.

On Courtney Dickens' February 10th letter I checked:

- *No homework*
- *Class work poorly completed*
- *Uncooperative*
- *Talking at inappropriate times*
- *Leave seat without permission*
- *Disruptive*
- *Rude*
- *Other—left classroom without permission, and extremely inattentive*

His May 1 letter was the same, except instead of no homework and class work, I checked poorly completed for both homework and class work. In addition I wrote, 'leaves the room without permission; cuts class on a regular basis; and please acknowledge the seriousness of this'.

One day I kicked him out of class (almost literally), because he was so very very rude and disrespectful to me. The AP, Ms. Esterman, took him to her office. Apparently she told him to write me a letter expressing his feelings for me and my teaching, this is what he wrote:

Dear Ms. Moline

This are ideas I have to make me a better role model To read when you come to class everyday to read and to go over things at least once a week and have a practice test and write the answer so we can study that when the test come will be ready.

I would like you to create a study so before the test we can study. I would like you to ready to peprare us for a test and a higher grade and also I would you to make it exicting.

If you do this thing for me, in return you will have respect and more.

My responsibility as a science student is the following..... .

I want you out of the school and bring ure Old teahcer Mr. Martelli from I have respect for Then I want to never call my houses If you have something to say say it to my face then I want miss Clemons

Courtney Dickens

If I were an AP and a student wrote me such a letter I would have thrown it back at him and have him sit there and redo it until he got it right. Instead this woman brought me the letter and presented it to me as one would present a trophy. The letter wasn't only poor in grammar, but it was scribbled on a sheet of copy paper and looked as thought it was done by a group of ants crawling around in ink. Am I crazy? Is it too much to expect that a student in the 7th grade should be able to write 3 legible, grammatically correct paragraphs to express his feelings?

On Christian Helmsley's February letter I noted that Christian would usually not complete homework or class assignments. Christian would instead play with toys he brought to school, and constantly leave his seat without permission. He was rude, extremely inattentive and uncooperative, and I also noted that he was fighting, disruptive, throwing objects in class, and eating in class.

His May 1st letter said he hadn't done homework or classwork, and he was uncooperative, talking continuously, and out of his seat continuously. I checked that I wanted the parents to speak to Christian, and make an appointment to see me. I never met Christian's parents in person, but I had several telephone conversations with them. I had even started to see an ounce of improvement.

Most of the times when I spoke to Christian's mother I got the sense that she didn't feel like being bothered. I got the impression that she felt that when he was in school he was my responsibility. When I spoke to his father I would get golden promises of improvement, but those promises were all quite empty.

I wrote Andrea Hansie's parents on February 10th to inform them that Andrea was not completing her homework or class assignments, she was uncooperative, she talked at inappropriate times, left her seat without permission, played around in class, and she was rude and extremely disruptive.

I met her mother on February 16th. Andrea apologized, and I was assured her behavior would improve. Andrea's mother told me not to be afraid to use the belt on her. She seemed not to realize that if I pulled off my belt and gave her daughter a good thrashing I would probably end up in prison for child abuse. I politely assured her that I was not in a position to spank her child. I believed the spanking that she was in for at home was more than enough.

It was hard to believe Andrea's behavior because she was by far the neatest and brightest student in the class. It was testament to how easy it is for a few bad apples to spoil the whole bunch.

Jimmy Holder's February letter noted that he did no homework or class assignments, he was uncooperative, talking at inappropriate times, calling out, leaving his seat without permission, and playing around in class. I also noted that he was rude, disruptive, and extremely inattentive.

Jimmy's mother wrote under comments, '*I have talked to Jimmy about his unacceptable behaviors, and appropriate measures of discipline will be taken if bad behaviors continue*'. I had a conference with Jimmy's parent on February 16th.

I sent 2 letters home for Prentice James. Prentice seemed like he belonged in special education. I think he probably got several social promotions without anyone taking the time to truly evaluate him.

Sharon Jones' February 10th letter stated that she did no homework or class assignments, she was uncooperative, talking at inappropriate times, out of her seat without permission, disruptive, playing around in class, and of course extremely inattentive. After I wrote this letter Sharon's behavior improved. She became one of the better students in the class.

Lisa Morales: I sent a February 10th letter to her home because she did no homework or class assignments, was uncooperative, talking at inappropriate time, out of her seat without permission, and generally disruptive. I spoke to her mother a number of times, and she began to improve just a little. I did schedule a meeting with her mother to which I got this response:

4–3-00

Dear Mrs. Moline;

This is Mrs. Morales and I'm writing you this letter to apologize for not being able to meet you yesterday. I couldn't come because I got sick. I would like to know if you could arrange another appointment for us to meet. I would like to know when could I come. Please write back.

Sincerely,

Mrs. Barbara Morales

In the letter I sent home to Jacqueline Menza's parents I wrote, 'leaves the classroom without permission; please acknowledge the seriousness of this; and Jasmine cuts class on a regular basis'.

I did meet Jacqueline's mother, and I was quite shocked at her manner. I also found out that she was ill, and had taken time out of her sick bed to meet with me. I reprimanded Jacqueline for putting her mother through that. It's unbelievable how little respect the children had for their parents.

I sent a letter home that said Mohammed Mozi did no homework, his class assignments were either not done or poorly done, he was uncooperative, talked at inappropriate times, left his seat without permission, played around in class, was extremely inattentive, and was generally rude and disruptive.

This child was Arabic, and I had a feeling that he couldn't understand half of the things I said to him in English. He was seriously misplaced at PS 999.

Stanley Ortega's letter indicated he did no homework, his class assignments were either not done or poorly done, he was uncooperative, talked at inappropriate times, and the usual—rude, disruptive, played around in class, and extremely inattentive. I sent the letter to a work address, and it was returned saying the parent didn't work there. Stanley was Mohammed's partner in crime, but whereas Mohammed tried to get work done, Stanley would just sit there and warm the chair all period long. Whenever I spoke to him, he would pout, utter an insolent remark, and return to his brooding.

Vincent Prodige's February 10th letter made note that he did no homework, his class assignments were either not done or incomplete, he was uncooperative, talkative, out of his seat without permission, fighting, and disruptive.
    Vincent's parent wrote this under comments, 'I will try my best to rectify this situation. Vincent will be disciplined'.

Clarise Wilts irritated me. It was the trashy way she carried herself, and the way she ran around with the little boys. The other girls in the class were quite neat, she was always dirty with her shirt out of her pants, and her hair was always unkempt. In her February 10th letter I noted that she left the room without permission, which meant she cut class. I added, 'this is a very serious matter, please acknowledge'.

So that was my middle school experience. It lasted less than 4 months when you take into account vacation time and maternity leave, but it felt like the most grueling year of my life.

THE FINAL CHAPTER?

Eyelashes are there to prevent dust and other small objects from getting onto the outer surface of the eyes. Yet, in a strange twist of fate, the eyelashes are the objects most often getting onto the surface of the eyes.

School personnel who help students cheat and engage in other forms of social promotion are like eyelashes—they are charged with ensuring that students achieve high standards of learning, but their actions actually deter high achievement.

In 2005 Caveon Test Security found that 700 Texas public schools had suspicious test scores. In a 2006 study 60% of high school students admitted to cheating on an exam at least once. (Newsweek article, October 15, 2007)

^{07}THE FINAL CHAPTER?

Northeastern High School, Upstate New York
(September 2004–January 2007)

It seems I never learn. I get out of teaching, and somehow I find myself right back in there, with great aspirations, and plans for making a difference.

Actually, in September of 2004 when I went to Northeastern High, I was in need of money after being unemployed for over 2 years. I managed the 2 years surprisingly well, but things were beginning to get tight.

One might think I just took 2 years off to relax, but the fact is I never stopped looking for work. I was experiencing one of the challenges of being an African American in the USA—your qualifications will get you into the interview, but your skin color will see to it that you are denied the job. Needless to say I went to several interviews, but did not secure a job until I was offered the teaching position at Northeastern near the end of August.

My first semester at the school I was starry eyed and bushy tailed, and so a lot of things just washed off my slick back. Although I was never truly inert to the contempt I felt in the eyes of the people around me—students and staff alike. I was also quite cognizant of the fact that I was the only black teacher in a school that was located in a county that based on the 2000 census was 97% white. My survival in such an environment is based on the fact that I can always look beyond skin color and consider people based on who they are and not what they are. I am also privy to the knowledge that skin color is a slight genetic adaptation that only has the significance that people attach to it.

The school was 'semestered'; which meant that I got a new set of students in the February semester, and said goodbye to the ones I had in September. The group of chemistry students I got in February of my first year was a teacher's dream. Since life cannot be without complications I was also assigned a bullshit course called unified science. It's the kind of course no science teacher wants to teach, but also the kind of course that schools keep around, because otherwise they will have to place students with poor skills, and piss poor attitude in a Regents science class.

The unified science course wasn't too bad; I had mostly seniors who needed the class to graduate, so they pretty much did whatever I told them to do. I worked them like crazy, and it went great. At the end of the semester, I had over 80% passing. The real treat was my chemistry class I had for the first time 100% passing on the Regents. I knew it had very little to do with me, but I was still thrilled.

There were a few in that unified science class of February 2005 that bear mentioning.

There was Sandra James who failed the course due to excessive absence, and came back to take it the following year, and failed again as a result of excessive absence. The first time I spoke with her mother she assured me that she would sort things out. It was the first time I ever got such a confident response from a parent that was so totally lacking in results.

There was Melinda McDonald, the special education girl for whom I had to wear a microphone attached to a telecommunication system that I shared with her. This was done because she was slightly deaf in one ear. The boys in the class liked to tease her. The interesting thing was that the ones who teased her the most were themselves special education students, and probably more needy than she was. I had a standing treat to send her and whoever messed with her to conflict mediation to sort out their differences. That threat ended the overt teasing of Melinda, but it did not end the surreptitious harassment which continued the entire semester.

One day Melinda stormed out of the room because she wrote 'dinosar' on the board instead of dinosaur, and the boys started going crazy. They were saying these really funny things and I tried to stop them, but in the midst of it I cracked a smile. Later Melinda came back and told me that she told the principal about what happened, and he defended me saying I would not have done such a thing. Normally I would not have done such a thing, but it was a rare lapse in judgment on my part; the sort of happening that's a reminder that I too am human and prone to mistakes.

I apologized profusely to Melinda, and she even broke into a laugh while we were discussing it. Melinda explained that the boys were surreptitiously teasing her while they wrote on the board. Apparently they claim she waddles like a duck, and so by writing duck and like animals on the board, they were actually making fun of her. Apparently the boys had been teasing her incessantly for years. I was not privy to all the information that she shared with me that day. The knowledge made me even more ashamed of my earlier behavior. As much as I apologized to Melinda, I don't think she ever truly forgave me.

Then there was Nelson Natolinino, whose father—a retired teacher who was a union representative, insisted that he would have a problem if his son failed because he didn't do homework. According to Mr. Natolinino, the District regulations called for homework that should not count towards the grade. When I went back to the regulations concerning homework, I found he was very wrong about it. Of course I didn't bother to tell him that. In any case, it was unlikely a student could ever fail my class solely on account of homework. I have had students who obtained above 80 averages without doing homework, which makes up a mere 10% of the student's grade. The idea is if a student is smart enough to excel without doing homework, then I don't think I should be the one to straddle such a student with homework.

The twins, Edwin and Irving Hedley, were also unforgettable. They were 2 wonderful young men who I could never tell apart. Another student once told me that she could tell them apart because one of the twins had a big mole on his nose. I thought this would have been useful to me until I realized that both boys had similar moles on their noses. I had one incident in which one of the twins was rude to me, and he came to me after class and apologized profusely. It was the only time in my teaching career wherein a student apologized for his poor behavior, and I could tell he was truly sorry.

I went back in September expecting another semester like the last one, and I got hit with the unified science class from south hell. I thought faith was going to smile on me, and I would for the first time escape having the class from south hell—NOOO. To compound things I was again treated with a unified science class in the spring semester. When I got the class in 2005 I was informed by the other science teachers that the class was given to teachers once every 3 semesters. My saving grace was always my chemistry class. I usually had one or 2 knuckleheads in the chemistry classes, but at least they had fairly good attitudes.

I found out early that this unified science class was the social promotion class. It was the class given to all the seniors who needed a science credit to graduate and who the counselors felt did not have what it took to pass a higher level Regents science, namely chemistry or physics. The course was disproportionately filled with students who had complicated social woes; needless to say they were more than a little crazy. I want to mention some of the crazier ones here.

Maury Bobbs was a giant loser. He was taking unified science in the 10th grade, and he was not special education. What that meant was that he was taking the class because he was lazy, a fact that he proved every day. Would you believe his mother was usually in the school working as a substitute teacher. He cursed like a sailor, and made it a practice to come to class with dirt on his shoes, then he would shake off the dirt, and leaves it right there at his desk.

One morning he came to class early, sat in his seat in the back of the room, and went about listening to his MP3 player. He had the volume up so loud that I could hear it all the way from my desk at the front of the room. By school rules he knew that electronic devices were not allowed. I told him to put it away or give it to me. That was my usual way of handling such situations; and for the most part students responded by putting away the electronic device. Maury instead told me, "class hasn't fucking started yet", and continued to listen to his MP3 player. Of course I went straight for my referral, and wrote him up.

He told the AP in charge of discipline, Paula Gillings, that what he actually said was fricking—right and my hearing is out of tune. Then there was the time I took the class to the library to work on a science project. Instead of doing research, Maury chose to use the computer to surf the web, look at pictures, and distract other students in the process. When I tried to get him to log off he told me, "I am working on my fucking project".

Maury was a little strange; he spent the entire semester just sitting in class doing nothing. When I met with his mother and guidance counselor, his response was that the work was too hard. I tried to ascertain how he determined it was too hard when he hadn't even tried. Speaking to his mother didn't seem to help. Maury was just one of the many students at Northeastern who just had no ambition

Another student that was seriously lacking any kind of motivation or drive was Delroy Bailey. Delroy did even less work than Maury. Delroy just sat in class and did nothing. If there was someone around who was interested in the very little that he had to say then he held a conversation. What was amazing about Delroy was his brother Duane who I taught chemistry the following year. Duane was doing chemistry in the tenth grade, and he was one of the smartest students in the class. At first I wondered about the relationship, and then I convinced myself there was no way 2 siblings could look so much alike and be so different academically. Then once I overheard a student asking Duane about Delroy. It turns out that Delroy dropped out of school, and was spending his days at home playing video games.

I did have a meeting with Delroy and his parents once, and the meeting was quite insightful. The father dominated the meeting, and it was obvious from his attitude that he didn't think as women the counselors, his ex-wife, or I had much to say that was worth his attention. He declared that Delroy would come and work with me after school to try to get back on track. Delroy showed up once, and didn't come back after that. I had a feeling the father was an abusive person. I guessed this from the manner in which he addressed his ex-wife, and also the manner in which he grabbed Delroy's hand when he tried to make a point of the fact that Delroy had a watch to tell him time, and as such should not be tardy so often.

Damien Towns got one referral from me, and determined that I had singled him out. I only wrote one referral on him, though I could have written many. The referral said what he did all the time—constant use of the F word; and constantly out of his seat and messing with supplies in the lab section. I usually had my chemistry lab set up in the lab section of the room, and Damien would agitate me by leaving his seat and going back there. It was the safety issue that really concerned me. The chemistry class used some pretty toxic chemicals; the chemicals were safe when handled in the manner and amounts used in the chemistry lab. However, with what I knew of Damien, I think he would go back there and hurt himself just to try to get me into trouble.

Anyway, I gave him an after school detention to go with the referral. The next morning when I came to work I was greeted by a call from his irate father accusing me of picking on his son. I was shocked and amazed, so I schedule a meeting with him. I really wanted to find out how he came to the conclusion that I was picking on his son.

In attendance at the meeting were Damien, his parents, his guidance counselor, his special education counselor, and the principal. Damien wasn't emotionally disturbed on record; he was special education because he had some sort of writing disability. During the meeting I tried to glean from the parents how they concluded that I was picking on their son. His mother claimed that her son got a 77 in my class, he wasn't a 77 student, and he had higher grades in all his other classes.

They brought up a couple of previous incidences. I once made a mistake on grading one of Damien's tests, instead of coming to me with the mistake, Damien went to his mother, and she took it to the principal, and then the principal wrote me a letter about it. Now, bear in mind, we are talking about a mistake that would gain Damien a point on a test, and still result in a failing grade. Then they also talked about Damien's poor paper for which he got a poor grade. Based on his learning disability he is supposed to have extra time on tests. This was a paper that was given months in advance, and was supposed to be typed; hence his handwriting disability didn't come into play. I had even confirmed as much with his counselor.

Then the father chimed in about how much he loves his children, and that he will die for them. I was wondering to myself if this father was aware that most days his son came to school smelling so bad that I stayed away from where he was working, or held my breath when I went by him. The parents claimed that my class had their son depressed, so much so that he was not eating right. When asked why Damien hadn't brought any of these problems to my attention, the mother claimed that she and her son find me unapproachable. They were telling this to a principal who was used to seeing students in my room all the time going over their work with me. The counselors asked why Damien did not take advantage of the other resources that were available, and Damien and his parents went mum.

I mentioned that I made arrangements to have a teacher's aide in the room with me, and that she had done a lot of work with Damien, though she was there to work with Collin Blackwell. I talked the school psychologist into having Marilyn Cunningham come in to work with Collin. I knew Collin did not need any help with science—what Collin really needed was help with self control. When Marilyn tried to work with Collin he would abruptly drive her away. Marilyn enjoyed being in the classroom, and she would spend her time sitting on the side of the room furthest away from Collin, and helping any student who asked for her help.

I knew that I would have someone else explaining things and working closely with the students. More important, I wanted to have a witness there. Interestingly enough during the period in which Marilyn was there, the students curbed their bad behavior—that worked for me too.

To get back to the story, the parents exhausted all avenues without showing that I was in any way singling their child out. Actually it was the mother and her son who seemed to have some kind of vendetta against me. Then they brought up the referral as proof. I mentioned that Damien was one of the few students in the class I rarely had any trouble with. I said my only concern was the fact that he kept leaving his seat and going to the back of the room where I had chemistry lab assignments set up. The mother boldly asked me how that was a bother to me, or some crap like that. I was so glad that the principal chimed in at that point to inform them of the safety issues involved—what a bunch of morons. Thus the meeting ended. It accomplished nothing, and was just a huge waste of my time.

I was so angry and confused about the whole ordeal that I spoke with Marilyn to see if maybe I was subconsciously targeting Damien. She was just as shocked by the accusation as I was.

Of all the students I met in my teaching career, Collin Blackwell was the one who made me seriously consider changing career; in the past it was poor administrators that inspired such feelings. He was also the only student I can recall who was always verbally abusive to me. In the second week of classes in September of 2005 he told me I was "fucking stupid". He went on cursing at me for about 5 minutes then he walked out of the class, and came back near the end of the period and continued to curse. Collin would tell me and other students whatever he felt like.

It was not uncommon for Collin to tell a student to "shut the fuck up", and if students tried to get him to calm down, his usual response was, "I don't give a fuck". He really didn't give a fuck, and after I met with the school psychologist I found out he didn't have to. Part of his individual education plan (IEP) made note of the fact that he had very little self control, and as such should be kept away from volatile situations. He had been informed that should he find that he was about to 'explode', then he should leave the room and go to his special education teacher. Collin rarely used that option, he found it more appealing to stay in the room and try to get into a confrontation with me.

Of course my usual response was to write a referral. I think the fact that I would simply write him up and have him suspended rather than get into an argument with him, made him return from suspensions even more determined to get under my skin. Also, I found out that Collin was from a household in which female opinions mattered very little. Such households were very common in the county where Northeastern was located, and it was not uncommon for the students to bring that background to their interaction with female staff in the school.

The students in unified science were a lot like the ones in general science at Hedley High School in that I wrote a ton of referrals on them. It wasn't uncommon for me to write a half a dozen referrals on a student in a semester (recall that the school is semestered). The students were always criticizing my opting for the referral all the time. They probably wanted to see me getting into confrontations with them. In that second year wherein I had unified science for both semesters, a number of fights took place in those crazy so-called science classes. I kept my distance, and called the main office to send people over. The students were amazed that I always refrained from approaching the fighting students.

Personally, I think those evil children were just hankering to see me get hurt. I never felt particularly safe in that building, and I was forever expecting to come outside and find that my car had been vandalized. Even though it added about 5 minutes to my travel time, most times I would travel around to the side of the building where the majority of the parking spots were occupied by staff.

Collin's most notable infarction was the day he told me to go back to Barmenia and plant weed, and he said it loud enough that the other chemistry teacher stayed in his classroom next door and heard it clear enough to identify Collin as the speaker. Amidst the pandemonium that was my class with Collin, I heard the statement, but was not able to discern who said it. It was amazing how different the class was with Collin versus the way it was when Collin was absent. I think when the other students saw his actions, and thought he was getting away with it they would proceed to see what they could get away with. Then when they found out that Collin was suspended, they would curb their actions for fear of getting like punishment. Collin's infarctions only went unpunished if I wrote a referral and the school's administration decided not to take action. I did find that Collin's referrals resulted in suspensions more often than other students guilty of similar infarctions.

Another student who was verbally abusive to me was Tom Princeton. The funny thing about Tom was he started out doing great—being respectful, following instructions, and getting good grades. Then near the end of the semester he made a wrong turn, and just went downhill from there.

One day in May, with little more than a month of classes left, I had to write him a referral. He told me I was a stupid teacher, and called me a retard. He left the room without permission, then came back and sat on my desk. When I told him to go sit down, he told me, "I am sitting down". He just went on harassing me, and being verbally abusive. Mrs. Gillings wrote on the referral that when she met with him about the referral he referred to me as a moron and a retard. He was suspended for 2 days.

Then later that month, he came to class, and just out of nowhere decided to smash the locking mechanism at the top of the door. I immediately made note of it, and he was given 2 days of after school detention.

Then on June second he snatched my book of hall passes from me because I refused to write him a pass to the bathroom. He took the passes to his desk, sat there and cursed me and called me names. I knew Tom did not want to actually go to the bathroom, he just wanted to be in the hall instead of in class. Then he went and sat on the lab desk, when I told him to sit in his seat he told me he could not because he needed to take a piss so bad. This referral was handled by the interim principal, Mr. Thank Kindade, who claimed Tom was honest and understanding of his wrong doings. He was given 2 days suspension.

I had no idea why but Tom was an angry and troubled child. I once heard him telling another student about the time he and a friend were arrested because they broke into someone's house. Apparently the owner of the house was away on vacation, and Tom and his friend broke into the house, ate up the food and messed the place up just for kicks.

Let's divert for a bit here and talk about the entrance of this Mr. Kindade. In the spring of my second year at Northeastern all the teachers were summoned to a meeting in the auditorium. It wasn't a regularly scheduled meeting, so out-of-the-loop people like me were at a loss. When we got to the meeting the principal, James Reese, enlightened us by informing us that it was his last day. Apparently, the school board had decided to remove Mr. Reese and have Kindade, who was serving as athletic director serve as interim principal. I was very upset by the whole situation because the staff didn't have so much as a slight say in the matter. After Mr. Reese left I felt even less comfortable at Northeastern. Mr. Reese was one of the few people there who was decent in his dealings with me, and he was the only person whose respect for me was not contrived.

I had a couple of unpleasant run-ins with Kindade while he was interim principal. All my run-ins with him involved him trying to get me to give passing grades to failing students. If you have read this book from the start, you can pretty much tell where this is headed—I do not subscribe to social promotion under any circumstance.

Jay Coombs was sent from Long Island to Northeastern with the hope that the move would take him away from bad company and drugs. The move definitely failed; Jay was a bad egg, and while at Northeastern he found some very bad company, and worked very hard to maintain his bad boy status.

In the first month of class he was involved in a confrontation with Britney Pedrosa. I called his number and found out he was living with his aunt because his parents were trying to get him to clean up his act.

By the second month of class I started to see less and less of Jay. I called his father in Long Island, we had a long talk, and I got the impression that things would change. My impression was false, nothing changed. Jay came to class, was disruptive, and did no work. I spoke with his father again. My calls to Jay's father were long distance to Long Island. His father told me he would travel up to talk with Jay in person.

When Jay came back to class after that allege meeting with his father, I saw the worst and last of him. Jay was in class telling students that he sells ecstasy. Britney asked, "do you really sell ecstasy?" Jay responded, "yeah I do, but only when I need money." I did not like the boldness of the admission, so I took the liberty of informing Mrs. Gillings. I don't know what action Mrs. Gillings took, but I did not see Jay again after that.

Britney Pedrosa was a time bomb. She was ranked last among the graduating seniors, and that fact became known throughout the school, and poor Britney was subjected to a lot of humiliation as a result. She was also very loud, and used foul language as though it came natural to her. During the first month of class I had to call her mother and write her a referral for cursing and being too talkative. She told a student to 'shut the fuck up', and when she saw me making a note to call her parent she added insult to injury by saying, "I don't care if she fucking calls home".

Britney was never openly disrespectful to me, and she never used foul language when she spoke directly to me, but her behavior in class still left much to be desired. As a senior, she was also very immature. She would pester some of the younger boys in the class; Stan Leach was her favorite victim. At one point she took off her shoes and placed her feet on his desk. Indeed, her antics were wild and unpredictable.

One day Britney came to class ranting about how she heard another classmate, Alison Shields, talking crap about her. She got pretty heated up as she spoke. I tried to get her to calm down, but my efforts were useless. Not too long after Alison came to class, and it wasn't long before they were mouthing off at each other. I tried to get them to calm down while I inched towards the phone. Alison's friend Helen moved Alison away from Britney to the other end of the room. I tried to get Britney to calm down, but she insisted on moving towards where Alison was. As soon as Britney moved towards Alison I picked up the phone and called the office.

Britney went over to Alison and started punching her. The time between the phone call and the wait for the office to send someone over was enough for those 2 girls to really go at each other. 2 other seniors jumped in there and parted them before the hall monitors got there. Alison socked Britney with some really good punches, but she cried the entire time. It was like someone who was being forced to do something evil that she definitely did not want any part of.

I never actually knew Alison's tale, but I was sure it was sad. An enduring lesson I learnt from Mr. Talbot of Berger High School is to not get too personal. I know many poor performing students have sad stories, but I tried not to hear any of it. Yes I know that's selfish of me, but it's just that I can't bear the thought of children suffering. I believe the worst thing that a society can allow is the suffering of children. I endeavor to ensure that for the period of time that students spend in my class they are happy and secure. That is the reason that I make a big deal of it when students disrespect me or their classmates.

Anyway, it seemed that Alison was not living with her parents. From the rumors, it seemed she was living at the home of another student in the school, who made it known that they were thinking of kicking her out. Once I got a call from Alison's parents stating that they wanted to get information on how she was doing in my class. I found it strange based on the rumor that I heard, so I raised the issue with Alison. She was adamant about me not contacting her parents about her. She stated that they abandoned her all that time, and then suddenly they were trying to become a part of her life. I thought that it might have been worth her while to give them a chance, but I kept my mouth close and stayed out of their business. I did not return the call to her parents, and they never contacted me again.

On the morning of the last day of school for the 2005–6 school year we came in to find at least a half dozen hens in the school's courtyards. No one knew who was responsible. Shortly after the start of school all the seniors were summoned to the auditorium for an emergency meeting—more like a group interrogation. Still no answers and no one came forward. Near the end of the day, with the hens still in the courtyards, an announcement was made for the owner of the hens to please remove them. Still nothing. Eventually, a member of the special education department took the hens to her home; she claimed they were Rhode Island Red, a quality breed.

Anyway, near the end of the last period of the day, Britney said, "I know who did it". I asked her who it was, and she whispered to me that it was Lesline Hemmings. Of course Lesline was not in school that day.

The most interesting thing about the incident was that Lesline did not graduate—probably because she failed my class. I saw her back in school the following September taking the class with Bill Pretzel. Lesline was an interesting case, because she was intelligent enough to do chemistry and do very well at it. The inane unified science class would have been a breeze for her if she had even made an attempt. What she did instead was start cutting class early until she eliminated her chance of getting a passing grade. Then she simply showed up intermittently, and sat around and did nothing.

As a result of Northeastern High School operating on a semester schedule, students were not allowed to have more than 10 unexcused absences for the semester. Once a student went above the 10-absence minimum, they were not able to get a passing grade for the class. The sad part about that arrangement was that those students had to spend the rest of the semester sitting in a class for which they had no chance of passing. The result was a lot of students who would sit in class, do no work, and be very disruptive. To prevent students from getting to the 10-absence point, there were documents that had to be sent home, and calls were to be made by the teacher. The system actually worked if you had a class with one or 2 chronic absentees, but in a class like the one I had where on any given day I could have up to 50% of the class absent, it didn't work so well.

The other problem was it was difficult to be certain that a student from my class was cutting, because there was a myriad of reasons that could be linked with those students' absences. There was a joint board of education campus for the 4 adjoining counties, and many of the students in the unified science class took vocational education classes there. The students would go to the board of education campus for one half of the day, and then be transported to the high school for the other half of the day. Also the computer system that kept track of attendance depended on data input from an attendance personnel, and this data entry was often backlogged.

In all my years of teaching Helen Cranberry was the only girl that I encountered with a really foul smell. At Northeastern the boys either had a foul smell or no smell at all. This Helen came to me one day smelling as though something just died inside her, and went about getting into my face with her abusive tone. All I could focus on was the stench emanating from her.

In the first month of class I wrote that she was disrespectful and insisted on leaving the room even though she was on the 'no passes no privileges' list. The list was put out on a daily basis, and had a start and end date for the students listed. If a student was on the list it meant they were not allowed to have a pass to leave the room; whatever they needed to do (use the bathroom, etc) had to be done in the 5 minute interval between periods.

Helen was always disrespectful and would curse in a manner you would not expect any self respecting person to. I once recorded where she said, "this class is so fucking stupid," and "Ms. Moline, how can you be so stupid?"

Like Danielle Hess at PS 999, Helen's bad behavior was matched only by the level of fear she exhibited regarding me calling her parents. Like Danielle she was constantly trying to make deals to get me not to call her home.

Ultimately I got tired of making deals with her, and I wrote her a referral listing 4 actions that were like trademarks for her:

1. Cursing in class, said, "that's fucking retarded".

2. Had a cell phone in class.

3. Left the room without permission. Said, "guess what, I am fucking walking out". Then she walked out.

4. Student was also very insubordinate, arguing with me even after I ask that we have the discussion after class.

You would think that such a write up would result in stern administrative action, but the result was a mere stay in the alternative instruction (AI) room.

The AI room at Northeastern was where students went when the administration felt that they were better off not being in the teacher's class. The term alternative instruction would imply that there was instruction taking place, but that was rarely the case.

Peter Henderson was a special education student, and the first one I encountered whom I felt was emotionally disturbed. As with all people who I think are emotionally disturbed, I was more than a bit terrified of Peter.

At one point Peter was arrested; I think the charge was attempted rape. It turns out Peter ambushed an elementary school girl on her way home from school. According to Peter he just wanted to talk to her; he was apparently infatuated with her. The other students questioned what right he had to be trying to talk to a student that much younger than him (Peter was a senior).

Peter was an extremely poor performer on written assignments, but if given the opportunity to give verbal responses he did better than the majority of the class. The problem with Peter was that he was stubborn, and would insist on doing things his way, though his way was usually incorrect. Also, he was afforded the opportunity to do his tests and other written assignments in an alternate setting, but he would often decline such services. He had all these delusions of grandeur that prevented him from accepting the simplest criticisms that would have proved helpful to him.

Peter's delusional attitude reminded me of Trevor St. Jemon, a chemistry student I had during my first semester at Northeastern. Trevor maintained that he was going to move to NYC and become a millionaire. He so believed in this self-established fate that he didn't put much effort into any other aspirations. Trevor's reality, like Peter's, was much bleaker than the delusional life he imagined—they were both trailer trash, for want of a more politically correct description.

Trevor once confessed that he cheated on all the Regents exams that he did well on. He tried to pass it off as a joke, but I believed him. When he went to take the chemistry Regents exam, he planted himself in a seat behind the highest performing student in his class. I quickly changed his seat.

I suspected Trevor had cheated his way to good grades all semester long. His punishment was getting a high grade for the class, but a failing grade on the Regents. In my last semester at Northeastern I heard that Trevor went about bragging about 2 things—that he would be getting a new BMW and that he was the one who flooded the chemistry lab. He never got the BMW, but I believe he may have been the one who flooded the lab.

A little over a month after I started working at Northeastern, the room in which I conducted chemistry classes and labs was flooded. The school's maintenance staff turned the water off in the building to do repairs. It also happened that the school chose that day to do an early dismissal drill. Everyone had to leave the building fifteen minutes before the usual dismissal time, and no one was allowed back into the building for at least a half hour. At some point after everyone had gone home they turned the water back on. Apparently, no one thought to check the taps in my classroom, and the tap at Trevor's desk was left on.

While my class was in the midst of a chemistry lab assignment they made an announcement that the water would be turned off in the building. I went around the lab and checked all the taps. I remember that Trevor wanted to wash his hand, and I allowed him to wash his hand in my office/prep room. When I think back over the events, I think I have always suspected Trevor. What I never suspected though was to find that the action was deliberate.

Of course the flooded classroom was not on my conscience as I think I lot of people at the school expected that it would be. I felt it was the responsibility of the maintenance staff to double-check the taps after turning the water back on. The school was insured so they did not lose out either. They filed a claim right after the incident, though at the point in time when I left, the only repair that had been completed was the replacement of some of the floor tiles, which took place in the month following the incident.

The big loser was the physics/earth science teacher from across the hall, Bill Pretzel, who had insisted on keeping a lot of his teaching supplies in the room. I think he kept his things there as a way of stating a claim for the room. The interesting thing was that the room was specifically designed for chemistry labs, and he was not licensed to teach chemistry. He even went as far as to insist on always conducting the earth science practical exam in the room, regardless of how inconvenient it was for me.

Anyway, on the Monday following the incident Bill was fit to be tied, because so many of his supplies were damaged. He got pretty mad at me because I came nonchalantly in to work that morning, and I did not get excited or agitated by his furious outbursts. The chair of the science department was also pleased, because she had been trying for years to get Bill to remove his supplies from the room.

After the incident Bill got mad at me because I exclaimed about the amount of work I had done to get the room organized. I couldn't understand why he was offended until the other chemistry teacher explained to me that the chemistry teacher who came before me did not make any changes to the room. Essentially Bill was teaching in a room that had an adjoining store room, yet he had a substantial amount of supplies stored in the classroom and office/prep room that was being used by another teacher.

That Bill was quite a character. Most people, myself included, felt pretty sure that Bill had a few screws loose. The main problem with Bill was that he had not an ounce of tact, which translated in the tacky way in which he related to students and staff in the building. On occasions when he tried his utmost to unnerve me all I did was to laugh at him like he just told me the funniest joke.

The one common theme at Northeastern was lack of respect, the students had a lack of respect for themselves, and their fellow students, and many students were blatant in the disrespectful manner in which they spoke to the staff. A lot of the staff allowed students to relate to them in the manner in which the student would relate to their peers. Most of the staff there did not show much respect for each other, and they were especially blatant in their disrespect of me. My response was to be completely oblivious to them, and their response was to deem me anti-social, and so the cycle went on.

One day I was in my classroom during my break reviewing a test with a couple of my students. One of the things that I tried very successfully at Northeastern was to have students review their test with me for an additional 5 points. It became an excellent way for me to privately tutor my students throughout the semester. While I was working with one student the other student was awaiting her turn with another classmate, a boy named Manuel.

In the midst of this activity, Bill stormed into my room, walked up to Manuel and said, "Your cell phone, give it to me." Manuel tried to say that he did not have a cell phone, but Bill insisted, and Manuel went into his pocket and turned over his cell phone. Then Bill stomped over to me and placed the cell phone on my desk, before storming out of the room. At the end of the tutoring session I gave the cell phone back to Manuel and told him to put it away in his locker.

Later that day Bill came to me and said, "Mrs. Gillings wants your kid's cell phone." I told him that I gave the cell phone back. He said, "Well you better go get it." I did not justify his statement with a response. Actually the kind of response that I had in store for him, I could not give him without belittling myself.

I heard that Bill was known throughout the school for 2 things, being blatantly disrespectful to coworkers, and taking things that did not belong to him. That explained why he had so many things that he needed 2 classrooms, 2 offices and a store room to hold it all. Can you believe that Bill used to be on a nuclear submarine?

Oh, let's get back to talking about Peter. He cut my class for quite a while, and I did not do much more than fill out the necessary paperwork. Ultimately the parent called to complain that the school allowed her son to cut class so many times. Of course when the school looked up the information on Peter, they found out that many notifications were sent to the parent, and I recorded calling the parent about the fact that Peter was cutting. Anyway Peter was given AI for a number of days to make up for the time he cut class. I did not see the purpose of the AI in that case, because Peter did not make any attempt to make up any of the assignments that he missed as a result of his cuts, and he was well on the way to getting a failing grade for the class. Also, Peter had already determined where he was going after high school; I think he said the military, but I can't be quoted on that.

Anyway, after Peter's cuts were dealt with, he was in a sense forced to attend my class. Needless to say, Peter was not thrilled by this turn of events. Peter became a complete nuisance in class. One day he came in and stated that he wanted to be suspended. He said he needed to get into a fight with someone so he could be suspended. John Paisley, who was insane for sure, but not deemed special education by the school, took up the challenge. John told Peter that he would be willing to throw his shirt at Peter as a way of instigating a fight. Peter told John to do it. John tossed his shirt at Peter, and Peter got up from his seat, went over to John's desk and started punching John. Of course the minute John's shirt hit Peter I placed a call to the main office. The office sent a couple of hall monitors over, Peter and John were removed from the room, and Peter got his wish—he was suspended for 3 days. One might think that such inane behavior was rare, but it was so commonplace I did not at the time think just how stupid the exchange between Peter and John was.

Like I said before, I am quite sure John was emotionally disturbed. His usual partner in crime, Orlando Castillo, was equally insane. Just about every time John came to class I had to either write him up and call his house, or I had to write him a referral.

His action was always the same idiocy. He would leave his seat and wander around the room. He would chew gum during lab assignments. Other times he would throw things across the room when he thought I was not watching. In the first month of class I gave the students lima beans for a term project they were supposed to complete. John asked for beans, and then proceeded to throw them across the room.

The bean plant project was a really neat assignment that I assigned every semester, and it was always amazing how poorly the students did with what was an extremely simple assignment. I think the fact that it required them to do ongoing work at home may have had something to do with it.

John was most famous for the huge spitballs that he would make and manage to get stuck to the ceiling tiles. This he would do in concert with Orlando and/or Stan leach. When I left Northeastern I left a number of John's/Stan's spitballs on the ceiling. I deliberately did not make any attempt to have the spitballs removed, I like having it there as evidence. Also, it served as a deterrent to stop them from putting more spitballs up there.

After the fight with Peter, I did not see much more of John. There were a number of times when I saw a note in the computer that said 'treatment facility'. Curiosity led me to ask what that meant, and I was told that it meant that John was in drug rehabilitation. How do you end up in rehab when you are in the 10th grade? Then again John was the one who said that no matter who you are you will end up in prison at some point in your life. I took that to mean that everyone he knew had experienced the prison system.

Orlando was a lot like John in the manner in which he would loiter around the room, look for things to mess with, and be generally annoying. John was obnoxious, but Orlando would inspire in me extreme sympathy, even when he was being rude.

In the second week of school I wrote that he was constantly out of his seat and playing with play dough. I also wrote him up because he had at least 3 unexcused absences. I called the number I had on file for him, and got a constant busy signal.

I always had the sense that Orlando, John and Jay were into drugs. As it turned out, I may have been right about John and Jay. There were lot of whisperings in the class about Orlando, but I was never able to eavesdrop enough to gather much. I could tell that whatever the rumor was it was extremely embarrassing.

Before the end of the first month of classes, I made note that Orlando was excessively absent. I guess the school must have been working on getting to the bottom of his absences because he showed up a couple of months later. He behaved okay for a little while, but you could tell it was a huge strain on him. At one point he asked me to write him a pass so he could go to the AI room. I told him I could not give him a pass to AI, and he tried pleading with me to no avail. Apparently he had some sort of rapport with Mr. Gregor, the teaching assistant who ran the AI room. I did try to find out from Mr. Gregor why a student would so adamantly insist on going to AI when he should be in class. Mr. Gregor feigned innocence but I could tell he knew more than he was telling me. My guess is he probably told Orlando to come and spend time with him in AI.

Maybe I should have done more of a followed up on that AI request from Orlando, because not too long thereafter I had to write him a referral that resulted in 4 days suspension. He was throwing spitballs on the ceiling. Then he went on to fool around during the lab session—he was wearing the microscope cover on his head, and kicking a sack around the room. Then he went up to my desk and started meddling with my items there. When I tried to talk to him he threatened me. He told me that he was holding himself back from hitting me.

Now here's the strange thing about Orlando's suspension. It did not occur right away; he was actually in class the next day running around the room, and hiding behind the lab counters. The sad part about that is he was not really hiding from anyone in particular. I wrote him another referral, and assigned him after school detention. Mrs. Gillings apparently spoke to Orlando about the first referral, and Orlando insisted he did not threaten me. Shortly after, another teacher wrote him a referral when he threw a chair in her class. She also made note that she felt threatened by Orlando, and so 9 days after the incident in my class Orlando was suspended.

Whereas John and Orlando were frequently absent, Stan Leach had very good attendance. I believe deep down Stan was a good child, but he had really poor self control. The other students in the class would call him a retard, or tell him that he was acting like he was on drugs. Stan would try really hard to behave in a manner that proved the assessments were correct.

I had to call his home during the first week of the semester because he was disruptive—his home number was not in service. The next day I asked Stan about it and he gave me his new home number. About a week later I had to call and talk to his mother because he was involved in a confrontation with Zeke Wilbur. Stan's mother told me that Stan had been having trouble with Zeke.

I wrote so many referrals on Stan that I started to wish I had a standard laminated referral for him that I could just turn in as needed. It would certainly have saved on paper and time.

In February I wrote him a referral for throwing beans and spitballs in class, and not doing his class assignments. I gave him AI for the following day, which he served. Then on March 8th I had to write him up for the same behavior, plus he was being disruptive. I note on the referral that he was given AI for the same behavior before. Mr. Gillings assigned him to AI for 2 days. Then on the 16th of March I gave him a referral for being tardy to class, and I assigned him after school detention.

Stan was never really late to the hallway where my class was located. He would just insist on standing in the hallway, and interfering with students walking by, and wait until the bell rang before he came into the classroom. I tried in vain to stop this practice, and the detention for being tardy was just another attempt.

It was amazing how different the situation was with the students in my chemistry class who were usually anxious to get to class. I was just a whole lot better at motivating my chemistry students than I was at motivating the students in unified science. It was no wonder that the state had licensed me to teach chemistry. If only I was allowed to teach just chemistry instead of all the other crap that have been dumped on me over the years I would have been one of the most successful chemistry teachers in New York State.

I have a passion for teaching chemistry. I remember when I used to do private tutoring in chemistry in the Bronx. After a couple of tutoring sessions my students would always have a completely changed view of chemistry.

In April I wrote Stan a referral that spanned 3 days because he was going crazy for 3 days straight. He called another student a "fucking retard", and complained aloud that another student was looking at his balls. He asked someone, probably Britney, if they were "fucking throwing shit" at him. Then in a conversation he said another student's opinion didn't count because "she's a lesbian". Of course when Mrs. Gillings spoke with him he denied that he made the statements. It's such a good thing that I always write what students say verbatim. Mrs. Gillings apparently told him she did not want to see another referral on him, so he was good for a little while.

Then in early May I had to write him up for going back to his usual antics of throwing spitballs on the ceiling, fooling around, and not doing his work. He was given AI. Then on May 19th he had a very telling referral. He pulled the desk away in an attempt to make his partner in crime, Walter Kroning fall. Then he claimed he did not do it and started cursing. It did not seem to matter that I and half the class saw him do it. Then he said, "don't blame that fucking shit on me". When his classmates asked that he stop all that cursing he said, "I don't care, I didn't fucking do it". Then he went on to say, "I will just tell Mrs. Gillings I didn't do it, and she will take it off the referral as she always does". Then he said, "yeah, that makes fucking sense", in reference to the referral. Again he got AI.

Is it me or is there a trend here. Stan does all this crap, and all he gets is AI; some students were suspended for less. If Stan used his time in AI to try to catch up with all his missed assignments, I could see some benefit to all the time he spent there.

The headache with the class had gotten so bad that I would schedule appointments for the afternoon so I could go in and teach my chemistry class, and then get a break from the crazies in unified science. On May 30th I was absent and the substitute wrote this about Stan:

Stan Leach did absolutely NO work + when I told him I planned to tell you that, he WALKED OUT of class. After about a minute, I called Mrs. Gillings' office. Mrs. Gillings came back with Stan—he had gone to complain that his partners weren't letting him get his work done. Walter was being a pain in the neck, but Stan wasn't doing any work. In the library 5th bell Stan said he lost all his work twice. First time, very early into the bell, Walter logged Stan off. Stan could not have lost much work because he had hardly started. Then Stan DELETED HIS OWN WORK later in the bell. It's 2:40 right now and he is just starting to handwrite something. When he tells you he couldn't get his work done because of Walter, HE IS LYING. He and Walter parted company @ 1:45—I moved Stan right when Walter logged him off. Stan has not been productive on his own.

On June 1st he was constantly cursing in class even after I spoke to him several times. I wrote him a referral and Kindade wrote on it "honest, respectful, and mitigating circumstances caused Stan to use profanity". He was given lunch detention. I know as much about lunch detention as a punishment at Northeastern, as I did about office detention as a punishment at Hedley High School in Cleveland. I would not doubt that Stan was honest, but respectful he was not. He did not respect me or his classmates, and he seem to have little or no respect for himself.

Of course you can see that Stan is having a buildup from doing all sort of antics and getting away scotch free. Naturally things got worst on the last referral. He was involved in a verbal confrontation with Britney. He called Britney "a fucking asshole", and told her, "you fucking pissed me off". Then he turned his attention to me and said, "write that down Ms. Moline, I said fuck". Then he said "I hate this fucking class so much", and told me to write it down. He was so out of control I had to call the office to have him removed. Kindade decided that Stan should spend the remainder of the year in AI. I was only too happy to see him go. We were at the point in time where I was actually having very little problems in the class, because most of the trouble makers had either left, or had decided to settle down so they didn't get written up anymore.

One of the big differences I noted between students in urban schools and those in the rural town where Northeastern was located had to do with the special education classification. Students would openly admit to having things like attention deficit disorder (ADD), and attention deficit and hyperactivity disorder (ADHD). When I gave a test many of the students in the unified science class were allowed to leave to take the test in an alternative setting because of their special education classifications. Based on their IEPs many of these students had to have the test read to them. To facilitate this activity I had these sheets that I had to fill in and give to the student to take to the alternate test site—usually what was called their resource room. In the resource room there was usually a special education teacher, and possibly a teacher's aide. One student I met was so smug with his special education classification that he proudly told me, "If I want someone to wipe my ass for me I can get it."

Students I taught in NYC had a much different take on special education classification. Student I taught in Cleveland would sooner admit to having a parole officer than to being special education. Ms. Hardy of Berger High School once told me that to get improvement in the behavior of the students in my class I should pick the most disruptive of the bunch, go see his guidance counselor, and tell the counselor that I don't think the student belong in a regular education setting. The counselor would then call the student down and inform the student of my assessment. I did this once, and saw a remarkable improvement in the student in question, and the class in general. I never tried it again though, it was just a little too risky.

It amazed me how willing the rural parents were to have their children diagnosed and medicated. Those children who were diagnosed with ADHD went from one extreme to the next—without medication they were wall-climbing maniacs, while with medication they were droopy and zombie-like.

Walter Kroning was such a child. I constantly had to call Walter's mother about his behavior. She would always get upset at me for calling her at work, but it wasn't upsetting enough to bring an improvement in Walter's behavior. When I finally had a meeting with her, she told me that Walter was diagnosed with ADHD, but hated to take his medication because he did not like the way it made him feel.

The first referral I wrote on Walter was on March 14th. I wrote that he passes gas in class on a regular basis, curses, and leaves his seat constantly. Walter would leave his seat, wander around the room to my desk, the lab station, the door to look outside, and other students' desk to disturb them. When I asked him to sit he would do so but only for a moment. I gave him AI, and I made a note that in a conference with his mother on the 9th she told me to give him a referral for future disciplinary problems.

I once wrote him a referral over a period of 3 days, April 10–12. On April 10th he told a student to 'shut the fuck up'. Said another student was trying to touch his balls. He was also instigating others to fight. On April 11th he was cursing in class and harassing Britney. He said, "I am going to fucking stab Britney." Then he said, "I fucking yelled at her because she ignored me." He also refused to sit in his assigned seat. On April 12th he was again harassing Britney. He called her a 'dumb ass' and a 'retard'. I wrote on the referral that in my conversation with Walter's mother she seems to prefer that the school deals with problems rather than call her at work. Mrs. Gillings indicated on the referral that Walter denied what was in the referral. She also wrote that if there was another referral Walter would be suspended. As you can see below there were 2 more referrals without any suspensions.

On May 16th I was absent and the substitute wrote him a referral because he signed out for the bathroom and was gone for half an hour. He got placed on no passes/no privileges, and also got 2 days of after school detention. It's interesting that I wrote about all kinds of abuse of the bathroom pass by students yet they were never placed on no passes/no privileges.

On June 8th he was involved in a confrontation with Britney Pedrosa, and his behavior was so bad I had to call the office to have him removed. After that there were no more referrals on Walter. He and the rest of the class had pretty much settled down. At the end of the semester Walter came close to passing but I gave him a failing grade. I think I probably wrote that he was eligible for summer school. When I say him the following school year he seemed a lot calmer, he had also grown a beard, and seemed a bit more mature.

Zeke was a senior, but about as immature a senior as Britney. Zeke was big, tall, and studious looking, but behind the façade he was a regular asshole that spent more time instigating confrontations between students than he did trying to get work done. Other times he would tease and otherwise disrupt other students. These antics would often lead to verbal confrontations between him and other students. By far his 2 favorite victims were Britney and Stan. On days when Zeke was not busy bothering other students, he would lay his head down and go to sleep. He was by far the laziest senior that I ever encountered.

Zeke was one of those students that Kindade tried to get me to socially promote. According to Kindade, he did not think that it was right for a one credit class to keep a student from graduating. This he stated when we had a meeting about Zeke's grade in my class. I made my dissension clear, and I could tell he made a mental note of it.

I will categorically affirm that I have never and will never apologize for not being party to social promotion. It is way beneath my principled way of thinking; it has always been beneath me, and will remain there. I must be real dense, but I fail to see how a student can derive any true benefit from social promotion.

I had a feeling that both Zeke and Helen copied their final project from someone else. I had no way of proving it of course, so I just let it go. I figured that one day their laziness would catch up with them. Now that I think about it, that may not necessarily happen since we live in a world where success is based more on one's willingness to kiss ass than on one's abilities.

Would you believe that Zeke indicated on his introductory card that in 5 years he expects to have a job and a family—well good luck with that! Then again Stan indicated that he expects to be in college, and most of the students in the class indicated that they thought it was import to be respectful. Words are like the air, it's free to all.

Try as I might it is hard to forget Elise Perry, the raunchiest girl I ever taught. Throughout the semester she just seemed to slip deeper and deeper into idiocy.

Elise was a fat girl, with a lot of fat girl insecurities. To make matters worst, she spent most of her time with a girl who was fatter, dressed worst, and was more insecure than her. Elise and her fatter friend were always getting into verbal confrontations with Collin Blackwell who would say the most horrid things about them.

My headache with Elise came mostly from the fact that she craved attention, and would do anything, no matter how wildly inane, to get this attention. One day I was absent, and the male substitute who was there made note that she was blowing up condoms in class. I thought maybe she had a balloon that looked like a condom, however when I asked Elise about it she quickly admitted to having had a condom. She claimed that she told the substitute that he should wear the condom. I was so upset by her insolent admission that I wrote her up.

Elise did not receive much in the way of punishment for the condom stunt, so a few days later she brought a tampon to class. I did not see her with the tampon, but a lot of attention was focused on her, so I knew something was up. During the break between the double periods of the class, she went out and set fire to the tampon. This was witnessed by another teacher who had her written up.

I don't think Elise was really a bad girl, she was more like a blatant scream for help. You may recall from before that acting out is what children do when their call for help is not answered. Needless to say there were these kinds of screams coming from at least a quarter of the student population at Northeastern.

There weren't too many crazies in my chemistry classes, and I think if I was allowed to teach only chemistry I would have felt a lot better about teaching at Northeastern. Nevertheless there were a few crazies that were assigned to my chemistry classes over the years.

In my third semester at Northeastern I had a special treat, I had Loxley Hinkle and Anthony Lynn in the same chemistry class. Anthony was obnoxious, but Loxley was special. Loxley would compliment me every chance he got, "Ms. Moline you are looking beautiful today", "Ms. Moline you are so wonderful", "Oh that's a nice suit you are wearing Ms Moline", "I love you Ms. Moline". One day during the break between the double periods Loxley went out and used a marker to write Ms. Moline between 2 hearts on his forehead. Then he went walking around in the hall so other students could see. I grew weary of these antics, and so I would try as much as possible to avoid Loxley. I was getting into my car after school one day, and I saw him heading my way. I quickly got in my car and pressed the power lock on the door. Loxley came over, kissed his palm, and planted it on the window next to me. He smiled at me, and I smiled back, and he went along his merry way.

As heavily as Loxley complimented me, that's how much he disrupted my class. I never saw Loxley's shoes properly laced; probably so he could kick them off at will. One day I was teaching, and as I walked across the front of the room, I stepped on something, I looked down and Loxley's shoes were sitting there in the front of the room, and he was sitting at his desk in his socks. One day while I was teaching I noticed that every time I turned my back to the class there were a lot of snickering. I knew instinctively that it had to have something to do with Loxley, so I tried to catch him in the act, but he was too fast for me. After school when I was doing my final walk-through of the room I found the reason.

The one last walkthrough at the end of the day was something I institute after the flooding of the room in my first semester. I actually had a dated checklist that I used to make sure that I checked every thing in the room on a daily basis. As testament to my efforts there was never another incident. It wasn't that the students didn't try to get me to have another incident. In my walk-through it was not uncommon for me to find sinks that had been plugged, and the water left running slow enough not to be noticed. Ultimately I hid all the plugs for the sinks, and made sure that I reported any sinks that were clogged.

To get back to the story, the reason for all the snickers was that every time I turn to the board Loxley would spit a tiny spitball onto a poster I had on the wall next to his desk. There must have been at least 30 little spitballs on the poster. I just took the poster down and discarded it.

I spoke to his mother a few times, and didn't see much improvement. It seemed his mother was just as exasperated with him as I was. One day I ran into Loxley and his mother at the local hardware store. His mother told me just how exasperated she was with him, and how different he was from her 2 older daughters who were both scholars in high school. Loxley was at the exit of the store waiting for his mother while she spoke to me. He called out, "Don't listen to her Ms. Moline, she's crazy." I could tell his mom just wanted to stomp on him for a few minutes, and I empathized with her.

Then there was the time Loxley was absent from school for a couple of days because he went hunting with his father. "Can you imagine Loxley with a gun," one of the other students in the class commented, I tried to imagine it, and it was indeed scary. The day before the hunt Loxley asked me, "Ms. Moline, if we catch deer do you want me to bring you back some venison?"

Loxley and Anthony seem to like starting fires in the lab. We had these clay pots in the lab that the students used to put small pieces of solid waste so they didn't clog the sinks. Anthony and Loxley thought that these pots were ideal places to have a nice fire going. I sent them to AI during lab period, and then let them come in and make up lab assignments on their own time in order for them to get the idea that I would not tolerate foolishness in the lab.

I still don't think the notion sank in because the following semesters I started hearing rumors about Loxley peeing in the sink. I told the students who asked me about it that it was just rumor; I told them that even Loxley was not that crazy. The truth is I don't think that peeing in the sink was beyond Loxley's scope of attention getting antics.

Loxley ended the semester in similar fashion with some interesting answers on the chemistry regents. For one question that he did not know the answer to he simply wrote, "because Boyle's law says chemistry is fun". There was a question that showed a picture of an electrolytic cell and asked what type of cell it was. Loxley's answer to the question, "what type of cell is this?" was "a good one".

Arlen Frank described himself as obnoxious and cool; I thought that an oxymoron, until I had experience with Arlen. He was rather obnoxious, but the other students seemed to think he was cool. The students were in awe of him because he took and got away with actions that they couldn't even dream of committing.

At one point Arlen was arrested for climbing on top of the school with another student. One of the inefficient things about Northeastern was in the actual construction. All of the schools in the district were single stories, which resulted in a lot of excesses in heating, plumbing, and electrical wiring. It also provided easy access to the roof, and ultimately some of the classrooms in the school. There were reports of students breaking into classrooms and stealing supplies. The prime targets were computer hardware.

Arlen stated on his introductory card that the one thing that he would change about the world was school curricula. He exemplified that notion in the way he constantly tried to defy the school rules and academic requirements.

Arlen had a lot of absences because he would decide to stay home and play video games instead of coming to school. As a result of the absences he fell way behind in the class. I spoke with his counselor, and Mrs. Gillings, and we managed to set up an arrangement for Arlen to meet with me and work on the assignments he was missing. Just when things were going great, Arlen went back to being absent again.

Students in the class told me that they would see Arlen in school. So I looked up Arlen's schedule, and went and talked with his other teachers. It turns out that though he was still attending my class, he had stopped going to most of his other classes a long time ago.

Then one day Arlen came in to see me to inform me that he had decided to drop out of school. I was so disappointed. I tried to convince him that he was making a big mistake, but he insisted he was making the best decision for him. He gave me a great big hug and left. I went and talked to Mrs. Gillings; I was so distraught. I asked about what would happen to Arlen now that he had made this awful decision. I was told that once his decision to drop out was final the school would not take any further action. In the midst of the conversation, I had a wild idea which I thought of out loud. I would have the students in the class send Arlen cards and letters on a daily basis until he came back to school. "That's a great idea," Mrs. Gillings exclaimed, and I had to agree.

The next morning I outlined my plan to the class, and they agreed it was a great idea. I reserved the last part of the class for making the first card. The students made a big card of hearts from construction paper. It was a very close class—they claimed that they were a band. Losing Arlen meant breaking up the band, and they couldn't bear to have that happen.

During my break I went and placed the card in an envelope, and dropped it off to be mailed. 2 days later Arlen came back to school. He claimed the card changed his mind, and his life. Though we were near the end of the semester, Arlen was back in school, and making plans to get back on track for the second semester. I don't know of Arlen's fate since I left Northeastern after the end of the semester. However, based on experiences I have had with students who changed their lives around, I have no doubt that Arlen is still on track.

Wesley Winter went without glasses almost the entire semester. As a result he had trouble doing his homework, and he did not complete the chemistry research paper. I spoke with the school doctor, and had it all arranged for him to get an eye exam and glasses at no cost. His parents refused to respond to give their consent for the exam, and the school could not proceed without it.

In addition, Wesley pissed me off because on the Regents exam he missed getting above a 90 because he didn't have a calculator, and he didn't bother to ask for one.

One of the most remarkable things about Northeastern was all the sad stories that we encountered. A student in one of my unified science classes was in a car accident. He was injured so bad he had to be airlifted to an out-of-town hospital.

In my first semester there, a student from one of my chemistry classes lost his father. His father worked at another high school, and fell to his death off scaffolding while working on wiring in that school's auditorium. A number of teachers were diagnosed with cancer, including one teacher who started the same time I did fresh out of college. You can begin to see how disheartening the job was with the combination of sad stories and possessed students.

I did not think that my morale could sink much lower, but when I returned in September of 2006 to find that Kindade had been appointed as the new principal my morale hit rock bottom. It was so reminiscent of September 2004 when I went back to Berger and found that my mentor had left, and Nellyann had it in for me. To say Kindade had it in for me would be an understatement.

The sad thing about it is that I honestly don't know what I did wrong. With Nellyann it was easy to guess that she was exacting vengeance because I filed a grievance. I keep thinking that Kindade hated me because I am black—that would seem like the only remaining explanation, but my logical mind keeps rejecting that conclusion. My only other impression is that he didn't like the stance I took regarding social promotion while he was interim principal. As he so shamelessly put it, "why should a 1 credit course keep a senior from graduating?"

I knew I could do no right when he criticized the lesson that resulted in my classes' best performance on a test in all my time there—100%. Our post obser-vation conference was reminiscent of the post observation conference I had with Nellyann during her vendetta. Kindade suggested that I take a course in public speaking, because he did not like my mode of delivery during the lesson.

I like to get my students to adjust to my way of speaking and doing things, rather than vice versa. I was never any good at hypocrisy, so as a teacher I chal-lenged myself to get my students to adjust to my way of doing things, and to enjoy the transition. This explains why the Berger students who I taught biology and chemistry to wanted me to be their physics teacher too.

In all honesty, I don't think that my way of doing things is so bad. Whereas the Northeastern School District's objective was 85% passing on Regents chemis-try, I was averaging over 90%. When I worked as a chemist in industry I devised a plan that saved the company about $10,000 per month; this I did in my first month on the job. I later computerized their entire production report saving them personnel time, and saving money in the long run.

As the similarities between Kindade and Nellyann started jumping out at me, I began to feel the onset of principal's revenge 3, and I decided to quit rather than go through that ordeal again. I bowed out gracefully, and my tormentors had their wish—the school's only black teacher was gone before she could gain ten-ure.

Writing this has made me realize just how much abuse I took in the 2 and a half years that I spent at Northeastern. Many of my friends and family have won-dered if I made the right decision in quitting when I did. This serves to let me know just how right that decision was. I can't even think of what it would have been like to endure several more years of such torture.

After I left Northeastern a great opportunity presented itself. I was offered a teaching position in London. The position was pending completion of my documentation, which included obtaining reference from my previous school. Shortly after contacting Northeastern, the people in London suddenly lost interest in hiring me. The people in London fabricated a story about concerns about a conviction on my police report. There were no convictions on my police report because I had never been arrested or charged with a crime—not even a misdemeanor.

I thought maybe Kindade had something to do with that turn of events, but again my logical mind refused to accept that. Then I interviewed for another teaching position; again I was offered the job pending their contacting my previous employer. The AP called me and told me that the principal's decision not to hire me was based on information they obtained from Kindade. I think the AP told me the details because he was disappointed about not being able to hire me. The AP was impressed with the fact that after our interview he asked me to teach a demo lesson to the chemistry class, and I hooked my laptop up to his projector, and taught a pretty good lesson. Plus, after the class many of the students kept asking if I were going to be their new teacher. Again I say, it's amazing how little children figure in the educational system.

I thought of taking legal action against Kindade; he was way out of line because he had only been principal for one of the 5 semesters I spent at Northeastern, and more important I did not list him as my reference from the school. I decided to forego legal action and go back to university with aspirations of changing careers.

I now truly believe that teaching in public high school in the United States is something that I must completely remove from my options. At this stage of my life daily torture is not an option I even want to consider.

POTPOURRI

*If we never give students the opportunity to shine,
how can we ever find out how bright they can be?*

POTPOURRI

Seating Plan (quick note to new teachers)

Assigning seats is a must I think, and the Delaney cards along with the Delaney book does wonders for this task. If you are in a school that does not use the Delaney Book and Delaney Cards, it's worth it to invest in them on your own. When you assign seats let the students know the seat assignments are not permanent, and you reserve the right to change things around. Another nice strategy is to constantly form groups in class, that way the students don't get to sit in the same seats among the same classmates for too long. Of course putting students in groups is something you do after you have gained some teaching experience, and you only do it with a class in which you know enough about the students to know they will work well in a group setting. One of the things I usually do is reserve some seats at the front. Students who continue to be troublesome get to come up front and sit with me. Sometimes the 'troublemaker' seat is located right next to my desk.

Note to Parents

It's important for parents to know a little about early childhood education. Parents can take a course or read a book. There are several books available at the library on the subject. Books can also be purchased in bookstores. The ideal book to buy is one that gives information on what to do in the form of a year by year guide. There are certain things that parents can do that can dramatically improve their child's academic performance. The investment in time and money will be well worth it when the child becomes a successful adult.

Also, if you don't speak English, take the time to learn. If it cost you a few hundred dollars to learn English, make the investment. At the very least it will help you gain better control over your children who are fluent in English. Some of the worst bilingual students I have taught are those whose parents have limited English proficiency. I can't tell you how frustrating it has been to try to explain to a parent just how poorly their child is behaving, while using that same child as the interpreter.

I just have to mention this, if a teacher calls you to complain about something that your child did in class, then your child did something worthy of reprimand. Teachers don't have time to go out of their way to call parents for no reason; we don't even have time to call parents to tell them how wonderful their children are doing. Another bit of advice for parents—don't overly restrict your child at home. You need to let your child be him/herself at home, that way you know your child. I have met children who are little devils, yet their parents think they are angels. I think this is because their parents are so strict with them at home that they don't get to do the things they want to. When these children get to a school which offers more freedom, they just go buck wild.

In the 1994–1995 school year I became aware that the ninth graders I had were significantly different from those I taught in previous years. I thought, "Oh my God! The crack babies have gotten to high school." In retrospect I realize that that explanation was nowhere near the truth. I had however developed this immense fear of the so-called "crack kids" that I had no qualms with this explanation. I heard teachers worrying about the time when crack kids would actually get to high school back when I started teaching in 1992. It was like an "end of the world" premonition. Many teachers insisted they did not want to be teaching when such an event came to pass.

You can well imagine my shock when I did some research and found that it wasn't the parent's use of cocaine that was a predictor of the child's performance in school, but rather the strongest predictor was the amount of interaction between the child and the parent and/or caregiver. I read several studies that all came up with the same conclusion, even in cases where babies were exposed to cocaine and crack cocaine while in the womb.

I suppose it is therefore safe to say the best gift a parent can give to a child is attention. For those parents who feel they must give expensive video games, how about playing the game with your child.

While taking courses in public health, I learnt about some very valuable research. It has been shown that the period 0–2 years is a period of immense brain activity. Scientists have concluded that it is a wise choice for parents to interact with their child extensively during this period. One suggestion is that parents read to their children. You can start reading to your child even before birth, and new research implies you can read to your sleeping child and have an effect.

I sang to my child while he was in the womb. I read to him during infancy. By the age of 6 months he knew the story *The Three Little Pigs* so well that when I told the story he would brace himself in anticipation of my huffing and puffing (in my character of big bad wolf). Later he would take the book and babble the story with his own set of dramatics. By age 3 he could read the story on his own. By age 4 he was a fluent reader.

What's really driving the benefit is not so much the reading, but the interaction between parent and child. So it could be a parent singing to the child, playing pat-a-cake or peek-a-boo, or any number of other fun parent-child interaction. If you don't know how to interact with your child, it's never too late to learn.

The golden rule of early childhood education is 'make it fun'. For example, when I read the *Three Little Pigs* to my son, I didn't read the story as it was in the book, which is rather boring. Instead I made up a more exciting story based on the pictures. I then dramatize it, changing my voice to match the little pig or the big bad wolf as necessary.

I often joke: "What if we had to get a license in order to become a parent?" The question is how many of us parents would get such a license. I know some people would try to bribe the licensing official.

We treat parenting as though it's our birthright. The ability to conceive and give birth may be a birthright, but parenting is a skill that has to be learnt, and I have watched enough talk shows to know there are many people who are lacking parenting skills (just kidding).

On a serious note, few people who have given birth actually take time to learn parenting skills. Maybe parenting skills should be a mandated class for graduation from college, and later for graduation from high school. I know I would have benefited more from a class on parenting than I did from the mandated *Development of Civilization* I took while attending University.

Great Teachers

In my time in the school system I have met some truly talented teachers. A lot of them have retired by now, but some of them are still teaching. 2 of those who are still teaching were recipients of *Teacher of the Year* awards in NYC. The first, Jesus Benito, I met at Berger High School. All his students, with whom he had amazing rapport, would almost always pass the Spanish Regents. The fact that Spanish was his first language and that of most of his students was a bonus, but 100% pass on any Regents is still quite a feat.

Jesus was given the award for teacher of the year, and his colleagues criticized that since he was Spanish and so were his students, his achievement wasn't worthy of teacher of the year. They did not consider the fact that in classes where the teacher and most of the students have English as their first language 100% passing on the English Regents is not commonplace. I tell you that kind of sour grapes couldn't even be used to make vinegar.

Another teacher of the year recipient, Mr. Sadler of Langley High School was known for getting 100% of his students to pass the physics Regents year after year. It occurred so often the surprise would be if a Langley High School student failed the physics Regents.

Some Success Stories

J was a student who was doing quite poorly in the first semester of Regents chemistry. At the end of the semester I sat him down and had a serious talk with him in which I threatened to bring his father into the discussion. I notice how adamant he was regarding his father being brought into the discussion. I decided to use that angle. I told him if he did not improve in the second semester I was going to have a serious talk with his father.

I notice he started picking up on his grades, and he started attending the 7:30 am lab classes on a regular basis. On open school night at the beginning of the second semester his father came in to see me, and I told him I felt J could do much better than he was doing. His father mentioned that he tried helping J, but J was reluctant to accept his help. I suggested that it might be worthwhile to get a tutor for J. I also recommended the purchase of the *Barron's Regents Review book for Chemistry*.

J's academic performance continued to improve throughout the second semester. I gave after school tutoring classes for chemistry students, and J attended all of them. Second semester saw J go from getting some of the lowest grades on chemistry tests to getting the highest grades in the class on just about every test. Also J's class participation improved from almost zero to being almost number one in the class.

In any case J's gradual improvement continued throughout the semester culminating in a passing grade on the chemistry Regents.

C took and failed non-Regents chemistry during the school year. He went to summer school and all they were offering was Regents chemistry—the more difficult course. I started tutoring C and realized with great dismay that I would have to start from scratch. C worked very hard, and showed a remarkable amount of discipline for a teenage boy. I could tell he was doing a lot of work on his own after I left in addition to homework that I set for him. It was unusual for me to give homework for a student I was tutoring privately, but I made an exception in his case.

On the last session that we had, when C gave me the fee for the session he gave me an additional $30–10$ was a tip from his mother, and the other $20 was a tip from him. C went on to pass the Chemistry Regent with flying colors. His mother was so proud she called and told me the good news.

In my first year at Berger, while working in the attendance office, I came across the name of a ninth grade student that I knew. He was excessively absent, and so I had to contact his parents to find out what was happening. I called and spoke to his mother who explained that she didn't know how to reach him. He had decided to drop out of school, and nothing she or the counselors did or said was making any difference. I asked to speak to the student. I had a nice long talk with him, and the next day he was back in school. Each day he would check in with me to let me know he was attending school. Of course everyone wanted to know what on earth I said to the child to make him return to school. Apparently he told his teachers that I was responsible for his return. I merely told him how bright he was, and how very deeply hurt I was by his not attending school.

More Student Notes

Dear Ms. Moline

I know that I was not your best student or your quietest but I did learn a few things that I am sure to use this summer when I begin June 29 (I guess he meant college). I just wrote this note to say thank you for being more than just a teacher but a friend.

Thank you

Jon Reight

Jon was one of my loud and mischievous students at Langley High School. He forgot to add to his note, "and by the way Ms. Moline, I would really appreciate a passing grade." "More than just a teacher but a friend" indeed!!!

I actually have a school newspaper with a picture of Jon standing next to Bill Clinton. At the time the picture was taken Bill Clinton was president of the United States.

5–2-94

Ms. Moline:

I know I did not do my best this marking period. I know I probably did not behave like I'm supposed to but I apologize. I know you probably failed me, and if you did I deserve it. But I want to work harder this marking period, starting today. But I can't do it by myself, I need your help. I hope you can still help me pass the class and the Regents.

Thank you.

Sincerely,

Armand Assart

P.S. I would like to talk to you after class.

I am pleased to say this Berger student went on to pass the chemistry Regents and the class.

3–6-96

Langley H.S.
Edmund Sparks

Dear Ms. Moline I am apologysin about yestarday in class when you came in side the classroom I acted like a jerk and I just want to apologys about the way I acted yesterda I shoulded never yell out and say what I said to you I know that there was no reason for me to disrespect you like that and I almost got the class in trouble too. But I just want you to accept my apology for acting like a jerk when you came inside the room yesterday and I want you and my science teacher to accept my apology for disrupting the class and trying to be funny by calling your name in a disrespect.

This letter I got from a student in Mr. Sadler's earth science class at Langley High School. I was not even aware that the student made remarks about me when I visited his room. It was that level of serious discipline that made me enjoy working at Langley. Catholic priests may be pedophiles but Italian men make great disciplinarians in city high schools.

2/10/00

Dear Ms. Clemons,

Please come to class 7C at once. I am unable to begin and complete my lesson because the students are very unreceptive.

Alison Juns

Well, this note from a student in 7C at PS 999 is very telling.

Becoming a Good Scientist

Becoming a good scientist is a good life skill for children to learn. It assures that people will not be able to quite easily pull one over on them when they become adults.

Who's a good scientist? A good scientist is someone who is willing to question everything before accepting it; the person with the inquiring mind. As teachers we work in an environment where the curricula can stifle such a 'good scientist'. Instead of teaching this very important life skill, we teach facts, or rather partial facts, which we expect students to accept without question. I say partial facts because that's what they are. By my estimate, high school science only give students about one tenth of the facts, if that much.

I ask the question, why give students 10% of the facts when they have no intention of going to college to learn the other 40% that they give there, or going on to research to try to gain another 20–30%.

Here's where parents can step in. As we know young children ask a million and one questions. The best time to foster this good scientist skill is when the child is 4 years old and asking all those questions.

What do you do? Well you give your child the gift that will keep on giving the rest of his/her life. Teach your child how to search for answers. Remember our rule of thumb—make it fun.

As an educator I encourage students to question what they read and what they hear, and to try and figure things out themselves. My favorite scientist is the student who likes to show his friends he can outsmart the teacher. Most experienced teachers have probably come across this student. This student will watch the Discovery Channel, and read relentlessly, so that while in class he can ask questions that will stump the teacher. For some strange reason this student gets a kick out of doing that. What I do with such a student is I openly admit that I don't know the answer, even when I do, then I promise to reward the student with extra credit if he does research and bring me back the answer.

Is this Psychology 101. No, this is Experience 101—the best darn Psychology teacher I ever had. I remember how much joy I got as a high school student when I read until I found that one bit of information I felt sure my science teacher did not know. Then the thrill of victory from hearing those 3 words fall from his lips, "I don't know". In retrospect I think my teacher just humored me as a way to get me to keep up my independent study. It worked like a charm.

Why encourage these good scientist skills? Let's think for a minute ... Where do most people get their information? Yes, from the media. I consider the media to be filled with bad scientist because they give information for rating rather than for learning. Consider this famous news story (Well I consider it famous because so many people have quoted it to me over the years)—drinking red wine reduces your chance of getting heart disease. Take the average person's interpretation—oh drinking can actually be good for you, yeah! Wouldn't you prefer that your child be the good scientist who questions this—Who did the study? Let me see the result. Is a lag time explanation possible?

A good scientist must be able to express himself orally and in writing. I often tell students, "If you are the greatest scientist in the world and no one knows but you, then no one cares." I try to get across to them that the way to let me know how smart they are is through oral and written expression.

EPILOGUE

In 1993 the Campaign for Fiscal Equity (CFE)—a non-profit organization which is a coalition of parent organizations, community school boards, concerned citizens, and advocacy groups-filed a constitutional challenge to New York State's school finance system. According to the lawsuit there was a funding gap that denied City students the opportunity for a sound basic education. In 2003, New York State Supreme Court ruled in favor of CFE that the State aid system was illegal because it robbed NYC students by more than $1 billion per year. I repeat, $1 billion per year. The State was ordered to undertake sweeping reforms. [07] As I complete this edit, the State and the City are locked in extended financial negotiations regarding additional funding for City school districts.

EPILOGUE

Education in Inner Cities: The Search for Solutions

The school system as it was designed to operate is excellent. The system is however extremely inefficient, because so much is lost in the implementation. So while the system struggles to adapt, our children fail as they struggle to survive a system in turmoil. Of course as long as there are concerned parents who are willing to force changes, all is not lost.

In 1991 Jonathan Kozol wrote a bestseller called *SAVAGE INEQUALITIES Children in America's Schools.* In addition to becoming a bestseller, the book spurred anger. It begged you to ask the question, "Why wasn't something done?" It even spurred you to action—made you want to be part of the solution. Unfortunately, one of the major criticisms of the book is that it offered very little of that precious commodity—solutions. It's quite reasonable to assume that the book was never meant to be a solution manual, but rather an eye opener that calls to action the educational system and those in it. The fact that the book has become almost standard reading in the teaching profession bears witness to this.

The same can be said of this book—it is not meant to be a solution manual. I felt the need to withstand the painful memories, and tell my story with the hope that it may inspire schools to change, and parents to become more vigilant.

One of the maladies that plague inner city school systems, whether they are in East St. Louis, Camden, Paterson, or New York, is favoritism. The other major problem, a direct symptom of the former is mismanagement. Kozol starts out by stating that he was fired from one of the poorest schools in Boston because he didn't follow a curriculum that he had never seen. He was then recruited by one of the wealthiest Boston suburban schools, "where the principal welcomed innovation." Excellence and innovation on the part of teachers are qualities that seem to threaten poor administrators. The Board in its infinite wisdom seems convinced teachers leave poor schools for greener pastures. Indeed, all the good teachers who I encountered who moved to better schools did so at the 'urging' of their principal.

Welcomed changes are taking place. However, sometimes changes take place so slowly as to be considered stagnating. Kozol speaks about "moving around the same old furniture in the house of poverty", another way of saying 'the more things change the more they stay the same'. So there arrive on the scene magnet schools and new vision schools—excellent in theory, but severely lacking in practice. It is one thing to have a vision on paper, but the ultimate objective should be to ensure that every child in the building knows the vision of the school just as well as they know the *Pledge of Allegiance.*

On the other hand, the hands of time are working against minority schools. Social policies concerning public education of minority children have been turned back over a hundred years. This becomes evident when one considers court cases from '*Plessy vs Ferguson*' in 1896, to present. Indeed we have come full cycle—we have segregated neighborhoods with segregated schools. Tax dollars are linked to public education making segregation and poor schooling just another part of state policy.

When I looked up information on East Saint Louis in 1999 after reading Kozol's book what I found were reports of the same kind of neglect and mismanagement that Kozol spoke of in his book. Likewise I doubt that much has changed in NYC. Yes they have moved around the furniture, in some cases painted the walls, and by raising salaries they have attracted some upscale tenants, they have even changed the name of the building, but it's still the same giant building with a lot of pretty messed up apartments, and the effort to raise student achievement is still lackluster at best.

Kozol makes constant reference to the link between child health and education. Issues such as abandoned buildings, homicide, homelessness, high infant mortality rates, high rates of childhood asthma, malnutrition, diabetes, dental problems, infrequent garbage pick-ups, lead exposure, presence of chemical and waste treatment plants next to schools all impact children's performance in school. High blood lead remains a concern for NYC children as it relates to IQ. 'Miseducation' and trouble with law enforcement go hand in hand, most prison inmates from inner cities are high school dropouts. The main cause of death for young people aged 15–24 in NYC is homicide, but based on 2004 data homicide is almost 8 times more common for blacks than for whites. (Note: When I started writing this in 1999 there were more homicide in NYC, and the number for blacks was only twice that of whites.

The work of Jenner and Pasteur in developing vaccines has been credited with wiping out numerous infectious diseases. A more important factor which is less frequently mentioned is that improvement in sanitation was the driving force behind the decline in many infectious diseases. If we were still dumping feces on city streets and dealing with rodent infestations, no amount of vaccine would have protected us from the scourge of diseases such as cholera and bubonic plague. I mentioned this here because I feel that we can do a lot more to improve student achievement in inner city schools by improving their communities far better than we can by simply injecting funds into the schools.

It's not enough to educate children, but the school system has to educate the communities from whence they come. The issues that concern the community must be addressed at forums within the community. Community school board and PTA meetings can be venues for such discussion. It would also help if PTA actually included teachers. After school programs should be established, not just for children, but for parents and their children. Parents so mobilize will begin to take their child's welfare seriously enough to begin to demand the best public education. Lawsuits can be filed against chemical companies who pollute the community. Pressure can be applied to industries that are located in minority communities yet pay little or no tax, and offer few jobs to residents. Liquor stores and gambling establishments abound in minority neighborhoods; this again speaks to the need to educate the community. It's said it takes a whole village to raise a child, but in the same tone the village must be equipped with the skills to raise that child.

[07]As I edit this manuscript, the current mayor of NYC, Michael Bloomberg, has plans of offering poor NYC parents financial incentives to take better care of their children. There are those who criticize this move, but I praise it. I have always given rewards to students who perform well. The last few years I have given financial rewards that were based on Regents chemistry grades. From my point of view it's not about the reward, it's about acknowledging the effort that my students make in performing to high standards.

Nevertheless, this is not to say that the school system can solve the problems of the student's community, but it should acknowledge them where they exist, and mobilize parents, students and teachers to advocate for change through elected officials, and other means. If the UFT campaigned for quality education for students in NYC as vibrantly as they campaigned for politicians, I dare say we may have gotten further than we are today. Maybe it's time for parents, teachers and students to have sit-ins until changes are made for our schools.

The New York Lottery claims it was created to fund public education. It's time to start asking questions about which schools get the money. A system needs to be put in place to ensure that areas where most lotto tickets are sold get a proportional share of the revenues. There are many wealthy individuals who went to school in poor New York City Districts. Alumni associations need to be looked at as sources of additional funding for poor schools. Such associations can provide individuals to act as mentors for young minority children. A career day, which features graduates of the school, and successful minority individuals in the school community can motivate and lift self esteem.

Lack of self-esteem among minority students is another issue. The situation is exacerbated by the fact that many of the teachers who teach our children have very little confidence in their abilities—the current focus on teacher accountability is a welcomed change. Partnership with businesses in the community can counter this. When students start work in a professional setting at an early age it builds confidence. Working in the grease of a McDonald or Burger King may earn students money, but it does little to build self-esteem and confidence.

The environment within which students are expected to learn is also at issue. Many schools in the inner cities suffer from disrepair, insufficient classroom and outdoor space, and outdated heating system. Now add to the turbid mix metal detectors, X-ray machines and in the case of NYC the NYPD. We offer these substandard conditions to minority students and then wonder why they are not inspired to learn.

Again and again Kozol expressed his exasperation at wealthy parents' insistence that it's not about money. High priced lawyers were hired to convince the public it's not about money. But it is about money. Academic excellence stems from having qualified teachers with a wealth of experience. There are New York suburbs where teachers are making six-figure salaries. Small class size is a factor; this means more teachers, and more teacher salaries and benefits. Providing teachers with resources—lab facilities, teaching aids and audiovisual equipment which complement teaching cost money.

One of the major mistakes of the system is to throw money at problems and hope they fix themselves. Education should be treated as a business, and money spent should be monitored for maximum efficiency based on the return on the investment. The Board's budget may be akin that of a Fortune 500 company, but any Fortune 500 company whose fund were as loosely spent as that of the Board would be sure to go under.

The Golden rule is 'He who has the gold makes the rules'. Legislation is costly; you need to have money to be able to afford lobbyists and/or lawyers to advocate for legislative changes. To have money you need to have a good education or be related to someone with money. Let's face it, the percent of CEOs of fortune 500 companies that are Ivy League graduates far exceed the percent of Ivy League universities. As an educator I have grasped the understanding that data runs education and likewise data is instrumental in facilitating change. Minority schools need to invest heavily in a team (possibly the school leadership team) which is equipped to gather data and write proposals that support the need for required changes.

Then there is the issue of appropriateness of the school curricula. Millions of dollars are spent to support different types of educational programs, but enough time and money is not invested in making the curricula relevant to the needs of children and their communities. To site a simplistic example, schools in disadvantaged areas should place great emphasis on teaching grant writing skills to students, as well as teaching them how to get legislative changes.

In one of his State of the Union addresses, President Bill Clinton, stated that one of the problems with trying to find solutions for education is that every problem that we encounter has been solved successfully elsewhere, it's just a matter of adapting the solution. NYC's school system has to be commended for taking steps to make changes to stamp out corruption and mismanagement. A big step in the right direction was the enacting of the changes in the *school governance laws*. The efforts are far from adequate, though I am optimistic that as time progress things will continue to improve. There are a number of areas that are still lagging.

- The appropriateness of staff development and staff developers.
- The appointment of qualified administrators.
- The negative impacts of unionism to the extent where it prevents the competitive hiring of competent individuals.
- The decline in discipline across the system.
- Providing adequate resources—computerization, audio-visual aid, lab facilities—to enable teachers to maximize their teaching of mathematics and science.

THE END

978-0-595-48208-5
0-595-48208-2